REA's Test Prep Books Are The Best!
(a sample of the <u>hundreds of letters</u> REA receives each year)

" I did well because of your wonderful prep books... I just wanted to thank you for helping me prepare for these tests. "
Student, San Diego, CA

" My students report your chapters of review as the most valuable single resource they used for review and preparation. "
Teacher, American Fork, UT

" Your book was such a better value and was so much more complete than anything your competition has produced — and I have them all! "
Teacher, Virginia Beach, VA

" Compared to the other books that my fellow students had, your book was the most useful in helping me get a great score. "
Student, North Hollywood, CA

" Your book was responsible for my success on the exam, which helped me get into the college of my choice... I will look for REA the next time I need help. "
Student, Chesterfield, MO

" Just a short note to say thanks for the great support your book gave me in helping me pass the test... I'm on my way to a B.S. degree because of you! "
Student, Orlando, FL

(more on next page)

(continued from front page)

" I just wanted to thank you for helping me get a great score
on the AP U.S. History exam... Thank you for making great test preps! "
Student, Los Angeles, CA

" Your *Fundamentals of Engineering Exam* book was the absolute best
preparation I could have had for the exam, and it is one of the major
reasons I did so well and passed the FE on my first try. "
Student, Sweetwater, TN

" I used your book to prepare for the test and found that the advice and the sample tests were highly relevant... Without using any other material, I earned very
high scores and will be going to the graduate school of my choice. "
Student, New Orleans, LA

" What I found in your book was a wealth of information sufficient to shore up
my basic skills in math and verbal... The section on analytical ability was
excellent. The practice tests were challenging and the answer explanations most
helpful. It certainly is the *Best Test Prep for the GRE*! "
Student, Pullman, WA

" I really appreciate the help from your excellent book. Please keep up
the great work. "
Student, Albuquerque, NM

" I am writing to thank you for your test preparation... your book helped me
immeasurably and I have nothing but praise for your *GRE* preparation."
Student, Benton Harbor, MI

(more on back page)

The Best Test Preparation for the

AP English

Language & Composition Exam

6th Edition

Dwight Raulston, Ph.D.
AP English Language Teacher
St. John's School, Houston, TX

Sally Wood, M.S.
Former AP and Dual-Credit Instructor of English
Aurora High School, Aurora, MO

Linda Bannister, Ph.D.
Professor and Chair, Department of English
Loyola Marymount University, Los Angeles, CA

Robert Liftig, Ed.D.
Adjunct Professor of Writing
Fairfield University, Fairfield, CT

Ellen Davis Conner, M.A.
Instructor of English
Clear Lake High School, Friendswood, TX

Luann Reed-Siegel, M.A.
Former Instructor of English
Linden High School, Linden, NJ

Research & Education Association
Visit our website at
www.rea.com

Research & Education Association
61 Ethel Road West
Piscataway, New Jersey 08854
E-mail: info@rea.com

The Best Test Preparation for the
AP ENGLISH LANGUAGE & COMPOSITION EXAM

Published 2008

Copyright © 2007 by Research & Education Association, Inc. Prior editions copyright © 2003, 2000, 1998, 1996, 1994 by Research & Education Association, Inc. All rights reserved. No part of this book may be reproduced in any form without permission of the publisher.

Printed in the United States of America

Library of Congress Control Number 2006933677

ISBN-13: 978-0-7386-0287-5
ISBN-10: 0-7386-0287-6

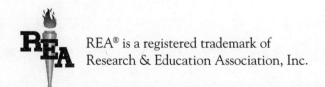
REA® is a registered trademark of
Research & Education Association, Inc.

CONTENTS

The AP Experts Behind Our Updated 6th Edition

Dwight Lloyd Raulston, Ph.D., is director of curriculum at St. John's School in Houston, Texas. A seasoned AP instructor, Dr. Raulston recently was cited in the College Board's "2006 Advanced Placement Report to the Nation" for an exemplary program that leads the world "in helping the widest segment of their total school population achieve an exam grade of 3 or higher in AP English Language and Composition." Dr. Raulston has received many academic honors, including Most Influential High School Teacher Recognition from the University of Texas and Massachusetts Institute of Technology and Outstanding Teacher Award from the University of Chicago, among others. Dr. Raulston received his B.A. (1975) and Ph.D. (1979) from Rice University.

Sally Wood, M.S., has taught Advanced Placement and dual credit courses, and is a certified exam reader for Educational Testing Service, a test-item writer for ACT, Inc., and the author of many academic and counseling articles for a wide range of educational publications. Ms. Wood has counseled college-bound students on such topics as academic preparation, test-taking, and college admissions. A four-time recipient of the Joplin Globe Distinguished Educator award, Ms. Wood is listed in *Who's Who in American Education* and is a long-time member of the Missouri State Teachers Association. She received her B.S. degree in 1971 and her M.S. in 1980.

About Research & Education Association

Founded in 1959, Research & Education Association (REA) is dedicated to publishing the finest and most effective educational materials—including software, study guides, and test preps—for students in middle school, high school, college, graduate school, and beyond.

REA's Test Preparation series includes books and software for all academic levels in almost all disciplines. Research & Education Association publishes test preps for students who have not yet entered high school, as well as high school students preparing to enter college. Students from countries around the world seeking to attend college in the United States will find the assistance they need in REA's publications. For college students seeking advanced degrees, REA publishes test preps for many major graduate school admission examinations in a wide variety of disciplines, including engineering, law, and medicine. Students at every level, in every field, with every ambition can find what they are looking for among REA's publications.

REA presents tests that accurately depict the official exams in both degree of difficulty and types of questions. REA's practice tests are always based upon the most recently administered exams, and include every type of question that can be expected on the actual exams.

REA's publications and educational materials are highly regarded and continually receive an unprecedented amount of praise from professionals, instructors, librarians, parents, and students. Our authors are as diverse as the fields represented in the books we publish. They are well known in their respective disciplines and serve on the faculties of prestigious high schools, colleges, and universities throughout the United States and Canada.

Today, REA's wide-ranging catalog is a leading resource for teachers, students, and professionals.

We invite you to visit us at *www.rea.com* to find out how "REA is making the world smarter."

Acknowledgments

In addition to our authors, we would like to thank Larry B. Kling, Vice President, Editorial, for his overall guidance, which brought this publication to completion; Pam Weston, Vice President, Publishing, for setting the quality standards for production integrity and managing the publication to completion; Diane Goldschmidt, Senior Editor, for editorial project management; Molly Solanki, Associate Editor, for preflight editorial review; and Jeff LoBalbo, Senior Graphic Designer, for coordinating pre-press electronic file mapping. Our cover was designed by Christine Saul, Senior Graphic Designer. We also gratefully acknowledge Kathy Caratozzolo of Caragraphics for typesetting.

STUDY SCHEDULE

AP English Language & Composition

STUDY SCHEDULE

AP English Language & Composition

The following study schedule will help you become thoroughly prepared for the Advanced Placement Examination in English Language & Composition. Although the schedule is designed as a six-week study program, you may wish to expand or condense it depending on how soon you will be taking the actual exam. Be sure to set aside enough time each week for studying purposes. Keep in mind that the more time you devote to studying for the AP English Language & Composition, the more confident and prepared you will be on the day of the exam.

Week	Activity
1	Read Chapter 1, "Excelling on the AP English Language & Composition Exam." This chapter will give you some background on the AP Examination in English Language & Composition. From this chapter you will learn about the format of the exam, and about scoring procedures and grade distribution.
2	Read Chapter 2, "Learning About the 'Other' Literature." This chapter will help you to develop critical reading skills. Do not rush through. Read carefully and take notes on the chapter for later review. Make flash cards of the main ideas of the chapter and of the glossary words.
3	Read Chapter 3, "Writing About the 'Other' Literature." This chapter provides instruction on analyzing, critiquing, and writing about the types of passages found on the exam. Again, take notes on the chapter and make flash cards of the main ideas.
4	Read Chapter 4, "Preparing for and Taking the AP Exam," and take Practice Exam 1. Be sure to simulate actual testing conditions, such as time constraints. After you finish the test, mark any confusing questions. Grade yourself and review the book's detailed explanations of the answers. Diagnose your weaknesses and turn back to the chapters for further review.
5	Take Practice Exam 2. Be sure to simulate actual testing conditions, such as time constraints. After you finish the test, mark any confusing questions. Grade yourself and review the book's detailed explanations of the answers. Diagnose your weaknesses and turn back to the chapters for further review.
6	Take Practice Exam 3. Be sure to simulate actual testing conditions, such as time constraints. After you finish the test, mark any confusing questions. Grade yourself and review the book's detailed explanations of the answers. Diagnose your weaknesses and turn back to the chapters for further review.

CHAPTER 1

AP English Language & Composition

Excelling on the AP English Language & Composition Exam

About This Book

This test-preparation guide has been written to help you learn how to do well on the Advanced Placement Examination in English Language & Composition. It will help you become familiar with the requirements of the examination and give you a chance to put your mastery of the AP exam to the test with a series of specially developed practice exams. The introductory sections of the book are devoted to explaining the test, reviewing and expanding your critical reading skills, and helping you learn how to approach writing essays and answering multiple-choice questions in the ways the AP examination will expect you to be able to do successfully.

This book provides three full-length practice exams with thorough explanations of every answer to help you pinpoint your problem areas. By taking these practice exams and devoting time to going through our targeted subject review, you'll be well prepared to succeed on the AP English Language & Composition Exam. In addition, this book includes a glossary of key literary terms with 65 entries, all fully defined.

About the Exam

The Advanced Placement Examination in English Language & Composition is geared toward the student who has studied the mechanics of writing and rhetoric at an advanced level and wishes to pursue college credit.

Take care not to confuse the AP Examination in English Language & Composition with the AP Examination in Literature & Composition. The **Literature** exam focuses on literature and literary criticism, while the **Language** exam deals with writing as a craft. This book is designed to help you prepare for the AP Examination in English Language & Composition *only*.

The AP English Language & Composition Exam is divided into two sections:

- *Section 1 – Multiple Choice (60 minutes—accounts for 45% of total score)*
  Five or six reading passages, with an average of 10 questions each.

- *Section 2 – Free Response (up to 120 minutes—accounts for 55% of total score)*
  Three essay questions.

The first section consists of five or six reading passages and sixty multiple-choice questions, which you will have one hour to complete. Each passage will be followed by an average of ten questions, and thereafter the passage will not be referred to again. Do not feel pressured to remember each reading; just digest them one at a time and move on. After reading the passage, you will have approximately one minute to answer each question.

The second section of the AP English Language & Composition Exam consists of three essay questions and is divided such that you will have forty minutes to write each essay. You will not be able to go back to an essay after the allotted time has elapsed. Note that each essay has very specific instructions, and most have a passage that you will read critically to answer the essay question. Your essays will be scored according to the essay structure, the clarity of your writing, and the extent to which you have answered the question.

Scoring the Exam

The multiple-choice section of the exam is scored by machine. Your score on this part of the exam is determined simply by adding the number of correct responses and subtracting one-quarter of a point for each wrong answer. Questions left blank do not count in any way—positive or negative—toward the score. The essay section of the examination is graded by well-trained human readers to ensure consistency. Each essay is read by more than one reader, and the scores of different readers are averaged together if they should disagree. Each essay is given a final grade from 0 to 9, and the total essay score is simply the total of these three essay scores. The maximum essay score is thus always 27, and each essay contributes equally to the essay score.

The multiple-choice section generally is weighted to account for about 45% of the total composite score, and the essay section is weighted to account for the remainder of the composite score. These weighted scores are then added together to get a composite score. These scores are broken down into ranges, and AP grades of 1 through 5 for the overall exam are assigned on the basis of the composite-score ranges. The exact composite-score ranges that correspond to each AP exam grade are adjusted slightly each year in accordance with statistical information that is gathered on the examination each year in order to keep year-to-year results as comparable as possible.

The following section explains how AP grades are calculated based on the multiple-choice section scores and the essay scores. You can use this section to help get a feel for how you might do on the exam. You can undoubtedly come up with various ways to see how your grade on the overall exam might be affected if you wrote two essays well but had real problems with the third one, for instance. You can also use the section to estimate what your exam score is likely to be based on how well you do on the practice exams given later in the book. Remember that this section simply gives you a general idea of what your exam score is likely to be. The actual scaling factors and composite-score ranges that the College Board uses to calculate the *actual* AP grades on each test annually will be somewhat different.

Multiple-Choice Scoring:

$$\underline{\hspace{4cm}} - (\tfrac{1}{4} \times \underline{\hspace{3cm}}) = \underline{\hspace{5cm}}$$

Number correct	Number incorrect	Raw score (rounded to nearest whole number)

Essay Scoring:

$$\underline{\hspace{3cm}} + \underline{\hspace{2.5cm}} + \underline{\hspace{2.5cm}} = \underline{\hspace{2.5cm}}$$

Question 1 (out of 9)	Question 2 (out of 9)	Question 3 (out of 9)	Essay score (rounded to nearest whole number)

As you can see, there is a deduction for guessing on the multiple-choice section, so you are discouraged from random guessing or filling in of answers. Depending on the number of multiple-choice questions, the Essay score is multiplied by approximately 3.3 to 3.8. This is called the Weighted Essay score. (If necessary, the Multiple Choice score is also weighted.)

Each section of the test is weighted according to time allotted to that section; that is, the Multiple Choice score counts approximately 60 points, and the Weighted Essay score counts approximately 90 points, to make a total of approximately 150 points. The Multiple Choice score is added to the Weighted Essay score to get a composite score, which is rounded to the nearest whole number. The composite score ranges are then determined for the final AP Grade. The following table is approximate, since the composite score range varies a few points from year to year.

Composite Score Range	AP Grade
101-150	5
90-100	4
70-89	3
50-69	2
0-49	1

The Composite Score

To obtain your composite score, use the following method:

_____ = _____ (weighted multiple-choice score—**do not round**)
multiple-choice
raw score

3.333 × _____ = _____ (weighted free-response score—**do not
free-response   round**)
raw score

Distribution of Grades

Distribution of grades varies from year to year and from testing to testing. The following table is an approximate distribution of grades for an AP English Language & Composition Examination and an approximation of the percentage of people earning the grade.

	Grade	Percent Earning Grade
Extremely well-qualified	5	10
Well-qualified	4	20
Qualified	3	35
Possibly qualified	2	30
No recommendation	1	5

Most colleges grant students who earn a 3 or better either college credit or advanced placement. Check with your high school's guidance office about specific requirements.

How to Use This Book

Read through the introductory material in chapters 1–5. The text in these chapters is designed to help you review what you've already learned, as well as expand your skills with some specific details and approaches to critical reading and writing that your English course may not have covered in as much detail. After studying the review material, it is *critical* that you take the three full-length practice exams included in this book and that you take them under as realistic a set of test conditions as possible.

If possible, try to find someone to score your essays for you, perhaps a friend who is also preparing for the exam. It's much easier to be objective about someone else's writing than your own. In the multiple-choice section, be sure to look carefully at the explanations for each question you missed. Remember, your goal in preparing for this exam is to score well on it. So, when you miss a question, don't try to convince yourself how your answer is "better" than the book's. Instead, try to see how the author of the question chose the answer that was given as the best choice. If you put yourself into the mindset of the people writing these sorts of questions, you'll have an easier time answering them correctly and your scores will improve.

It is important to note that critical reading is a skill and that while memorization may suffice for the mastery of literary terminology, practice is your only means to master critical reading. Chapters 2 and 3 of this book have been designed to help you hone your critical reading and writing skills. Once you have practiced these skills, move on to Chapter 4, which coaches you for the format and time limits of the AP exam. If the test date is near, it may be a better idea for you to start with the coaching chapter and practice tests since they provide direct instruction for the exam format. Ideally, it's best to use the six-week study schedule in the front of this book.

How to Contact the AP Program

To obtain a registration bulletin or to learn more about the Advanced Placement Examinations, contact:

The College Board Advanced Placement Program
P.O. Box 6671
Princeton, NJ 08541-6671
Phone: (609) 771-7300
Website: *www.apcentral.collegeboard.com*
E-mail: *apexams@info.collegeboard.org*

CHAPTER 2

AP English Language & Composition

Learning About the "Other" Literature

What Is Literature?

Although much of what you have read in literature classes would surely qualify as great poetry, novels, and short stories, these types of works are, in fact, only a part of what makes up good writing—and literature. In fact, an entire genre—nonfiction—is sometimes minimized or even overlooked in literature courses. Yet nonfiction essays (including persuasive pieces such as editorials and political speeches) include some of the most powerful works written in the past few hundred years.

Indeed, as a part of the AP Course in English Language & Composition, students may be exposed to a variety of these "other" literatures. Students may read the works of autobiographers, diarists, biographers, historians, critics, essayists, journalists, political commentators, scientific writers, and nature writers, among others. Whatever the discipline, excellent prose pieces share certain characteristics of style and arrangement. Similarly, there are strategies for critical reading that are useful for any prose passage.

A Brief Look at the Significance of the Essay

The "other" literature most often takes the form of an essay. Students in the AP Course in English Language & Composition study essays written by writers from a variety of disciplines and periods. Over the past 400 years, many compelling essays have captured the audiences of their day with their powerful ideas and styles. The development of the essay as an art form is particularly interesting precisely because great essay writers have sprung from fields as diverse as politics and biology, education and art history. This fact speaks to the importance of conveying ideas in writing. The literary tradition of the essay has been shaped by thinkers who, regardless of their training, felt strongly about issues and ideas and who had an impact on their audiences.

Despite its power to change people's thinking, the essay has not enjoyed the prestige of fiction, poetry, and drama. Montaigne, a sixteenth-century lawyer and writer, generally agreed upon by scholars to be the father of the essay, helps us understand why. Montaigne articulated the problematic nature of the form when he defined the essay very loosely, saying anything could be included in it and that it could start and stop wherever it pleased. An essay could consequently include history and personal experience, fact and fiction, scientific discovery and philosophical musing. The "proper" length of an essay is nowhere specified, though it is generally read in one sitting. Essays are often written in the first person and thus are easily seen as an expression of the author's persona or voice as well as the author's thoughts. An essay's style, therefore, is as significant as the information and opinion it contains. Essays are often superb examples of the marriage of form and content, the hallmark of great literature. It is indeed appropriate to consider essays the "other" literature.

Strategies for Critical Reading of Prose Passages

Critical reading is a demanding process. Linguists and language philosophers speak passionately of the importance of true literacy in human affairs. It is not enough merely to comprehend: true literacy lies in the ability to make critical judgments, to analyze, and to evaluate. It is with this end in mind—true literacy—that any reader should approach a text.

What Critical Readers Do

If you can summarize the main points of an essay, that's a start. If you can recall the plot twists in a short story or articulate the line of reasoning in an argument, that's a start. But if you are able to offer an informed opinion about the purpose and merits of a text, then you are on the road to true literacy.

The AP Examination in English Language & Composition seeks to identify critical readers, readers who not only can describe *what* happened in a text they've read, but *why* it happened and *how* it happened.

More specifically, as a critical reader, you will:

- summarize and outline complex material,

- critically examine a text's reasoning,

- analyze the way a text achieves its effects, especially through stylistic choice,

- evaluate a text, deciding whether it is accurate, authoritative, and convincing,

- determine a text's significance,

- compare and contrast different texts,

- synthesize information from one or more related texts, and

- apply concepts in one text to other texts.

As a critical reader, you'll be an active participant, not a passive recipient. It may help to envision yourself in a dialogue with the author and other critical readers. As rhetorician and critic Mikhail Bahktin argues, language operates in a dialogic mode, where receivers are just as essential to effective transmission of messages as senders.

There are six strategies a critical reader can employ to participate fully in the "re-creative act" that is reading.

1. Get the facts straight.

2. Analyze the argument.

3. Identify basic features of style.

4. Explore your personal response.

5. Evaluate the text overall and determine its significance.

6. Compare and contrast related texts.

1. Get the Facts Straight

Read actively, pencil in hand, underlining important phrases or noting key points in the margin. Briefly record your reactions, questions, and conclusions. Though you may not have time to annotate a prose passage thoroughly during a test, if you rigorously practice annotating beforehand, you'll begin to do it more easily and with less written back-up during the actual exam.

Your first task as a critical reader is to put the essay you're about to read into context. Doing so involves looking carefully at the title (if one is given), looking for the time of composition of the piece, as well as any biographical information given about the writer.

Your first task as a successful test-taker is to make sure you know what you are being asked to write about. *Before you begin to read the essay*, read the essay prompt carefully and underline it. That way, you'll have an understanding of how you'll be using the information you're acquiring during the reading in order to write your response to the prompt.

As you read, underline key phrases in the passage or make marginal notes of what seem to be the most important ideas and details that are mentioned. If it helps you focus your thoughts, jot down the major idea and slant of the passage in a single sentence at the end of the piece.

There are really four activities you perform in order to "get the facts straight":

a. **Previewing** – Looking over a text to learn all you can *before* you start reading. (This is, of course, much more difficult with excerpts.)

b. **Annotating** – Marking up the text to record reactions, questions, and conclusions. (Hint: It's especially useful to underline what you think the thesis is.)

c. **Outlining** – Identifying the sequence of main ideas, often by *numbering* key phrases.

d. **Summarizing** – Stating the purpose and main idea, the "essence" of a text.

Once you've got the facts straight, you're ready to tackle the analytic and evalua-tive aspects of critical reading. Before addressing those, let's test your ability to get the facts.

Here's an essay titled "Education of Women" by William Hazlitt, an essayist and scholar who wrote during the early nineteenth century. Try your hand at previewing, annotating, outlining, and summarizing it. Then look at the following pages, where a proficient critical reader has done those operations for you. Compare your responses and see where you can improve. Remember, you don't have to take copious notes to get to the essence of a text.

Education of Women

We do not think a classical education proper for women. It may pervert their minds, but it cannot elevate them. It has been asked, Why a woman should not learn the dead languages as well as the modern ones? For this plain reason, that the one are still spoken, and may have immediate associa-tions connected with them, and the other not. A woman may have a lover who is a Frenchman, or an Italian, or a Spaniard; and it is well to be pro-vided against every contingency in that way. But what possible interest can she feel in those old-fashioned persons, the Greeks and Romans, or in what was done two thousand years ago? A modern widow would doubtless prefer Signor Tramezzani to Aeneas, and Mr. Conway would be a formidable rival to Paris.[1] No young lady in our days, in conceiving an idea of Apollo, can go a step beyond the image of her favorite poet: nor do we wonder that our old friend, the Prince Regent,[2] passes for a perfect Adonis in the circles of beauty and fashion. Women in general have no ideas, except personal ones. They are mere egoists. They have no passion for truth, nor any love of what is purely ideal. They hate to think, and they hate every one who seems to think of anything but themselves. Everything is to them a perfect nonentity which does not touch their senses, their vanity, or their interest. Their poetry, their criticism, their politics, their morality, and their divinity, are downright affectation. That line in Milton is very striking—

'He for God only, she for God in him.'

Such is the order of nature and providence; and we should be sorry to see any fantastic improvements on it. Women are what they were meant to

---

[1] Hazlitt was a theatre critic and had accused a popular Italian tenor, Tramezzani, of overacting in his love scenes. He also criticized actor William Conway in the role of Romeo.

[2] The Prince Regent was George, Prince of Wales. His father, George III, had recently been declared insane.

be; and we wish for no alteration in their bodies or their minds. They are the creatures of the circumstances in which they are placed, of sense, of sympathy and habit. They are exquisitely susceptible of the passive impressions of things: but to form an idea of pure understanding or imagination, to feel an interest in the true and the good beyond themselves, requires an effort of which they are incapable. They want principle, except that which consists in an adherence to established custom; and this is the reason of the severe laws which have been set up as a barrier against every infringement of decorum and propriety in women. It has been observed by an ingenious writer of the present day, that women want imagination. This requires explanation. They have less of that imagination which depends on intensity of passion, on the accumulation of ideas and feelings round one object, on bringing all nature and all art to bear on a particular purpose, on continuity and comprehension of mind; but for the same reason, they have more fancy, that is greater flexibility of mind, and can more readily vary and separate their ideas at pleasure. The reason of the greater presence of mind which has been remarked in women is, that they are less in the habit of speculating on what is best to be done, and the first suggestion is decisive. The writer of this article confesses that he never met with any woman who could reason, and with but one reasonable woman. There is no instance of a woman having been a great mathematician or metaphysician or poet or painter: but they can dance and sing and act and write novels and fall in love, which last quality alone makes more than angels of them. Women are no judges of the characters of men, except as men. They have no real respect for men, or they never respect them for those qualities, for which they are respected by men. They in fact regard all such qualities as interfering with their own pretensions, and creating a jurisdiction different from their own. Women naturally wish to have their favourites all to themselves, and flatter their weaknesses to make them more dependent on their own good opinion, which, they think, is all they want. We have, indeed, seen instances of men, equally respectable and amiable, equally admired by the women and esteemed by the men, but who have been ruined by an excess of virtues and accomplishments.

—William Hazlitt (1815)

1. Get the Facts Straight

A. Previewing "Education of Women"

A quick look over the text of "Education of Women" reveals a few items worth mentioning. As is often the case in essays, the opening sentence gives the basic slant of the piece: it will argue against education for women. The use of "we" as a subject suggests the author is speaking—or feels he is speaking—for a broad audience, so the essay is most likely related to an opinion piece or editorial in a newspaper. It will have a definite point of view and is unlikely to be even-handed in its treatment of the subject. The date of the piece—1815—reminds you of what you may remember from your history courses: the piece was written well before women had significant legal rights or opportunities of being independent.

B. Annotating "Education of Women"

An annotation records reactions, questions, and conclusions. Underlining key phrases may help you find the theme. Here are excerpts from Hazlitt's essay with underlining and annotations alongside to facilitate easy reference.

Education of Women

We do not think a classical education proper for women. It may pervert their minds, but it cannot elevate them. It has been asked, Why a woman should not learn the dead languages as well as the modern ones? For this plain reason, that the one are still spoken, and may have immediate associations connected with them, and the other not. A woman may have a lover who is a Frenchman, or an Italian, or a Spaniard; and it is well to be provided against every contingency in that way. But what possible interest can she feel in those old-fashioned persons, the Greeks and Romans, or in what was done two thousand years ago? A modern widow would doubtless prefer Signor Tramezzani to Aeneas, and Mr. Conway would be a formidable rival to Paris.[1] No young lady in our days, in conceiving an idea of Apollo, can go a step beyond the image of her favorite

1. **Thesis:** the author is against a traditional education for women.

2. Such an education is actually harmful to women.

3. Women learn modern languages to be able to speak to their lovers—women have a shallow purpose for education.

4. Allusion to "poor" actors of the day (see footnote) who are preferable to historical figures (Aeneas, Paris)—women have little interest in history or politics, only romantic self-gratification.

poet: nor do we wonder that our old friend, the Prince Regent[2], passes for a perfect Adonis in the circles of beauty and fashion. <u>Women in general have no ideas, except personal ones.</u> They are mere egoists. They have no passion for truth, nor any love of what is purely ideal. <u>They hate to think,</u> and <u>they hate every one who seems to think of anything but themselves.</u> Everything is to them a perfect nonentity which does not touch their senses, their vanity, or their interest. Their poetry, their criticism, their politics, their morality, and their divinity, are downright affectation. That line in Milton is very striking—

'He for God only, she for God in him.'

Such is the order of nature and providence; and we should be sorry to see any fantastic improvements on it. <u>Women are what they were meant to be;</u> and we wish for no alteration in their bodies or their minds. They are the <u>creatures of the circumstances in which they are placed,</u> of sense, <u>of sympathy and habit.</u> They are exquisitely susceptible of the passive impressions of things: but <u>to form an idea of pure understanding or imagination,</u> to feel an interest in the true and the good beyond themselves, <u>requires an effort of which they are incapable. They want principle,</u> except that which consists in an adherence to established custom; and this is the reason of the severe laws which have been set up as a barrier against every infringement of decorum and propriety

5. Women don't think, are selfish, frivolous.

6. Women's destiny—creatures of circumstance, habit. Women can't change.

7. Women only respond to their environment; they do not have original ideas but simply respond passively and only to what they feel concerns themselves.

8. They "want" principle...They "want" imagination...Want means lack, not desire.

in women. It has been observed by an ingenious writer of the present day, that <u>women want imagination.</u> This requires explanation. They have <u>less</u> of that imagination which depends on intensity of passion, on the <u>accumulation of ideas and feelings round one object,</u> on bringing all nature and all art to bear on a particular purpose, on continuity and comprehension of mind; but for the same reason, <u>they have more fancy,</u> that is <u>greater flexibility of mind,</u> and <u>can more readily vary and separate their ideas at pleasure.</u> The reason of that greater presence of mind which has been remarked in women is, that they are <u>less in the habit of speculating on what is best to be done, and the first suggestion is decisive. The writer of this article confesses that he never met with any woman who could reason, and with but one reasonable woman. There is no instance of a woman having been a great mathematician or metaphysician or poet or painter: but they can dance and sing and act and write novels and fall in love,</u> which last quality alone makes more than angels of them. <u>Women are no judges of the characters of men, except as men. They have no real respect for men, or they never respect them for those qualities, for which they are respected by men.</u> They in fact regard all such qualities as interfering with their <u>own pretensions,</u> and creating a jurisdiction different from their own. Women naturally wish

9. They don't synthesize ideas but rather "separate" them. Does this mean they can't compare issues, seeing things only in isolation?

10. Women go with the first idea, don't reason through alternatives. Where is his evidence?

11. The evidence is that the author has met only "one reasonable woman"! How absurd!

12. Women have accomplished little intellectually; they are only talented in artistic areas and in falling in love.

13. Women only respect aspects of men that men themselves do not respect.

to have their favourites all to themselves, and flatter their weaknesses to make them more dependent on their own good opinion, which, they think, is all they want. We have, indeed, seen instances of <u>men,</u> equally respectable and amiable, equally admired by the women and esteemed by the men, but <u>who have been ruined by an excess of virtues and accomplishments.</u>

14. Women flatter men and try to make them dependent on the woman's good opinion of them.

As these notes suggest, the primary point of Hazlitt's essay—that he is against education for women—is supported by "evidence" that few today would consider persuasive. The essay is full of overstatement as well as prejudice presented as fact. By the end, it has even veered away from its own point—about education for women—to indulge in a diatribe about how being around women is bad for men in general!

Your notes during an actual examination will probably not be complete sentences; they may be just a word or two in the margins. But they should indicate areas where you think the writer is making a major point or going way off track, where you see evidence for his/her point, where you see that there is a problem with the "evidence," and where you either agree with or question a point the essay is making. Your underlinings should help you identify and discuss the main ideas when you write your own essay in response to the given prompt.

C. Outlining "Education of Women"

Notice that the statements you have underlined as well as your marginal notes have effectively created an outline of the major points of the essay and your response to them! While you are practicing for the Advanced Placement Examination, it's a good idea for you to write out an outline based on these underlinings and notes. During the actual exam, you likely won't have time to do so. But you should at least glance over your underlinings and notes before you start to write your response so that you are familiar with the major points you will be critiquing in your essay.

D. Summarizing "Education of Women"

As you read the outline you wrote or as you re-read the underlinings you made and the notes you jotted down, you should see that Hazlitt's essay is clearly an opinionated discussion of why women are not suited for education. Women are "born to" certain frivolous qualities of mind and behavior and lack the mental capacity to reason, particularly in any principled fashion. The outline of key points and supporting statements leads you rather pointedly to this conclusion. It also becomes clearer how much Hazlitt relies on "accepted" opinion and his own experience rather than demonstrable proof.

We have just undertaken previewing, annotating, outlining, and summarizing the elements of "Get the Facts Straight." Very often at the conclusion of this stage of critical reading, the reader begins to get a handle on the text. The remaining five strategies after "Get the Facts Straight" seem to flow readily and speedily. To recap, these remaining five strategies are:

2. Analyze the argument.

3. Identify basic features of style.

4. Explore your personal response.

5. Evaluate the text overall and determine its significance.

6. Compare and contrast related texts.

Let's apply these remaining five strategies to Hazlitt's "Education of Women."

2. Analyze the Argument

An analysis examines a whole as the sum of its parts. Another brief look at the outline of "Education of Women" reveals the parts of Hazlitt's argument. In short, women should not be educated because they lack the qualities education enhances. They lack the capacity to entertain ideas because they have no passion for truth and hate to think. Women are naturally predisposed to acting precipitously rather than thoughtfully, with the use of reasoning. Evidence for these statements may be found in the lack of female contributions to human knowledge. Women can "perform" and fall in love, but they can do little else. In short, things that require judgment are not suitable activities for women.

Hazlitt's essay has a rather simple argumentative structure. He declares that women are not educable and then provides "reasons" why. Hazlitt's "reasons" are primarily opinions, offered without any backing except the assertion that women have achieved little. By the end of the essay, he is totally off-topic, having moved from discussing the education of women to asserting that they are inferior human beings who bring out the weaker sides of men and are thus dangerous to them.

Analysis reveals that Hazlitt's essay has little to offer in support of the opinion it presents. Further, its statements seem more an emotional outpouring than a reasonable explanation. (Careful readers will also note how difficult it is to view Hazlitt's remarks in an unprejudiced fashion—the twentieth-century reader will, in all probability, find his assertions a bit ridiculous.)

3. Identify Basic Features of Style

Stylistically, Hazlitt's essay may be described as a series of blunt statements followed by reflection on how the statement is manifested in his culture. Hazlitt draws on anecdotal support—his observations of the women of his day, a line from Milton, and his own lack of knowledge of women's accomplishments. His essay seems a collection of accepted or common knowledge: he writes as though his "reasons" are generally agreed upon, undisputed statements of fact. This structure suggests that because something is widely believed, readers should accept it. Thus, the tone is both authoritative and perhaps a bit annoyed—annoyed with the problems women present.

Hazlitt's diction is largely straightforward, more plain than flowery. A few of the words and phrases he chooses have powerful or dramatic connotations, such as "pervert," "mere egoists," "perfect nonentity," "downright affectation," "hate to think," and "no passion for truth." But he relies largely on ordinary language and sentence structure. Only occasionally does he indulge in a sophisticated use of language. For example, in the sentence "The writer of this article confesses that he never met with any woman who could reason, and with but one reasonable woman," Hazlitt shifts the modal verb "could reason" to the adjective "reasonable" with memorable effect. By and large, however, his sentences are simple declaratives, not difficult to read or interpret and not especially memorable stylistically.

This is an appropriate time to mention that most of the literary and rhetorical terms used in this discussion and the others that follow are included in the glossary at the end of these chapters on critical reading and writing.

4. Explore Your Personal Response

While nineteenth-century readers—especially men—might have nodded in agreement as Hazlitt offered reasons women shouldn't be educated, many contemporary readers are likely to be surprised by his statements, perhaps even offended by them.

Review your responses in the annotations to the text. They will help re-create your personal reactions and the causes for those reactions. Do not always expect to agree with, or even to appreciate, a writer's point of view. You will find yourself disagreeing with texts rather regularly. The important thing is to be certain you can account for the sources and causes of your disagreement. Much of reader disagreement with Hazlitt's essay rests in what we would consider a more enlightened perspective on the abilities of women. An awareness of historical context does help explain "Education of Women," but it probably doesn't enhance contemporary sympathy for Hazlitt's position.

5. Evaluate the Text Overall and Determine its Significance

Determining the significance of the text you've read is important in your academic courses and in the synthesis question that characterizes the AP English Language and Composition Exam from 2007 onward. On other questions, you may not have the background knowledge necessary to put the text you're given into context. Still, any time you can do so, you will have contributed something significant to your response that many other students will not have done.

In this particular case, Hazlitt's essay "Education of Women" was a product of early nineteenth-century sensibilities. Its chief significance today is as a representative of its time, an indicator of a social and intellectual climate much different than our own. As a citizen of the Romantic period preceding the Victorian age, Hazlitt expresses an understanding of women that today we would deem, at the very least, incomplete.

6. Compare and Contrast Related Texts

A complete analysis of Hazlitt's essay would include a comparison of other essays of his, if available, on the subject of women and education. It would also be useful to examine other early nineteenth-century essays on this subject, and lastly, to contrast Hazlitt's essay with present-day essays that argue for and against the education of women. Such a detailed analysis, involving much research into external sources, is not feasible on any timed examination. However, the basic *principle* behind the idea—to synthesize information from several sources in order to better understand a basic idea or proposal—is now the source of the *synthesis question* on the new (from 2007) AP English Language and Composition Exam. This type of question is similar to the *Document Based Questions* on various Advanced Placement History Examinations and requires reading several excerpted sources for information on a common topic and then writing an essay that takes information from three of those sources to support its thesis. On other essays and in the multiple-choice section of the AP English Language and Composition Exam, the need to bring in information or perspectives from more than one work is very limited.

The very *active* reading strategies employed on Hazlitt's essay "Education of Women" can be used with any text to help you "re-create" it with optimal effectiveness. That is to say, you as a reader should be able to approximate very closely the original authorial intentions as well as understand the general audience response and your more particular individual response. The AP Course in Language and Composition is designed to help you practice these skills, while the AP Examination in English Language and Composition tests your mastery of them. In order to gain further valuable practice with these critical reading strategies, you may wish to read the following short essays. Remember to work with the six strategies in sequence. They are:

1. Get the facts straight.

    a. Preview

    b. Annotate

    c. Outline

    d. Summarize

2. Analyze the argument.

3. Identify basic features of style.

4. Explore your personal response.

5. Evaluate the text overall and determine its significance.

6. Compare and contrast related texts.

Read the following sample essays, each with brief comments by a professional reader employing the six strategies. These comments should enable you to check your own responses for accuracy and thoroughness. Once you become familiar with these strategies, they should become almost second nature to you and easy to employ. This familiarity is your best tool for success on the AP Examination in English Language and Composition.

Sample Essay #1

Female Suffrage

I have read the long list of lady petitioners in favor of female suffrage, and as a husband and a father I want to protest against the whole business. It will never do to allow women to vote. It will never do to allow them to hold office. You know, and I know, that if they were granted these privileges there would be no more peace on earth. They would swamp the country with debt. They like to hold office too well. They like to be Mrs. President Smith of the Dorcas Society,[1] or Mrs. Secretary Jones of the Hindoo aid association, or Mrs. Treasurer of something or other. They are fond of the distinction of the thing, you know; they revel in the sweet jingle of the title. They are always setting up sanctified confederations of all kinds, and then running for president of them. They are even so fond of office that they are willing to serve without pay. But you allow them to vote and to go to the Legislature once, and then see how it will be. They will go to work and start a thousand more societies, and cram them full of salaried offices. You will see a state of things that will stir your feelings to the bottom of your pockets. The first fee bill would exasperate you some. Instead of the usual schedule for judges, State printer, Supreme court clerks, etc., the list would read something like this:

OFFICES AND SALARIES

President Dorcas Society	$4,000
Subordinate Officers of same, each	2,000
President Ladies' Union Prayer Meeting	3,000
President Pawnee Educational Society	4,000
President Of Ladies' Society for Dissemination of Belles Lettres among the Shoshones	5,000
State Crinoline Directress	10,000
State Superintendent of Waterfalls	10,000
State Hair Oil Inspectress	10,000
State Milliner	50,000

You know what a state of anarchy and social chaos that fee bill would create. Every woman in the commonwealth of Missouri would let go everything

[1] The Dorcas Society was a benevolent religious organization for women.

and run for State Milliner. And instead of ventilating each other's political antecedents, as men do, they would go straight after each other's private moral character. (I know them—they are all like my wife.) Before the canvass was three days old it would be an established proposition that every woman in the state was "no better than she ought to be." Only think how it would lacerate me to have an opposition candidate say that about my wife. That is the idea, you know—having other people say these hard things. Now, I know that my wife isn't any better than she ought to be, poor devil—in fact, in matters of orthodox doctrine, she is particularly shaky—but I still would not like these things aired in a political contest. I don't really suppose that woman will stand any more show hereafter than—however, she may improve—she may even become a beacon light for the saving of others—but if she does, she will burn rather dim, and she will flicker a good deal, too. But, as I was saying, a female political canvass would be an outrageous thing.

Think of the torch-light processions that would distress our eyes. Think of the curious legends on the transparencies: "Robbins forever! Vote for Sallie Robbins, the only virtuous candidate in the field!"

And this: "Chastity, modesty, patriotism! Let the great people stand by Maria Sanders, the champion of morality and progress, and the only candidate with a stainless reputation."

And this: "Vote for Judy McGinniss, the incorruptible! Nine children— one at the breast!"

In that day a man shall say to his servant, "What is the matter with the baby?" And the servant shall reply, "It has been sick for hours." "And where is its mother?" "She is out electioneering for Sallie Robbins." And such conversations as these shall transpire between ladies and servants applying for situations. "Can you cook?" "Yes." "Wash?" "Yes." "Do general housework?" "Yes." "All right; who is your choice for State Milliner?" "Judy McGinniss." "Well, you can tramp." And women shall talk politics instead of discussing the fashions; and they shall neglect the duties of the household to go out and take a drink with candidates; and men shall nurse the baby while their wives travel to the polls to vote. And also in that day the man who hath beautiful whiskers shall beat the homely man of wisdom for Governor, and the youth who waltzes with exquisite grace shall be Chief of Police, in preference to the man of practiced sagacity and determined energy.

Every man, I take it, has a selfish end in view when he pours out elo- quence in behalf of the public good in the newspapers, and such is the case with me. I do not want the privileges of women extended, because my wife already holds office in nineteen different infernal female associations and I have to do all her clerking. If you give the women full sweep with the men in political affairs, she will proceed to run for every confounded office under the new dispensation. That will finish me. It is bound to finish me. She would not have time to do anything at all then, and the one solitary thing I have shirked up to the present time would fall on me and my family would go to destruction; for I am *not* qualified for a wet nurse.

—Mark Twain (1867)

Commentary on Mark Twain's "Female Suffrage"

Although this essay by famous American humorist Mark Twain also casts women in a less than favorable light, it is done in a light-hearted, hyperbolic fashion rather than with Hazlitt's straightforward seriousness. Contemporary readers are much less likely to take offense at Twain's intentional overstatement. His humorous, manufactured legislative offices, for example, "State Milliner" (hatmaker) and "Crinoline Directress" (petticoat manager), are intentionally facetious. This exaggerated style is a clue to Twain's intentions. Rather than mounting a serious argument about the unsuitability of women for legislative office, Twain is spoofing the results of women voting and holding office. The reader doesn't come away with the impression that Twain feels real rancor towards women, or completely lacks respect for their abilities, as Hazlitt seems to. A brief look at some textual evidence reveals why this is so.

Twain's list of "Offices and Salaries" created by women who vote and "go to the legislature" (take office) is delightfully silly. "Superintendent of Waterfalls" is not biting satire, but openly, lightheartedly ludicrous. Later Twain compares men and women politicians, saying that "instead of ventilating each other's political antecedents, as men do, they [women] would go straight after each other's private moral character." And he parenthetically adds, "I know them—they are all like my wife." Here Twain is actually commenting on the superiority of the feminine perspective on suitability for office. Moral character is certainly a better measure of a person running for public office than their political connections. Twain's aside, which is generalizing from a particular, is an obvious humorous ploy, since Twain would not marry until three years after this essay was written.

Twain also compares the woman legislator to a "beacon light for the saving of others." He extends this metaphor when he predicts that "she will burn rather dim, and she will flicker a good deal." This metaphor may be interpreted as a suggestion that women are fallible and inconstant; still, they *are* a "beacon light" for others.

Twain ends the essay with a prediction that women will "talk politics instead of…fashion" and "neglect the duties of the household," and "men shall nurse the baby while their wives travel to the polls to vote." Furthermore, Twain's own circumstances will change. "That will finish me. It is bound to finish me." (Repetition for comedic effect is particularly well done here.) "She would not have time to do anything at all then, and the one solitary thing I have shirked up to the present time would fall on me and my family would go to destruction; for I am *not* qualified for a wet nurse." Twain's joking about male selfishness is nicely capped with a final punch line. Twain's essay is marked by a number of stylistic features that contribute to his hyperbolic humor. Though only a few examples have been mentioned, it is readily clear that Twain's essay is meant as a playful jibe, poking as much fun at men as it does women.

Sample Essay #2

The Handsome and Deformed Leg

There are two sorts of people in the world, who with equal degrees of health, and wealth, and the other comforts of life, become, the one happy, and the other miserable. This arises very much from the different views in which they consider things, persons, and events; and the effect of those different views upon their own minds.

In whatever situation men can be placed, they may find conveniences and inconveniences: in whatever company, they may find persons and conversation more or less pleasing; at whatever table, they may meet with meats and drinks of better and worse taste, dishes better and worse dressed; in whatever climate they will find good and bad weather; under whatever government, they may find good and bad laws, and good and bad administration of those laws; in whatever poem or work of genius they may see faults and beauties; in almost every face and every person, they may discover fine features and defects, good and bad qualities.

Under these circumstances, the two sorts of people above mentioned fix their attention,—those who are disposed to be happy, on the conveniences of things, the pleasant parts of conversation, the well-dressed dishes, the goodness of the wines, the fine weather, etc., and enjoy all with cheerfulness. Those who are to be unhappy, think and speak only of the contraries. Hence they are continually discontented themselves, and by their remarks sour the pleasures of society, offend personally many people, and make themselves everywhere disagreeable.

If this turn of mind was founded in nature, such unhappy persons would be the more to be pitied. But as the disposition to criticize and to be disgusted, is perhaps taken up originally by imitation, and is unawares grown into a habit, which though at present strong may nevertheless be cured when those who have it are convinced of its bad effects on their felicity. I hope this little admonition may be of service to them, and put them on changing a habit, which, though in the exercise it is chiefly an act of imagination, yet has serious consequences in life, as it brings on real griefs and misfortunes. For as many are offended by, and nobody well loves this sort of people, no one shows them more than the most common civility and respect, and scarcely that; and this frequently puts them out of humor, and draws them into disputes and contentions. If they aim at obtaining some advantage in rank or fortune, nobody wishes them success, or will stir a step, or speak a word, to favor their pretensions. If they incur public censure or disgrace, no one will defend or excuse, and many join to aggravate their misconduct and render them completely odious.

If these people will not change this bad habit, and condescend to be pleased with what is pleasing, without fretting themselves and others about the contraries, it is good for others to avoid an acquaintance with them, which is always disagreeable, and sometimes very inconvenient, especially when one finds one's self entangled in their quarrels.

An old philosophical friend of mine was grown from experience very cautious in this particular, and carefully avoided any intimacy with such people. He had, like other philosophers, a thermometer to show him the heat of the weather, and a barometer to mark when it was likely to prove good or bad; but, there being no instrument invented to discover, at first sight, this unpleasing disposition in a person, he for that purpose made use of his legs; one of which was remarkably handsome, the other by some accident, crooked and deformed. If a stranger, at the first interview, regarded his ugly leg more than his handsome one, he doubted him. If he spoke of it, and took no notice of the handsome leg, that was sufficient to determine my philosopher to have no further acquaintance with him. Everybody has not this two-legged instrument; but everyone, with a little attention, may observe signs of that carping, fault-finding disposition, and take the same resolution of avoiding acquaintance of those infected with it. I therefore advise those critical, querulous, discontented, unhappy people, that if they wish to be respected and beloved by others, and happy in themselves, they should *leave off looking at the ugly leg*.

—Ben Franklin (1780)

Commentary on Ben Franklin's "The Handsome and Deformed Leg"

Ben Franklin, noted inventor, philosopher, and eighteenth-century statesman, wrote prolifically on the morals of his time. In this essay he sets up a dichotomy and proceeds to investigate it. The dichotomy involves two sorts of people—those "who are disposed to be happy" and those "who are to be unhappy." Stylistically, Franklin is adept in this essay at stringing sets of opposites together in long list-like constructions. The second paragraph of the essay, for example, creates a rather comprehensive catalogue of the circumstances of life, in both its positive *and* negative aspects. Franklin uses this list to set up situations which people invariably react to. His essay is, in short, a commentary on the quality of those reactions.

Franklin calls his essay a "little admonition" and offers it as a service to others. Franklin is famous for his prescriptions for happy life, and this essay fits well within that category.

A few words about Franklin's title are well worth mentioning. Previewing the text inevitably focuses in on this rather perplexing title: the reader wonders whether Franklin intends it literally or figuratively. The answer comes in the concluding paragraph, which is an anecdote based on a philosopher friend's deformity. This fellow, lacking an instrument like a thermometer or barometer to discover unhappy, disagreeable people, made use of his legs—one handsome, one crooked and deformed. This philosopher felt that persons with a "carping, fault-finding disposition" would regard "his ugly leg more than his handsome one" and would even "speak of" the ugly leg. The philosopher would then "have no further acquaintance with him." Franklin concludes the anecdote and his essay with his advice: "I therefore advise those critical, querulous, discontented, unhappy people, that if they wish to be respected and beloved by others, and happy in themselves, they should *leave off looking at the ugly leg.*" The title and the anecdote are now linked, and Franklin's advisory essay is firmly rooted, via analogy, in the reader's mind.

Sample Essay #3

The following text is an excerpt of a long essay by Charles Lamb.

A Bachelor's Complaint
of the Behaviour of Married People

As a single man, I have spent a good deal of my time in noting down the infirmities of Married People, to console myself for those superior pleasures, which they tell me I have lost by remaining as I am.

I cannot say that the quarrels of men and their wives ever made any great impression upon me, or had much tendency to strengthen me in those antisocial resolutions which I took up long ago upon more substantial considerations. What oftenest offends me at the houses of married persons where I visit, is an error of quite a different description;—it is that they are too loving.

Not too loving neither; that does not explain my meaning. Besides, why should that offend me? The very act of separating themselves from the rest of the world, to have the fuller enjoyment of each other's society, implies that they prefer one another to all the world.

But what I complain of is, that they carry this preference so undisguisedly, they perk it up in the faces of us single people so shamelessly, you cannot be in their company a moment without being made to feel, by some indirect hint or open avowal, that *you* are not the object of this preference. Now there are some things which give no offence, while implied or taken for granted merely; but expressed, there is much offence in them. If a man were to accost the first homely-featured or plain-dressed young woman of his acquaintance, and tell her bluntly, that she was not handsome or rich enough for him, and he could not marry her, he would deserve to be kicked for his ill-manners; yet no less is implied in the fact, that having access and opportunity of putting the question to her, he has never yet thought fit to do it. The young woman understands this as clearly as if it were put into words; but no reasonable young woman would think of making this the ground of a quarrel. Just as little right have a married couple to tell me by speeches, and looks that are scarce less plain than speeches, that I am not the happy man,—the lady's choice. It is enough that I know I am not: I do not want this perpetual reminding.

The display of superior knowledge or riches may be made sufficiently mortifying, but these admit of a palliative. The knowledge which is brought out to insult me, may accidentally improve me; and in the rich man's houses and pictures,—his parks and gardens, I have a temporary usufruct at least. But the display of married happiness has none of these palliatives: it is throughout pure, unrecompensed, unqualified insult.

Marriage by its best title is a monopoly, and not of the least invidious sort. It is the cunning of most possessors of any exclusive privilege to keep their advantage as much out of sight as possible, that their less favoured neighbours, seeing little of the benefit, may the less be disposed to question the right. But these married monopolists thrust the most obnoxious part of their patent into our faces.

Nothing is to me more distasteful than that entire complacency and satisfaction which beam in the countenances of a new-married couple,—in that of the lady particularly: it tells you, that her lot is disposed of in this world: that *you* can have no hopes of her. It is true, I have none: nor wishes either, perhaps: but this is one of those truths which ought, as I said before, to be taken for granted, not expressed.

The excessive airs which those people give themselves, rounded on the ignorance of us unmarried people, would be more offensive if they were less irrational. We will allow them to understand the mysteries belonging to their own craft better than we, who have not had the happiness to be made free of the company: but their arrogance is not content within these limits. If a single person presumes to offer his opinion in their presence, though upon the most indifferent subject, he is immediately silenced as an incompetent person. Nay, a young married lady of my acquaintance, who, the best of the jest was, had not changed her condition above a fortnight before, in a question on which I had the misfortune to differ from her, respecting the properest mode of breeding oysters for the London market, had the assurance to ask with a sneer, how such an old Bachelor as I could pretend to know anything about such matters!

But what I have spoken of hitherto is nothing to the airs which these creatures give themselves when they come, as they generally do, to have children. When I consider how little of a rarity children are,—that every street and blind alley swarms with them,—that the poorest people commonly have them in most abundance,—that there are few marriages that are not blest with at least one of these bargains,—how often they turn out ill, and defeat the fond hopes of their parents, taking to vicious courses, which end in poverty, disgrace, the gallows, etc.—I cannot for my life tell what cause for pride there can possibly be in having them. If they were young phoenixes, indeed, that were born but one in a year, there might be a pretext. But when they are so common—

I do not advert to the insolent merit which they assume with their husbands on these occasions. Let *them* look to that. But why *we*, who are not their natural-born subjects, should be expected to bring our spices, myrrh, and incense,—our tribute and homage of admiration,—I do not see.

"Like as the arrows in the hand of the giant, even so are the young children"; so says the excellent office in our Prayer-book appointed for the churching of women. "Happy is the man that hath his quiver full of them." So say I, but then don't let him discharge his quiver upon us that are weaponless;—let them be arrows, but not to gall and stick us. I have generally observed that these arrows are double-headed: they have two forks, to be sure to hit with one or the other. As for instance, where you come into a house which is full of children, if you happen to take no notice of them (you are thinking of something else, perhaps, and turn a deaf ear to their innocent caresses), you are set down as untractable, morose, a hater of children. On the other hand, if you find them more than usually engaging,—if you are taken with their pretty manners, and set about in earnest to romp and play with them,—some pretext or other is sure to be found for sending them out of the room; they are too noisy or boisterous, or Mr. _____ does not like children. With one or other of these forks the arrow is sure to hit you.

I could forgive their jealousy, and dispense with toying with their brats, if it gives them any pain; but I think it unreasonable to be called upon to *love* them, where I see no occasion,—to love a whole family, perhaps eight, nine, or ten, indiscriminately,—to love all the pretty dears, because children are so engaging!

—Charles Lamb (1825)

Commentary on the Excerpt from Charles Lamb's "A Bachelor's Complaint of the Behaviour of Married People"

Lamb's essay opens with a summary of his essential thesis, and the remaining text is an amplification of that thesis. Lamb objects to married people for several reasons. He says first that they are too loving but clarifies this by saying loving in and of itself is not the real issue, rather married people's carrying their "preference [for one another] so undisguisedly" that they make single people feel that they "are not the object of this preference." In short, Lamb's problem is not the married state itself, but the air of superiority married people attach to it and the propensity of married people to display their "state" for the improvement of single folk. He goes on to say that the "display of married happiness has none of these palliatives: it is throughout pure, unrecompensed, unqualified insult." Here he does more than lament marriage's "superior" stance: he almost seems envious of it.

Lamb is fond of elevated diction. Words like palliative ("reduction of pain or intensity"), usufruct ("enjoyment"), and patent (meaning "contract") appear throughout Lamb's text. Similarly, his syntax is often rather complicated, sometimes masking his satiric barbs under an elitist syntactic respectability. Take this sentence as an example: "The excessive airs which those people give themselves, rounded on the ignorance of us unmarried people, would be more offensive if they were less irrational." This "more-less" construction accuses the married folk of several sins: excessive airs, ignorance, and irrationality. In fact, it is only this irrationality that saves them from being even more offensive. This jab satirizing the married state is framed in a sentence requiring rather careful processing to achieve understanding. Lamb seems to relish poking fun in this complex way.

Lamb includes a humorous anecdote about a "young married lady of his acquaintance." In fact, this young married woman was married less than two weeks (a fortnight), when she "sneered" about Lamb, "old Bachelor" that he was, "pretending" to know about breeding oysters for market. The reader is expected to smile here at the young woman's lack of experience at being married, but also at the foolish notion that marriage somehow dispenses an immediate knowledge of commerce that bachelors aren't privy to. Lamb laughs gently, not acerbically. His tone is bemused, not intolerant.

The selection ends with a commentary on the further airs married people put on when they have children. Lamb speaks so disparagingly of children that his remarks have become funny. Lamb laments, "If they were young phoenixes…but when they are so common——." The mythical phoenix, which rises up from its own ashes every five hundred years, is contrasted with those "so little a rarity," children. Lamb finds a rather involved way of stating that children are abundant. He then alludes to Christ's nativity when he speaks of parents expecting homage, indeed "spices, myrrh and incense," from appropriately doting single people. Here Lamb suggests that parents consider their children nothing less than divine. He ends with the elaborate metaphoric joke comparing children to arrows, double-headed arrows, "to be sure to hit with one or the other (head)." The explanation of the metaphor follows. When you enter a house full of children and fail to notice them properly, you are "untractable, morose, a hater of children," the first half of the double-headed arrow. But if you play with them in earnest (the second half of the arrow), they are sent out of the room. Guests cannot be too popular with the children; parental jealousy sets in. This is clearly a no-win situation for the unsuspecting single person. The double-headed arrow strikes, one way or the other.

Lamb's style, deliberately old-fashioned, is the voice of a bemused observer. He is less didactic than he is a satirist of the foibles he observes. In this essay, married people are the targets.

Conclusion

These commentaries are far from complete, but they begin to apply the most significant of the six critical reading strategies. Students preparing for the AP Examination in English Language and Composition should test their responses against these brief commentaries, and then move on to other essays, always attentive to the marriage of form and content that is the hallmark of excellent prose.

CHAPTER 3
AP English Language & Composition

Writing About the "Other" Literature: A Critical Dialogue

Critical Writing

As we discussed in the chapter on critical reading, *literature* is a term encompassing much more than the traditional genres of fiction, poetry, and drama. While some traditional literary genres are included, the AP Course in English Language & Composition and the AP Examination in English Language & Composition both feature a variety of other types of literature, chiefly nonfiction, especially the essay. In addition to demonstrable skill in critical reading of essays, biographies, journalistic prose, and political, historical, and scientific treatises, students are expected to write about these texts effectively. The primary form written responses take is the critical essay.

Writing as Dialogue

The critical essay may be thought of as a written dialogue with another text. The writer responds to the effects created by a text he or she has read, not with a mere overflow of feeling, but with a keenly critical eye, looking to the *how* of the text under scrutiny as well as the *what*. Most readers of *Beloved*, the Pulitzer Prize-winning novel by Toni Morrison, will vividly recall moments when the text overwhelmed them emotionally. When Sethe, a black mother, tries to kill her own children rather than give them up to slavers, reactions of fear, pity, love, and even loathing are reported. Though these reactions to the text are sincere, they are "monologues," involved in the text of *Beloved* only indirectly. The critical writer becomes involved directly and enters into dialogue with the text by attempting to discern how it created the responses it did. The critical writer may also take issue with a text. In each case, however, whether the reader agrees or disagrees with the important points in a text, the sense of dialogue is of primary importance to writing critically about a text. Without such a sense of strong interaction with the text as it unfolds, the written response will be either a superficial expression of emotion or a banal summary of what took place. Dialogue is crucial to critical writing. In the previous chapter on critical reading, much useful information is afforded the critical writer as well.

It is good practice to apply the six strategies for critical reading to any text that you eventually have to write about. These six strategies are the beginning of the dialogue you'll enter into with any text. Putting your dialogue into words is the next challenge and the focus of this chapter.

Writing for the AP Examination

The English Language and Composition exam assumes that students are fluent in standard English syntax and grammar. They are also expected to be able to organize their thoughts in coherent, well-expressed expository prose. Most will be amply familiar with the standard five-paragraph theme with its introduction, three body paragraphs, and conclusion. Beyond an ability to use this basic form, however, students need to be aware of the different stylistic effects created by different syntactic and lexical choices. That is to say, when students choose a particular word or construct a very short or very complex sentence, they need to be in control of their choices, realizing how these choices affect their readers. They need to be aware of the effects of the text on the audience. This awareness is useful in both the analysis *and* creation of expository prose.

Fiction and poetry are natural locations for observing syntactic choice and diction, but exploring the rhetoric of nonfiction reinforces the strategies the AP Exam expects students to employ in their own prose. A key skill in writing about nonfiction is the ability to analyze stylistic strategies. In addition to analyzing prose style, students are asked to write argumentative essays (with appropriate support/evidence) in response to various readings. These readings are often excerpts rather than whole essays and thus offer additional challenges.

Strategies for Analysis and Argument

Since rhetorical analysis and argumentation are the two important expository forms, this chapter presents strategies for improving your work in these two forms. In short, you will gain more practice in creating dialogues with the texts you are asked to read and write about. These dialogues may be analytic or argumentative, but in both cases they employ critical acumen and style. Thus, the following chapter has two sections:

1. Analytic Writing: A Critical Dialogue

2. Argumentative Writing: A Critical Dialogue

1. Analytic Writing: A Critical Dialogue

Most competent writers know that an essay has three basic parts: a beginning, a middle, and an end. But that basic organizational scheme may be stretched and altered in many ways. Think of an essay draft as an unconditioned athlete. With practice, even ordinary people of average ability can stretch and tone their muscles until they are capable of impressive feats of athletic endurance, flexibility, and strength. Similarly, with practice, an essay can become much more than an ordinary five-paragraph theme. That essay, through proper attention to style, can become a toned and effective piece of rhetoric. ("Rhetoric" is meant here in its best sense—effective, compelling communication—rather than in its pejorative sense of sham or false persuasion.)

Starting with Style

In order to flex your essay-writing muscles, you must consider matters of style. Good analytic writing focuses both on a text's substance and style and is itself written in an appropriate style.

Writing critically *about* style and writing critically *with* style are our first concerns. Bearing in mind our framework of the dialogue, let's enter into a dialogue with a particular text and its style. In the following essay by Washington Irving, "The Voyage," several interesting stylistic strategies may be noted. In order to analyze Irving's work, you must be attentive to how these stylistic strategies support his thesis. In fact, voice, style, tone, and other rhetorical considerations are usually well-chosen reflections of an author's purpose and subject. Entering into a dialogue with a text can reveal how form and content reinforce one another—thus adding to the impact of the text.

Irving's essay is printed on the next page and the analytic response, in the form of a dialogue, follows. In order to prepare for your own analysis (and to better understand the professional analysis given), you should read Irving's essay using the same critical reading strategies recommended in the previous chapter. By

1. getting the facts straight,

2. analyzing the argument,

3. identifying basic features of style,

4. exploring your personal response,

5. evaluating the text overall and determining its significance, and

6. (to the extent you can) comparing and contrasting related texts,

you will muster a wealth of data about the text that will enable you to compose an astute analysis.

The Voyage

Ships, ships, I will descrie you
Amidst the main,
I will come and try you,
What are you protecting,
And projecting,
What's your end and aim.
One goes abroad for merchandise and trading,
Another stays to keep his country from invading,
A third is coming home with rich and wealthy lading.
Halloo! my fancie, whither wilt thou go?

Anon.

To an American visiting Europe, the long voyage he has to make is an excellent preparative. The temporary absence of worldly scenes and employments produces a state of mind particularly fitted to receive new and vivid impressions. The vast space of waters that separates the hemispheres is like a blank page in existence. There is no gradual transition by which, as in Europe, the features and population of one country blend almost imperceptibly with those of another. From the moment you lose sight of the land you have left, all is vacancy until you step on the opposite shore, and are launched at once into the bustle and novelties of another world.

In traveling by land there is a continuity of scene, and a connected succession of persons and incidents, that carry on the story of life, and lessen the effect of absence and separation. We drag, it is true, "a lengthening chain" at each remove of our pilgrimage; but the chain is unbroken: we can trace it back link by link; and we feel that the last still grapples us to home. But a wide sea voyage severs us at once. It makes us conscious of being cast loose from the secure anchorage of settled life, and sent adrift upon a doubtful world. It interposes a gulf, not merely imaginary, but real, between us and our homes—a gulf subject to tempest, and fear, and uncertainty, rendering distance palpable, and return precarious.

Such, at least, was the case with myself. As I saw the last blue line of my native land fade away like a cloud in the horizon, it seemed as if I had closed one volume of the world and its concerns, and had time for meditation, before I opened another. That land, too, now vanishing from my view, which contained all most dear to me in life; what vicissitudes might occur in it—what changes might take place in me, before I should visit it again! Who can tell, when he sets forth to wander, whither he may be driven by the uncertain currents of existence; or when he may return; or whether it may ever be his lot to revisit the scenes of his childhood?

I said that at sea all is vacancy; I should correct the expression. To one given to day-dreaming, and fond of losing himself in reveries, a sea voyage is full of subjects for meditation; but then they are the wonders of the deep, and of the air, and rather tend to abstract the mind from worldly themes. I delighted to loll over the quarter-railing, or climb to the maintop, of a calm day, and muse for hours together on the tranquil bosom of a summer's sea; to gaze upon the piles of golden clouds just peering above the horizon, to fancy them some fairy realms, and people them with a creation of my own;—to watch the gentle undulating billows, rolling their silver volumes, as if to die away on those happy shores.

There was a delicious sensation of mingled security and awe with which I looked down, from my giddy height, on the monsters of the deep at their uncouth gambols. Shoals of porpoises tumbling about in the bow of the ship; the grampus slowly heaving his huge form above the surface; or the ravenous shark, darting, like a spectre, through the blue waters. My imagination would conjure up all that I had heard or read of the watery world beneath me; of the finny herds that roam its fathomless valleys; of the shapeless monsters that lurk among the very foundations of the earth; and of those wild phantasms that swell the tales of fishermen and sailors.

Sometimes a distant sail, gliding along the edge of the ocean, would be another theme of idle speculation. How interesting this fragment of a world, hastening to rejoin the great mass of existence! What a glorious monument of human invention; which has in a manner triumphed over wind and wave; has brought the ends of the world into communion; has established an interchange of blessings, pouring into the sterile regions of the north all the luxuries of the south; has diffused the light of knowledge and the charities of cultivated life; and has thus bound together those scattered portions of the human race, between which nature seemed to have thrown an insurmountable barrier.

We one day descried some shapeless object drifting at a distance. At sea, everything that breaks the monotony of the surrounding expanse attracts attention. It proved to be the mast of a ship that must have been completely wrecked; for there were the remains of handkerchiefs, by which some of the crew had fastened themselves to this spar, to prevent their being washed off by the waves. There was no trace by which the name of the ship could be ascertained. The wreck had evidently drifted about for many months; clusters of shell-fish had fastened about it, and long seaweeds flaunted at its sides. But where, thought I, is the crew? Their struggle has long been over—they have gone down amidst the roar of the tempest—their bones lie whitening among the caverns of the deep. Silence, oblivion, like the waves, have closed over them, and no one can tell the story of their end. What sighs have been wafted after that ship! What prayers offered up at the deserted fireside of home! How often has the mistress, the wife, the mother, pored over the daily news, to catch some casual intelligence of this rover of the deep! How has expectation darkened into anxiety—anxiety into dread—and dread into despair! Alas! not one momento may ever return for love to cherish. All that may ever be known, is, that she sailed from her port, "and was never heard of more!"

The sight of this wreck, as usual, gave rise to many dismal anecdotes. This was particularly the case in the evening, when the weather, which had hitherto been fair, began to look wild and threatening, and gave indications of one of those sudden storms which will sometimes break in upon the serenity of a summer voyage. As we sat round the dull light of a lamp in the cabin, that made the gloom more ghastly, everyone had his tale of shipwreck and disaster. I was particularly struck with a short one related by the captain.

"As I was once sailing," said he, "in a fine stout ship across the banks of Newfoundland, one of those heavy fogs which prevail in those parts rendered it impossible for us to see far ahead even in the daytime; but at night the weather was so thick that we could not distinguish any object at twice the length of the ship. I kept lights at the mast-head, and a constant watch forward to look out for fishing smacks, which are accustomed to lie at anchor on the banks. The wind was blowing a smacking breeze, and we were going at a great rate through the water. Suddenly the watch gave the alarm of 'a sail ahead!'—it was scarcely uttered before we were upon her. She was a small schooner, at anchor, with her broadside towards us. The crew were all asleep, and had neglected to hoist a light. We struck her just amid-ships. The force, the size, and weight of our vessel bore her down below the waves; we passed over her and were hurried on our course. As the crashing wreck was sinking beneath us, I had a glimpse of two or three half-naked wretches rushing from her cabin; they just started from their beds to be swallowed shrieking by the waves. I heard their drowning cry mingling with the wind. The blast that bore it to our ears swept us out of all farther hearing. I shall never forget that cry! It was some time before we could put the ship about, she was under such headway. We returned, as nearby as we could guess, to the place where the smack had anchored. We cruised about for several hours in the dense fog. We fired signal guns, and listened if we might hear the halloo of any survivors: but all was silent—we never saw or heard anything of them more."

I confess these stories, for a time, put an end to all my fine fancies. The storm increased with the night. The sea was lashed into tremendous confusion. There was a fearful, sullen sound of rushing waves, and broken surges. Deep called unto deep. At times the black volume of clouds over head seemed rent asunder by flashes of lightning which quivered along the foaming billows, and made the succeeding darkness doubly terrible. The thunders bellowed over the wild waste of waters, and were echoed and pro-longed by the mountain waves. As I saw the ship staggering and plunging among these roaring caverns, it seemed miraculous that she regained her balance, or preserved her buoyancy. Her yards would dip into the water: her bow was almost buried beneath the waves. Sometimes an impending surge appeared ready to overwhelm her, and nothing but a dexterous movement of the helm preserved her from the shock.

When I retired to my cabin, the awful scene still followed me. The whistling of the wind through the rigging sounded like funeral wailings. The creaking of the masts, the straining and groaning of the bulk-heads, as the ship labored in the weltering sea, were frightful. As I heard the waves rush-ing along the sides of the ship, and roaring in my very ear, it seemed as if Death were raging round this floating prison, seeking for his prey: the mere starting of a nail, the yawning of a seam, might give him entrance.

A fine day, however, with a tranquil sea and favoring breeze, soon put all these dismal reflections to flight. It is impossible to resist the gladden-ing influence of fine weather and fair wind at sea. When the ship is decked out in all her canvas, every sail swelled, and careering gayly over the curling waves, how lofty, how gallant she appears—how she seems to lord it over the deep!

I might fill a volume with the reveries of a sea voyage, for with me it is almost a continual reverie—but it is time to get to shore.

It was a fine sunny morning when the thrilling cry of "land!" was given from the mast-head. None but those who have experienced it can form an idea of the delicious throng of sensations which rush into an American's bosom, when he first comes in sight of Europe. There is a volume of associations with the very name. It is the land of promise, teeming with everything of which his childhood has heard, or on which his studious years have pondered.

From that time until the moment of arrival, it was all feverish excitement. The ships of war, that prowled like guardian giants along the coast; the headlands of Ireland, stretching out into the channel; the Welsh mountains, towering into the clouds; all were objects of intense interest. As we sailed up the Mersey, I reconnoitered the shores with a telescope. My eye dwelt with delight on neat cottages, with their trim shrubberies and green grass plots. I saw the mouldering ruin of an abbey overrun with ivy, and the taper spire of a village church rising from the brown of a neighboring hill—all were characteristic of England.

The tide and wind were so favorable that the ship was enabled to come at once to the pier. It was thronged with people; some, idle lookers-on, others, eager expectants of friends or relatives. I could distinguish the merchant to whom the ship was consigned. I knew him by his calculating brow and restless air. His hands were thrust into his pockets; he was whistling thoughtfully, and walking to and fro, a small space having been accorded him by the crowd, in deference to his temporary importance. There were repeated cheerings and salutations interchanged between the shore and the ship, as friends happened to recognize each other. I particularly noticed one woman of humble dress, but interesting demeanor. She was leaning forward from among the crowd; her eye hurried over the ship as it neared the shore, to catch some wished-for countenance. She seemed disappointed and agitated; when I heard a faint voice call her name. It was from a poor sailor who had been ill all the voyage, and had excited the sympathy of everyone on board. When the weather was fine, his messmates had spread a mattress for him on deck in the shade, but of late his illness had so increased, that he had taken to his hammock, and only breathed a wish that he might see his wife before he died. He had been helped on deck as we came up the river, and now was leaning against the shrouds, with a countenance so wasted, so pale, so ghastly, that it was no wonder even the eye of affection did not recognize him. But at the sound of his voice, her eye darted on his features; it read, at once, a whole volume of sorrow; she clasped her hands, uttered a faint shriek, and stood wringing them in silent agony.

All now was hurry and bustle. The meetings of acquaintances—the greetings of friends—the consultations of men of business. I alone was solitary and idle. I had no friend to meet, no cheering to receive. I stepped upon the land of my forefathers—but I felt that I was a stranger in the land.

—Washington Irving (1819)

Analytic Writing: A Critical Dialogue with Washington Irving's "The Voyage"

Irving begins his essay "The Voyage" by quoting an old poem—no author is mentioned. The poem muses about sailing ships and the various purposes for which they set to sea. This prefatory poem helps set the tone of Irving's essay. The critical reader/writer in dialogue with the text would begin by asking, "Why did Irving choose this introduction?" One answer seems readily apparent: the subject of the essay is a sea voyage, and Irving is simply setting the scene. However, the poem's focus on the purposes of sea voyages may be a link worth remembering and considering as the essay unfolds. Now that we have launched into our dialogue, let's change to a format that will help us visualize the reader's interaction with the text. From now on, the analytic questions and comments will come from a "Reader" and the "Text" of "The Voyage" will answer.

Reader: The text of "The Voyage" is an account of Irving's Atlantic crossing. There are several moments when Irving gives information about his feelings on the journey.

Text: Yes, in the third paragraph Irving speaks rather wistfully of America, "now vanishing from [his] view, which contained all most dear to [him] in life": he worries about what "vicissitudes" might occur in his absence and what changes might occur in himself. He wonders when he may return and even *if* he will return to "revisit the scenes of his childhood."

Reader: But Irving's trepidation isn't so powerful that it prevents him from sailing. The tone here, Irving's "voice," is best described as a mixture of wistful fondness for the familiar and a fearful curiosity about the future. This ambivalence is mirrored in the physical fact of Irving's sailing—he is between the old and the new.

Text: Irving begins by describing his daydreams at sea, romanticizing the "piles of golden clouds just peering above the horizon, to fancy them some fairy realms, and people them with a creation of my own;—to watch the gentle undulating billows, rolling their silver volumes, as if to die away on those happy shores."

Reader: These musings on the clouds and waves are a departure from Irving's earlier abstract philosophizing. Here, he is caught up in the wonders of the sea and waxes almost poetic. In fact, the following two paragraphs are filled with images and descriptions: the fourth paragraph is a series of metaphors about sea creatures (monsters gambol like lambs, porpoises are tumblers, sharks are spectres). The language here ("fathomless valleys," "shapeless monsters," "wild phantasms") is reminiscent of that used in the supernaturally charged "Legend of Sleepy Hollow," Irving's most famous work. Paragraph five is another philosophical ascent, speculating on a sail on a distant horizon. Here Irving harks back to the introductory poem of his opening. The sail is called a "fragment of the world, hastening to rejoin the great mass of existence." The sail, which stands for all types of sea-going vessels, brings the continents into contact with one another. Many purposes exist for travel by sea, but Irving sees them all as a way of binding "together those scattered portions of the human race." Perhaps he sees himself as a participant in the great cycle of connective journeys.

Text: Paragraph six describes passing the wreck of an unknown ship. Poignant details, like "the remains of handkerchiefs, by which some of the crew had fastened themselves to the spar, to prevent their being washed off by the waves," are abundant in this section.

Reader: Yes, Irving asks where the crew is and speaks sadly of their "bones whitening" in the deep. When he speaks of the "sighs wafting after that ship," and the "prayers offered up at the deserted fireside of home," it's not difficult to imagine the anxiety of Irving's own friends and relatives as he set out on his long, dangerous voyage. The description of the wreck indirectly suggests Irving's fearfulness. More of the same is found in the Captain's anecdote, which follows.

Text: The Captain's story of the large ship hitting and sinking the small schooner seems all the more pathetic because of the unprepared, sleeping crew, who "start from their beds to be swallowed shrieking by the waves."

Reader: These stories of shipwreck increase Irving's fear and end his fanciful musing on the sea. When a storm blows in, Irving describes its awful progress a bit melodramatically. "As I heard the waves rushing along the sides of the ship, and roaring in my very ear, it seemed as if Death were raging round this floating prison, seeking for his prey: the mere starting of a nail, the yawning of a seam, might give him entrance." Irving's mortality is an overwhelming preoccupation. In these lines, Death might enter through any crack: Irving certainly has let him in through his imagination.

Text: Irving now turns to the "gladdening influence of fine weather and fair wind at sea." And shortly thereafter, land is sighted. Irving then returns to his theme of New World citizen sailing back to the Old World. He speaks of the "delicious throng of sensations which rush into an American's bosom, when he first comes in sight of Europe…It is the land of promise, teeming with everything…"

Reader: Irving is now filled with buoyant expectation. "Teeming," "stretching," "towering," and "rising" are some of the words that he uses to convey the enormous possibilities that await him. Why does he then shift gears and end with the sad reunion between the poor, ill sailor and his wife waiting at the dock?

Text: An answer might be found in the final line, "But at the sound of his voice, her eye darted on his features; it read, at once, a whole volume of sorrow."

Reader: So even in the happy moment of arrival, a scene of anxious sorrow intervenes. In fact, Irving shares this sorrowful mood. "I alone was solitary and idle. I had no friend to meet, no cheering to receive. I stepped upon the land of my forefathers—but I felt that I was a stranger in the land." So, at least the sick sailor is met at the dock by a loved one; Irving's voyage, however, ends with all the anxious fear strangers feel.

The above hypothetical dialogue between a reader and the text of Washington Irving's "The Voyage" pinpoints a number of revealing stylistic strategies. The stylistic choices Irving makes reflect his attitudes toward his subject and lead the reader to the essence of his text. Through this analysis, which focuses on style, it is readily clear that Irving was anxious about this voyage, a feeling that manifested itself in several ways and never left him, even when he was safely on shore. The anxiety felt on a sea voyage, though tempered by joyful expectation, may be seen as a reflection of his anxiety at visiting the Old World. Indeed, all Americans abroad in the early nineteenth century probably experienced it and would appreciate Irving's extended metaphor of a perilous sea voyage.

You will not, of course, have time to write out any such dialogue when you take the AP English Language and Composition Exam. Instead, you will do what has been pointed out in Chapter 2: you will underline key points of the essay and jot down notes and questions to yourself in the margins or on the test page as you read. These underlinings, notes, and questions will be the skeleton of the dialogue you had with the text while you read it. And they will serve as notes to yourself as you write in the test booklet your own essay that responds to the specific prompt presented to you by the essay question in the AP English Language and Composition Exam.

Exercise: Using the dialogue on Irving's "The Voyage," write a brief analysis (500 words) that incorporates the key elements of textual evidence and reveals Irving's reasons for writing. Remember, purpose is a significant determiner of style. Put another way, we infer an author's purpose in writing from the *style and tone* s/he chooses and the way in which that style is implemented in the writing through *diction (word choice), use of specific detail, imagery, and general use of language.*

2. Argumentative Writing: A Critical Dialogue

Argument is a quintessential human skill. Almost from the cradle, human beings manifest disagreement, sometimes very vocally! But argument, and argumentative writing, is not simply skillful disagreement. Essays that argue a particular point usually also involve the analytic skills emphasized in the previous section. The AP Examination in English Language and Composition asks students to respond to a text by taking an opposing stand. To respond effectively and advance a successful argument, you need to analyze the opposing argument as part of your response.

This section offers practice in responding to argumentative texts, including performing the analysis that is so crucial to mounting a successful counter argument. The AP Exam frequently presents students with an argumentative text or an excerpt of an argument and asks you to take the opposing view, sometimes regardless of your personal feelings on the subject. Students are also asked to compare and contrast two arguments to determine the more effective of the two.

In order to address all these possibilities in this review chapter, you will be presented with two arguments on a similar topic, a comparative analysis of their relative strengths and weaknesses, and instruction in composing your own argumentative response. Thus, the several skills of argumentative writing are all included.

As in the previous section, you should view the writing process as a critical dialogue. This methodology helps articulate the essential issues you will analyze and oppose. You will also be given a brief review of sound argumentative essay structure and a few of the writing devices that regularly appear in effective argumentative essays. In addition, you will find many useful rhetorical and literary devices in the glossary at the end of this chapter.

The two arguments to analyze and to compare follow. Presented chronologically, the first essay excerpt, taken from "Idleness an Anxious and Miserable State," was written in 1751 by Samuel Johnson, a famous eighteenth-century literary critic and essayist. The second essay excerpt, taken from Robert Louis Stevenson's "An Apology for Idlers," was published in 1876 and has since become a classic. Robert Louis Stevenson is a noted American author, perhaps most famous for *Treasure Island*.

Idleness an Anxious and Miserable State

Who knows if heav'n, with ever-bounteous pow'r,
Shall add tomorrow to the present hour?

I sat yesterday morning employed in deliberating on which, among the various subjects that occurred to my imagination, I should bestow the paper of today. After a short effort of meditation by which nothing was determined, I grew every moment more irresolute, my ideas wandered from the first intention, and I rather wished to think, than thought upon any settled subject; till at last I was awakened from this dream of study by a summons from the press; the time was now come for which I had been thus negligently purposing to provide, and, however dubious or sluggish, I was now necessitated to write…

There was however, some pleasure in reflecting that I, who had only trifled till diligence was necessary, might still congratulate myself upon my superiority to multitudes, who have trifled till diligence is vain; who can by no degree of activity or resolution recover the opportunities which have slipped away; and who are condemned by their own carelessness to hopeless calamity and barren sorrow.

The folly of allowing ourselves to delay what we know cannot be finally escaped, is one of the general weaknesses, which, in spite of the instruction of moralists, and the remonstrances of reason, prevail to a greater or less degree in every mind…

It is indeed natural to have particular regard to the time present, and to be most solicitous for that which is by its nearness enabled to make the strongest impressions. When therefore any sharp pain is to be suffered, or any formidable danger to be incurred, we can scarcely exempt ourselves wholly from the seducements of imagination; we readily believe that another day will bring some support or advantage which we now want and are easily persuaded, that the moment of necessity which we desire never to arrive, is at a great distance from us.

Thus life is languished away in the gloom of anxiety, and consumed in collecting resolutions which the next morning dissipates; in forming purposes which we scarcely hope to keep, and reconciling ourselves to our own cowardice by excuses, which, while we admit them, we know to be absurd. Our firmness is by the continual contemplation of misery, hourly impaired; every submission to our fear enlarges its dominion; we not only waste that time in which the evil we dread might have been suffered and surmounted, but even where procrastination produces no absolute increase of our difficulties, make then less superable to ourselves by habitual terrours…

To act is far easier than to suffer; yet we every day see the progress of life retarded by the *vis inertiae*, the mere repugnance to motion, and find multitudes repining at the want of that which nothing but idleness hinders them from enjoying…

There is nothing more common among this torpid generation than murmurs and complaints; murmurs at uneasiness which only vacancy and suspicion expose them to feel and complaints of distresses which it is in their own power to remove. Laziness is commonly associated with timidity…

Among all who sacrifice future advantage to present inclination, scarcely any gain so little as those that suffer themselves to freeze in idleness. Others are corrupted by some enjoyment of more or less power to gratify the passions; but to neglect our duties, merely to avoid the labour of performing them, a labour which is always punctually rewarded, is surely to sink under weak temptations…

The certainty of life cannot be long, and the probability that it will be much shorter than nature allows, ought to awaken every man to the active prosecution of whatever he is desirous to perform. It is true, that no diligence can ascertain success; death may intercept the swiftest career; but he who is cut off in the execution of an honest undertaking, has at least the honour of falling in his rank, and has fought the battle though he missed the victory.

—Samuel Johnson (1751)

An Apology for Idlers

Just now, when everyone is bound, under pain of a decree in absence convicting them of *lèse*-respectability[1], to enter on some lucrative profession, and labour therein with something not far short of enthusiasm, a cry from the opposite party who are content when they have enough, and like to look on and enjoy in the meanwhile, savours a little of bravado and gasconade. And yet this should not be. Idleness so called, which does not consist in doing nothing, but in doing a great deal not recognised in the dogmatic formularies of the ruling class, has as good a right to state its position as industry itself…

Where was the glory of having taken Rome for these tumultuous barbarians, who poured into the Senate house, and found the Fathers sitting silent and unmoved by their success? It is a sore thing to have laboured along and scaled the arduous hilltops, and when all is done, find humanity indifferent to your achievement. Hence physicists condemn the unphysical; financiers have only a superficial toleration for those who know little of stocks; literary persons despise the unlettered; and people of all pursuits combine to disparage those who have none.

[1] A play on *lèse-majesté*, a crime or offense committed against a king.

But though this is one difficulty of the subject, it is not the greatest. You could not be put in prison for speaking against industry, but you can be sent to Coventry for speaking like a fool. The greatest difficulty with most subjects is to do them well; therefore, please to remember this is an apology. It is certain that much may be judiciously argued in favour of diligence; only there is something to be said against it, and that is what, on the present occasion, I have to say...

It is surely beyond a doubt that people should be a good deal idle in youth. For though here and there a Lord Macaulay may escape from school honours with all his wits about him, most boys pay so dear for their medals that they never afterwards have a short in their locker, and begin the world bankrupt. And the same holds true during all the time a lad is educating himself, or suffering others to educate him. It must have been a very foolish old gentleman who addressed Johnson at Oxford in these words: "Young man, ply your book diligently now, and acquire a stock of knowledge; for when years come upon you, you will find that poring upon books will be but an irksome task." The old gentleman seems to have been unaware that many other things besides reading grow irksome, and not a few become impossible, by the time a man has to use spectacles and cannot walk without a stick. Books are good enough in their own way, but they are a mighty bloodless substitute for life. It seems a pity to sit, like the Lady of Shalott, peering into a mirror, with your back turned on all the bustle and glamour of reality. And if a man reads very hard, as the old anecdote reminds us, he will have little time for thought.

If you look back on your own education, I am sure it will not be the full, vivid, instructive hours of truantry that you regret; you would rather cancel some lack-lustre periods between sleep and waking in the class. For my own part, I have attended a good many lectures in my time. I still remember that the spinning of a top is a case of Kinetic Stability. I still remember that Emphysteusis is not a disease, nor Stillicide a crime. But though I would not willingly part with such scraps of science, I do not set the same store by them as by certain other odds and ends that I came by in the open street while I was playing truant. This is not the moment to dilate on that mighty place of education, which was the favourite school of Dickens and of Balzac, and turns out yearly many inglorious masters in the Science of the Aspects of Life. Suffice it to say this: if a lad does not learn in the streets, it is because he has no faculty of learning. Nor is the truant always in the streets, for if he prefers, he may be out by the gardened suburbs into the country. He may pitch on some tuft of lilacs over a burn, and smoke innumerable pipes to the tune of the water on the stones. A bird will sing in the thicket. And there he may fall into a vein of kindly thought, and see things in a new perspective. Why, if this be not education, what is?

Extreme *busyness*, whether at school or college, kirk or market, is a symptom of deficient vitality; and a faculty for idleness implies a catholic appetite and a strong sense of personal identity. There is a sort of dead-alive, hackneyed people about, who are scarcely conscious of living except in the exercise of some conventional occupation. Bring these fellows into the country, or set them aboard ship, and you will see how they pine for their desk or their study. They have no curiosity; they cannot give themselves over to random provocations; they do not take pleasure in the exercise of their faculty for its own sake; and unless Necessity lays about them with a stick, they will even stand still. It is no good speaking to such folk: they *cannot* be idle, their nature is not generous enough; and they pass those hours in a sort of coma, which are not dedicated to furious moiling in the gold-mill...

If a person cannot be happy without remaining idle, idle he should remain...

And what, in God's name, is all this pother about? For what cause do they embitter their own and other people's lives? That a man should publish three or thirty articles a year, that he should finish or not finish his great allegorical picture, are questions of little interest to the world...

The ends for which they give away their priceless youth, for all they know, may be chimerical or hurtful; the glory and riches they expect may never come, or may find them indifferent; and they and the world they inhabit are so inconsiderable that the mind freezes at the thought.

—Robert Louis Stevenson (1876)

A Critical Dialogue on "Idleness an Anxious and Miserable State" by Samuel Johnson and "An Apology for Idlers" by Robert Louis Stevenson

Reader: These two essay excerpts really present varying perspectives on idleness. Is it too easy to say Johnson is against it and Stevenson is for it?

Text:[2]   Not really. That is, in a superficial sense, the basic point of departure. Finding the thesis in each essay will clarify their opposition.

Reader: Essentially, Johnson believes that idleness is evil because it means missed opportunity.

Text: Yes, he says idlers can never "recover the opportunities which have slipped away" and that they are "condemned by their own carelessness to hopeless calamity and barren sorrow."

Reader: Stevenson's message is much less "moralizing" in tone and substance. He thinks idleness is okay if it makes you happy.

Text: He actually goes further than that, saying that "extreme *busyness*…is a symptom of deficient vitality; and a faculty for idleness implies a catholic appetite and a strong sense of personal identity."

Reader: How can I summarize the differences, then? Well, it boils down to the purpose of life. Johnson seems to value producing and doing most highly. Stevenson wants to stop and smell the roses. I see value in *both* approaches to idleness. If I were to construct a counterargument, I might suggest that there is a time for idleness and a time for productivity. Stevenson seems to recognize that better than Johnson, perhaps because Johnson had such a hard time with indolence in his own life. He can't give himself a break!

    But western civilization has a powerful work ethic and idleness for its own sake would be hard to justify. If I were going to support my moderate position, I'd probably look for authoritative backing, the testimony of great thinkers on the value of idleness, perhaps an example or two of a "eureka" experience that accompanied an afternoon of daydreaming. I would also, however, provide examples of people who were too often idle and managed to do nothing with their lives.

Text: Though Johnson might agree with that tactic, Stevenson might retort, but if they were happy, what does it matter?

Reader: Ah ha! Now I've got *my* conclusion. I think true happiness is impossible when inactivity is complete or total. I guess I'll need evidence from psy-

---

[2] "Text" in this dialogue refers to *both* the Johnson and Stevenson excerpts.

chologists or sociologists on the value of work—all work, physical and mental. I have my own definition of idleness now.

The hypothetical dialogue between a reader and the texts written by Johnson and Stevenson should help you "walk through" the process of analyzing and responding to arguments. In your own argumentative essay you should be aware of (and able to make use of) the many rhetorical and literary strategies that will bolster your case. Remember to peruse the Glossary, where these strategies are defined.

A Brief Review of Argumentative Structure

Composing an argument is a little like preparing a debate. You should approach the subject by first carefully defining it *and* by trying to figure out how someone with the *opposite* perspective on the issue might define it. Sometimes it's at this level, definition, that the real controversy is revealed. Certainly that was true of the two essays on Idleness.

The next step is to look for reasoning and evidence that supports your definition (or understanding) of the issue. At this stage in your preparation, make sure that your own argument is a sound one. Good evidence for what you want to say can take a variety of forms, and it's important to avoid basing your arguments on faulty reasoning. (Check the glossary for examples of both sound and faulty reasoning as you write practice essays of this type.) As you construct your own argument for the essay you're about to write, your job is to make clear *how* and *why* you arrived at the position you did. The essay reader must be able to follow your logic readily and should find your evidence compelling if you are to earn a high score on the AP Exam.

The next step involves covering your opponent's objections. In any argument, two or more positions may legitimately exist. Rather than discount your opposition out of hand (since this merely alienates; it doesn't win arguments), you should make a reasonable effort to deal with the major points of conflict and demonstrate where the opposition errs.

Lastly, your argument should offer a solution to the issue's problem(s). No reader likes to read an argument that complains without offering alternatives.

To make the above recommendations clearer, an outline of argumentative strategy is provided below.

Argument Outline

1. State premise or thesis; define issue(s)

   a. provide details about the nature of the issue

   b. articulate how your definition differs from the opposition; analyze their argument carefully

    c. define by denotation, connotation, division, example, and/or cause and effect

2. Offer reasoning and evidence

    a. provide readers with the logic that led you to your conclusion

    b. offer supporting evidence (comparison, analogy, authority, quotation, statistics, personal experience, etc.)

    c. check your reasoning and evidence for fallacies

3. Cover the opposition's objections to your position

4. Offer a solution or alternative

By following this outline you can create a reasonable, well-founded argument. Remember, careful analysis of your opponent's argument is the starting point for success—in any argumentative essay and on the AP Examination in English Language and Composition.

CHAPTER 4

AP English Language & Composition

Preparing for and Taking the AP Exam

The Advanced Placement English exams developed by the College Board are rigorous and challenging. A good score on an AP exam can be useful in two ways. For tests taken before your senior year in high school, a good score can be an asset when *applying* to colleges. For all tests, regardless of when they are taken, a good score can result in your getting *credit* or *placement* out of courses when you arrive at college. You should be aware that at many universities, *different departments have different policies for the awarding of credit or placement based on AP scores.* In other words, a university may give a certain placement and amount of credit for a 4 on the AP Biology Examination and a different placement and amount of credit for a 4 on the AP English Examination. Also, of course, different universities vary in how they award credit or placement. Thus, you *must* check a university's website (or published literature) to see how it awards credit and placement for specific scores on AP examinations.

Format of the AP English Language & Composition Examination

The AP English Language & Literature Examination is divided into two parts, multiple-choice and essay. The multiple-choice section has approximately 60 questions divided among five or six reading passages (the exact number varies from year to year). There will be from five to fifteen questions per reading passage. You are allowed 60 minutes for the objective portion. Generally speaking, the test is geared so that most good students can finish within the time limits. The second part of the AP English Language & Composition Examination consists of three essay questions, and you will be allowed 120 minutes to complete this portion of the examination. You will be given interim time limits for each individual essay question.

Changes Effective on the May 2007 Exam

Note the following changes in the AP English Language and Composition Examination. Additional information is available from the College Board's website, *http://apcentral.collegeboard.com/*

Free-response section. From 2007 onward, the free-response section of the exam contains, as one of three mandatory questions, an essay that asks students to synthesize ideas from various sources to either support an argument or analyze an issue. This question will cite four to seven sources and contain a prompt that calls upon these sources; for the most part, at least one of these sources will be shown as an image (e.g., photograph, cartoon, charts or graphs, etc.). Examinees must write essays that use three or four of the sources in an argumentative or analytical response, as necessary; the sources must be used in support of the examinee's argument or position. A 15-minute reading period is provided to accommodate the required reading.

Multiple-choice section. From 2007 onward, some items in the multiple-choice section refer to documentation and citation of sources. While examinees need not memorize any particular style (e.g., MLA, Chicago, APA, etc.), they will need to use information from citations that may indeed follow a given style. Some passages—"at least one," says the College Board—will be from a published work (book, journal, periodical, etc.) that incorporates footnotes or a bibliography; the documentation questions will be based on such passages.

Critical Reading of Prose Passages

There are usually five or six prose passages in the multiple-choice portion of the AP English Language & Composition Exam. The passages are taken from a variety of time periods and sources; therefore, contemporary pieces are mixed with excerpts from earlier centuries. At least one selection will be written from the first person point of view, others being from third person point of view—objective, omniscient, or limited omniscient. Some passages will be casual, and some will be formal.

As you read each passage in the multiple-choice portion of the practice tests in this book, ask yourself the questions below. Not all of these questions will apply to every selection, of course. You should practice with these questions regularly in your reading. You would do well, for example, to have a copy of these questions as you read novels recommended by the College Board for the AP test.

Genre

1. Is the passage persuasive? Although essays range widely in subject matter, they will vary in tone and style from serious to satirical, from humorous to tragic, and from light inquiry to active—even aggressive—assertion. Typically, these nonfiction essays seek to fulfill the four purposes of academic nonfiction prose: describe, explain, inform, or persuade. More often than not, authors will use all their skills and all their minor purposes (i.e., describing, explaining, or informing) to support their ultimate purpose: to persuade you to some point of view.

Authors of persuasive passages generally appeal either to your *emotions* about a particular topic or to *reason* in order to persuade you to their point of view. When you look at a persuasive passage, try to find the places in the essay where the author is appealing to emotion as well as the places where an appeal to *reason* or *logic* is made. You should make sure to include in your essay an assessment of those appeals (for emotion, are people likely to agree with the emotions the author is trying to raise? And for logic, is the logic that is presented actually valid?) as you critique the passage.

2. Is the passage an excerpt from a work of fiction, a novel or short story? These passages tend to be a description of character or location, seldom a philosophical commentary. Sometimes a character's dialogue with another may be given to you to analyze.

Organization

1. If the passage is descriptive, is it organized spatially or by order of importance? What is the overall effect?

2. If the passage is narrative, is the chronological order of events interrupted by flashback, foreshadowing, episodic events? Is the plot framed or circular?

3. If the passage is expository, are any of the following devices or methods used: definition, cause and effect, deductive order, inductive order, comparison/contrast, division and classification, examples, extended example, analogy?

4. If persuasion is used, what methods does the author use to bolster the argument? Does the author deal with opposing evidence? Where is the thesis—at the beginning or at the end? Does the author fall into any logical fallacies?

Setting

1. Where does the story take place?

2. Is the description real or imaginative or a combination of both?

3. What are the details of weather, countryside, building(s), language, actions, dress?

4. What imagery is used (appeals to the senses, or from history, literature or mythology)?

5. How does the setting create mood?

6. How does the setting affect the character(s)?

7. Is personification used to describe buildings or society, weather, or nature? Are there any other figures of speech used in the description of setting?

8. How does the setting create or tie in with conflict or symbolism?

9. Is setting important to the theme?

10. How does the setting create mood or conflict?

Plot and Conflict

1. What is the conflict (self versus others, self versus self, human versus nature, humans versus God or fate)?

2. What is the situation at the beginning? How does this relate to the conflict? theme? character development?

3. Upon what past action, if any, is the plot dependant?

4. Is the plot **episodic** (one scene following another with the only linking device that of a change in time or place) or **paradigmatic** (i.e., a sort of logical puzzle, such as a mystery, or an inescapable design whose outcome is inevitable, such as those associated with myth)?

5. What is the first complicating incident? What is the climax? Are problems resolved in the falling action?

6. Is there a resolution or denouement?

7. Are there any subplots? If so, how do they tie in with the main plot?

8. How is suspense maintained, particularly once the climax has passed? Does the author continue the revelation of clues? Is the identity of a key character withheld? Does the dialogue or action become more intense?

9. Is the main thrust of the literature comic or serious?

10. If the literature is primarily serious, do any scenes offer comic relief?

11. If the literature is primarily humorous, are there any serious scenes? What is the point of the author's satire?

12. Is there flashback or foreshadowing?

13. Are there any parallel plots?

Character

1. Who is the main character?

2. What is the character like (list three adjectives to describe the character)?

3. Do you like the character? Does the character seem to be ethical or unethical?

4. Who or what are the **protagonist** (character trying to accomplish something) and **antagonist** (character or force opposing the protagonist)?

5. What are the motives of the character(s)?

6. Does the character have a good self-knowledge? If not, is he or she unreliable, self-deluding, or complacent?

7. Is the character in the process of changing, or is the character static?

8. Does the character reflect on a past dilemma? Is that dilemma resolved? How?

9. Do minor characters play an important role? Do they **complement** (appear similar), or do they serve as a **foil** (opposite personality or traits)? Do any provide comic relief or commentary?

10. How does the central character view the setting, conflict, other characters?

11. What are the **ethics** (moral position or beliefs) of the central character? Is the character being pressured to compromise?

12. Is the story one of changes: initiation, symbolic birth or rebirth, fertility, or death?

13. Are any of the characters symbols or stereotypes?

    For example, do some characters seem to stand for an idea or other abstraction, such as Love, Innocence, Truth, or Greed? Do some characters appear to be stereotypes of their role, such as the spinster, the mad scientist, the country doctor, the wayward youth, the ingenue?

Point of View

"Point of View" in this sense is the literary device the author uses to narrate the fiction. This device is not to be confused with the author's attitude, or point of view (discussed below), toward the subject or theme. Typically, the point of view from which the fiction is told is that of some narrator or other, who then also may become an important character in the narration of the story, helping the plot to move forward, or in fact, functioning as a central figure in the development and outcome of the story. You should examine carefully the nature and character of the fictional narrator of the story, who is not the same person as the historically and biologically real author of the fiction, e.g., David Copperfield is the fictional narrator of the novel of that name, and Charles Dickens is the author. They are not the same!

1. What sort of narrator does the author employ: omniscient, limited omniscient, first person, third person?

2. If there is a first person narrator, does he or she provide an accurate self-analysis?

3. In an omniscient or limited omniscient point of view, in whose mind does the author dwell the most?

4. If the point of view is objective, what effect is created? Is it cold, unemotional, logical, or scientific?

5. With which character does the point of view encourage you to sympathize or relate?

Theme

1. What is the passage's theme?

2. Is the theme **explicit** (stated) or **implicit** (implied)?

3. Is there a universal truth, or simply a comment upon a particular situation or location?

4. How are the other elements of fiction—setting, character, plot, irony, symbolism, tone, mood—related to the theme?

Tone and Mood

1. What is the mood created by the **selection** (effect upon the reader)?

2. What is the **tone** (author's attitude toward the subject)?

    This question may ask you to consider and decide how the *author* seems to feel toward the subject of a fiction. Be careful to make distinctions between how the *narrator's* attitude toward the subject and how the *author's* attitude may differ or coincide. Is the *narrator*, for example, sympathetic towards a character that the *author* treats as a symbol of Greed? Imagine the way that suggests how the author feels about the narrator! Be sure to review all the elements (character, plot, diction, imagery, and setting) and how they interact before you decide on how the *author* feels toward the theme or subject of the fiction.

Words Useful in Describing Tone

admiring	detached	inflammatory	petty
angry	determined	informative	pretentious
apprehensive	didactic	insipid	respectful
bantering	diffident	insolent	restrained
benevolent	disdainful	ironic	sardonic
biting	disgusted	irreverent	satiric
bitter	dramatic	learned	scholarly
candid	ecstatic	lugubrious	scornful
clinical	effusive	mock-heroic	sentimental
colloquial	elegiac	mocking	solemn
compassionate	facetious	mock-serious	somber
complimentary	factual	moralistic	sympathetic
concerned	fanciful	mournful	taunting
condescending	flippant	neutral	threatening
confident	hopeful	nostalgic	turgid
contemptuous	impartial	objective	urbane
contentious	incisive	patronizing	urgent
cynical	indignant	pedantic	worshipful

Language and Style

The narrator's language and style give you clues about the personality of a character in a fiction. The author may also use a consistent set of metaphors and symbols during the descriptive passages in a pattern to generate specific feelings in the reader. For example, metaphors of the sea ("voyaging across the seas of conflict," "arriving on the shores of decision") may be used to suggest some universal relationship of the theme to life or, say, overwhelming odds.

Be careful, when relevant, to distinguish among the narrator's, other characters' and the author's tone. They may be varied.

1. What is the word choice? Is it colloquial, idiomatic, scientific, Latinate, formal, concrete, abstract, scholarly, or allusive?

2. To what senses does the author appeal?

3. What literary devices of sense does the author use (personification, metaphor, simile, allusion)?

4. What literary devices of sound does the author use (alliteration, assonance, consonance, repetition)?

5. Does the language have rhythm?

6. Are the sentences long or short? Where does the author use short sentences or fragments for special emphasis? Where are there long sentences or run-ons for special effect?

7. Are the sentences simple, compound, complex, or compound-complex? Where does the author use sentence variety to emphasize an idea?

   See the glossary for detailed examples of the terms cited in questions 8 and 9.

8. What specialized sentence structure does the author use? The following are emphatic types of sentence structures: balanced, freight-train, inverted, parallel, periodic. Also, the author can employ anaphora, antithesis, asyndeton, chiasmus, negative-positive restatement, polysyndeton, tricolon.

9. Do any sentences begin or end with a significant word or phrase? Do any sentences have the main idea "hidden" in the middle, in an interrupter, so as to create surprise or suspense?

10. Does the author use colors to enhance moods, characterize someone in the story, or to develop the setting description (e.g., are there many references to red or shades of red to heighten the mood of danger or of bloody action)? Consider Poe's classic "Masque of The Red Death."

11. What are the best-worded phrases or best-chosen words?

An Explanation of Style

Style is the habitual, repeated patterns that differentiate one writer from another (or, one singer or painter from the other, for that matter). Salvador Dali painted in the surrealist style, with his most famous painting being "The Persistence of Memory," which shows the clocks and watches dripping and oozing off the sides of tables and over a bare tree limb. Claude Monet painted in the impressionist style, with bits of color that blend together to form a coherent whole only if the viewer stands back from the picture; Monet was interested in the use of color to form an impression, rather than the absolute realistic portrayal of a scene. In literature, Hemingway is well known for his terse, sparse, objective style indicative of the isolation of people in the twentieth century; Hawthorne for his flamboyant, exaggerated word pictures that create a mood of horror or fearful introspection.

So, the first part of style is the repetition of patterns. The other component of style is deviation from the customary patterns. Hemingway, for example, deviates from his usual short sentences and few descriptive words when he describes nature. In those passages, you will find long, flowing sentences and lyrical descriptions of nature, such as a river, to show the peace that people obtain when they escape the jarring, destructive effects of civilization and is comforted by the healing beauty of nature.

Expectation (the pattern) and **surprise** (the deviation from the pattern) are the component parts of style. A discussion of style is also a discussion of the **well-chosen word or phrase**. A discussion of the well-chosen word or phrase depends on your ability to be discriminating about language and to recognize good writing.

The AP English Language and Composition Examination tests your knowledge of style in two ways: through multiple-choice questions that closely analyze reading passages, and through essay questions that ask you to demonstrate your ability to analyze style in a passage.

The *most important* thing about discussing style is to show its relationship to the theme or main idea of a passage. A discussion which does no more than list fancy terms and give examples of each will not get a good grade on the AP test. The graders wish to see how you interpret the link between theme and language, or between characterization and language, or between description of setting and language. The graders wish to see that you can recognize and discuss (in essay format) or identify (in multiple-choice questions) how style highlights the central idea, characterization, setting, symbolism, and how, in a well-written piece of literature, all elements interrelate. In an essay analyzing style, it is not enough to discuss theme or to discuss style—you must relate each to the other in a fluid, organized manner.

For example, if the **theme** is about fertility and success, does the author have the story setting in the spring and use **images** of blossoming, growth, or fruition? Are the **characters** getting married? Is the **tone** optimistic, hopeful, humorous? Does the **word choice** have connotations of positive, safe, or loving feelings? Is the **plot** one that climaxes in marriage, good fortune, or renewal? Your job is to understand and, in your essay response, to show **how** the author blends these elements to produce an experience of the **theme** viscerally, emotionally, and intellectually.

To discuss style in detail, you should be familiar with the terms listed under "Language and Style."

Colloquial word choice is not standard formal usage and employs idiomatic or slang expressions; this word usage develops a casual tone. Scientific, Latinate (words with Latin roots or origins), or scholarly language would be formal and employ standard rules of usage. Concrete words form vivid images in the reader's mind, while abstract language is more appropriate for a discussion of philosophy. Allusive style uses many references to history, literature, or other shared cultural knowledge to provoke or enlighten the reader. Appeals to the senses make the writing more concrete and vivid. Since prose does not have a natural rhythm, an obvious metrical pattern in a passage signals an important idea.

Authors also employ other poetical devices in their writing to emphasize important ideas. Any time the author cares enough to use similes or metaphors, or any of the other common poetic or rhetorical devices, it is because the author wants to draw attention to that particular characteristic and perhaps suggest a more complex relationship to the implied or stated theme. Therefore, you should pay attention, too.

See the "Glossary of Literary and Rhetorical Terms" on page 85 for a list and explanation of common literary tropes.

If the author suddenly or obviously varies sentence structure or length of a sentence, you should take note. Short sentences (seven or fewer words) or fragments usually signal important ideas. You should look out for them. If, in the midst of a variety of sentence structures and lengths, the author inserts two or three short, simple sentences, you should notice this change as being significant. Most certainly, a detail or action will appear in these sentences that the author considers crucial.

Faulkner is an author who uses the interrupter to foreshadow details that later become significant. Humorous writing employs the interrupter for contrast or to give the author's real point.

An author can pick from a variety of specialized sentence patterns or structures to create emphatic sentences. Most sentences in the English language are **loose** sentences; that is, the main idea appears at the beginning of the sentence (subject first, then predicate, then additional modifiers) and much of the predicate part of the sentence can be cut off without serious damage to the main idea. Any time an author wishes to call attention to an important idea, he or she can use a different sentence structure. These different structures are called **emphatic** because they emphasize the ideas contained therein.

In analyzing an author's style, then, seek out patterns, habitual wording or phraseology, and then attempt to spot variations from the norm. Suppose an author employs many rather lengthy, balanced sentences with the frequent use of parallelism and anaphora, and the word choice is formal and Latinate. You can then make intelligent observations about the formal, balanced style. If this same author then includes one or two short sentences, a metaphor, and an inverted word order, you can point out these constructions and discuss the importance of the ideas contained in and signaled by these constructions. In addition, you should be on the lookout for the well-chosen word, for the compelling turn of a phrase. Don't forget: all discussion of style should show the relation to the tone or theme of the selection.

Logic and the AP Exam

Occasionally, an AP Literature and Language multiple-choice question will ask about logic or logical fallacies.

Formal logical arguments can be inductive or deductive. Inductive argumentation lists cases, examples, and facts, and then ends with a logical conclusion (particular to general). Deductive argumentation begins with a statement of opinion and proceeds to prove it with cases, examples, facts (general to the particular). The basic form of the deductive argument is a three-part format known as a **syllogism**. The syllogism, you may recall, has a major premise, a minor premise, and a conclusion. If your audience accepts your premises, then your conclusion is usually accepted.

Here's an example:

Premise One: Most Americans love violence.

Premise Two: Football is violent.

Conclusion: Therefore, most Americans love football.

Sound reasoning can be undermined by logical fallacies. The following is a list of common logical fallacies you are expected to know for the AP English Language and Composition Examination. While you do not need to know the specific names of each fallacy, you should definitely be able to identify when the reasoning an author uses in a passage is faulty. Likewise, you want to be sure *not* to use faulty reasoning when writing your own essay responses!

Attacking the Person

This argument, often called an *ad hominem* argument, attacks the personality of the individual instead of dealing with the arguments and issues.

Example: John Smith can't tell us anything about the faithfulness of dogs because he has no faith at all in anything.

Begging the Question

Assumes something to be true that needs proof. The arguer uses as proof the very argument that needs proving.

Example: The reason George is so smart is that he is very intelligent.

> (In other words, A is true because A is true. Just a minute, here! I've got to show why George is intelligent—the condition that stands in need of proof can't be the source of the proof! "Intelligent" is just a synonym for "smart," not evidence for it.)

Creating a False Dilemma

Uses a premise that presents a choice which does not include all the possibilities.

Example: People hate politics because politicians often lie.

> (The premise that "people hate politics" is not necessarily true; somebody is sitting in those chairs in Washington.)

Since rabbits are often responsible for destroying suburban lawns, homeowners should shoot rabbits on sight.

Describing with Emotionally Charged Terminology

Uses vocabulary carrying strong connotative meaning, either positive or negative.

Example: Senator Jones is a commie, pinko, bleeding heart liberal who hates his mother, babies, apple pie, *and* the American way.

(This form of the tactic—name-calling—is perhaps most common. Poor Senator Jones is getting a terrible review; apparently, he hates all the things we love and is the things we hate, so our emotions are likely to be *transferred* from them to him by association, whether they are true about him or not.)

Either/Or Fallacy

Does not allow for any shades of meaning, compromise, or intermediate cases.

Example: Either we abolish cars, or the environment is doomed.

(Probably other factors contribute to this possibility besides cars.)

Generalizing from Insufficient Evidence

(Hasty generalization) uses too few of the examples needed to reach a valid conclusion.

Example: Only motivated athletes become champions.

(Maybe not. What are the other factors in becoming champions? Good health? Superior genes?)

Circular Reasoning

This argument attempts to prove something by showing that because a second event followed a first event, the second event is a result of the first event.

Example: He went to the store to buy shoes, and therefore, the house burned down.

(I doubt it. Probably somebody lit a match. Buying shoes doesn't make a house burn down.)

Answering Multiple-Choice Questions

Reading attentively takes practice. Use the following tips while you practice.

1. Scan the reading passage to determine the subject of the passage, the major points, and perhaps the general tone of the passage.

2. Read the questions (not the answers, yet!) to get a sense of what to be looking for when you go back and read the passage more carefully.

3. If it helps you focus, circle the key word or phrase in each question as you read it.

4. Since all questions count the same amount, don't spend too much time on any one question!

5. If you can eliminate some of the choices, it's usually to your advantage to make an educated guess when you get down to a choice of only two possible answers.

6. If you're not sure, remember that your first guess is usually correct, so don't go back and "second-guess" yourself.

7. As you take the practice exams, it's *critical* that you go back and read the *reasons* for each question you missed. These will help you see the mind-set of the people writing these sorts of questions. It is sometimes the case with some of the subtler questions that different people will make different choices of what the "best" answer is. So, if you want to score well on the test, it's important that you try to figure out *why* the given answer was chosen instead of simply insisting that "your answer was good, too!"

Study these tips carefully before you take a multiple-choice practice test. With enough practice, you will get a sense of how the authors approach these sorts of questions, and possibly even predict answers based on your having read the passages and looking carefully at the questions before you see the possible choices.

Rewriting

This question type does not always occur on each year's tests, but it is important for you to be familiar with it just in case. This rewriting section is part of Section I of the test when it occurs, and it is usually the very first 12 to 15 questions of the test. The following pages will more than adequately prepare you for this rather specialized set of questions.

A rewriting question consists of a grammatically correct, well-written sentence and directions to make a specific structural change while maintaining the meaning of the sentence. The directed change will refer to one or a few words that will spawn other changes in another part of the sentence in a cause-and-effect relationship. Your answer choices will include various versions of the "effect" part of the new sentence.

Sentence: Arriving before he was expected, he turned the tables on the party givers.

Directions: Change <u>Arriving</u> to <u>He arrived</u>.

     (A) and so he turned
     (B) and turned
     (C) and then turning
     (D) and had turned
     (E) and there he had turned

The rewritten sentence should be: "He arrived before he was expected and turned the tables on the party givers," making (B) "and turned" correct. Answer (A) is incorrect because it introduces a cause-and-effect element into the sentence; since it changes the meaning of the sentence somewhat, it is a poor choice. Choice (C) is incorrect because using it produces a sentence fragment—a sentence with no independent clause; turning a grammatically correct sentence into one that is incorrect is *always* a bad idea! Choices (D) and (E) are incorrect because they change the sequence of events in the sentence, trying to put "turning the tables" *before* the arrival of the person. Changing the meaning of the sentence is always a poor choice!

Your primary goals in answering these questions revolve around the formulation of the new sentence. The new sentence should carry, as much as possible, the same meaning as the test's original sentence. It should be the most fluid and natural of the choices in its construction and phrasing. The new sentence must adhere to the requirements of standard written English. And finally, your new sentence should be well-written—concise, logical, and idiomatic.

The questions of this section fall into definable types, which mostly draw on sentence structure as a basis for change. In the example given on the previous page, the original sentence has a dependent clause, "Arriving ... expected," and an independent clause, "he turned ... givers." The directions instruct a conversion of the dependent clause into an independent clause. A quick glance at the answer options—the repeated "and ... (verb)"—tells us that the original independent clause will remain independent, even if it shares the subject with the other predicate. "And" is a conjunction, joining equal things.

Like most of these question types, the exam has a mirror image of such questions. Holding to the principle that to know something well you must be able to do it backwards and forwards, another type of question requires you to rewrite two independent clauses as a dependent clause and an independent clause. The conjunction will be eliminated, and you must recognize which answer will properly convert one of the clauses into a dependent clause.

In certain instances, dependent-independent conversions as a type will help you find the answer. When an independent clause is converted to a dependent clause, another clause from the sentence must become an independent clause. Look at the following example.

Sentence: Such topics as the role of fraud and its detection were not addressed in the debate on welfare reform, which idealistically concentrated on incorporating recipients back into the work force.

Directions: Begin with <u>Rather than address</u>.

    (A)   detection, the debate that
    (B)   detection in the debate, it
    (C)   detection, the debate
    (D)   detection, instead the debate
    (E)   detection, concentrating

The original clause "Such ... reform" is independent, but changing the beginning to <u>Rather than address</u> will make it dependent. The original clause "which idealistically ... work force" was dependent and must now become the independent clause in the new sentence. Answers (A) and (E) require the "work force" clause to be dependent, with their use of "that" and the use of the gerund ("ing" ending on "concentrate"). It would be incorrect to have two dependent clauses and no independent clause in the sentence. Choice (D) is punctuated in such a way that what should be an introductory dependent clause is made into a fragment, which is an error. Choices (B) and (C) both allow for both an independent and a dependent clause in the sentence. But (B) is awkwardly phrased, with an indefinite "it" as the subject of the independent clause. Of the two grammatically correct sentences, choice (C) is better written, so it should be the answer that is chosen.

The fourth and final type that depends on the status of clauses is the conversion of a description to an independent clause.

Sentence: His seemingly offhand remark struck many in the group with pangs of self-doubt.

Directions: Change <u>struck</u> to <u>but it struck</u>.

    (A)   remark seemed
    (B)   remark, and it seemed
    (C)   remark which seemed
    (D)   remark, seemingly
    (E)   remark, despite seeming

The change to <u>but it struck</u> requires that the original subject of the sentence now become an entire independent clause. To accomplish this, "seemingly offhand remark" becomes "remark seemed offhand." Only answer (A) places "remark" as a subject in any clause.

The next two types of questions are derived most directly from good reading and writing. The sentence "Mutual hostility was the result of his uncaring actions" uses a linking verb, which is a nonactive sentence structure that equates the subject and its object, making it reversible to "The result of his uncaring actions was mutual hostility." The noun "result" has another usage as a verb, and some test questions will require you to change the first sentence above to "His uncaring actions resulted in mutual hostility." Because so many words have both noun and verb forms, these sentences vary greatly and can be very complicated. However, they tend to hinge on a linking verb that will be replaced by a former noun.

The last potentially difficult question form requires a transition from a passive sentence, in which the subject receives the action, to an active sentence, in which the subject performs the action. An active sentence is often considered to be more aggressive than a passive sentence, so their alternating uses are important to authors stylistically.

Sentence: The little boy was overcome with fear only a few minutes into his fruitless search for his mother.

Directions: Begin with <u>Fear</u>.

    (A)   searched for
    (B)   fruitlessly searching

(C)   was overcoming

(D)   overcame

(E)   had overcome

In the original sentence, the boy did not perform any action, but was acted upon. He was overcome. The word "fear" had the action, but the sentence was written passively. To begin the new sentence with <u>Fear</u> will require you to make the sentence active for the sake of avoiding an awkward construction. You can immediately eliminate choices (A) and (B) since "fear," the new subject of the sentence, is not doing the searching—the boy is! The correct choice is (D) because "fear overcame the boy..." Choices (C) and (E) can be eliminated because they are the wrong tenses. In (C), the tense is progressive, implying that fear was in the process of overcoming the boy more and more during the whole time he was searching, which changes the meaning of the sentence. Likewise, in (E), the meaning of the sentence is changed since the tense is past perfect, implying that fear had already overcome the boy *before* he started searching. Be aware that some test questions may instead require a conversion from active to passive.

Some simpler types of questions test very basic rules. The Should-If question contrasts these constructions, requiring you to know their appropriate connections to "would" and "will." "Should you forget, I would be furious" becomes "If you forget, I will be furious." The quote to non-quote question requires a conversion from "He said, 'My dog has fleas'" to "He said that his dog has fleas," which hits on the punctuation of quotes and the points of view of pronouns. The Most-Few question is another case of points of view, or optimism vs. pessimism. It requires a conversion from "Most know little" to "Few know much." The answer options on Most-Few questions strenuously test your ability to maintain the meaning of the original sentence.

Identifying these basic question types will help you to orient yourself when you come to each new question. You will know from the type of question what form the rewritten sentence should take and thereby eliminate two or three of the incorrect answer choices. From this point, you will have the time to test the remaining answers in your mind. Discerning the correct answer will depend on your ability to recognize good writing. You will be able to practice more examples of these types of sentence changes in the practice examinations.

Questions about the Speaker

For these questions, you are asked to make observations about the speaker or author. You are asked to judge how the speaker views himself or herself, what effect certain objects or events have on the speaker, what is important to the speaker, and how the speaker obtains/has obtained information about the world.

Questions usually appear in the following format:

In lines _____ the speaker depicts himself/herself as _____.

In lines _____ the speaker depicts himself/herself as all of the following EXCEPT _____.

For the speaker, _____ (subject) has the effect of _____.

For the speaker, _____ (subject) is _____ (evaluation of meaning or importance).

Which of the following is probably the main source of the speaker's knowledge of _____?

In "_____" (quotation containing action or description) the author is _____ (conclusion about that action or description).

Questions about Attitude

For these questions, you are asked to determine or make judgments about the attitude of the speaker or author toward the subject being described or discussed. You may be asked to do the following:

- identify a shift
- analyze the effect of the author's attitude
- decide what the author believes
- determine the atmosphere/mood
- determine the tone/atmosphere

Questions usually appear in the following format:

The shift in point of view has the effect of _____.

The author's attitude toward _____ can be described as _____.

The speaker assumes that the audience's attitude will _____.

The author believes/apparently believes _____.

The point of view indicated in _____ is that of _____.

The atmosphere is one of _____.

In "_____" which of the following most suggests a humorous attitude on the part of the author?

The passage is an appeal for _____.

Questions about Word Choice and Selection of Details

For these questions, you are asked to analyze the fine points of language and specific word choice. You are asked to determine the meaning of a word/phrase/sentence, identify elements of fiction, analyze important details or quotations, determine meaning of a word or phrase from the context, identify parts of a sentence, such as subject of a verb or antecedent of a pronoun, or analyze the style of a passage.

Sometimes, you will be asked to tell the meaning of a word in the context of the paragraph. You may not have seen the word before, but from your understanding of the writer's intent, you should be able to figure out what it is s/he's after.

For example, read the following paragraph:

Paris is a beautiful city, perhaps the most beautiful on Earth. Long, broad avenues are lined with seventeenth and eighteenth century apartments, office buildings, and cafés. Flowers give the city a rich and varied look. The bridges and the river lend an air of lightness and grace to the whole urban landscape.

In this paragraph, "rich" most nearly means

(A) wealthy.
(B) polluted.
(C) colorful.
(D) dull.

If you chose (C) "colorful" you would be right. Although "rich" literally means "wealthy" (that is its **denotation**, its literal meaning), here the writer means more than the word's literal meaning and seems to be highlighting the variety and color that the flowers add to the avenues—that is, richness in a figurative sense.

The writer is using a non-literal meaning, or **connotation**, that we associate with the word "rich" to show what s/he means. When we think of something "rich," we usually also think of abundance and variety and color, not just plain numbers.

Questions about word choice and selection of details usually appear in the following format:

Which of the following best describes what _____ symbolizes?

The _____ sentence/paragraph/section is unified by metaphors of _____.

The style of the passage can best be characterized as _____.

"_____" signals a shift from _____ to _____.

The _____ paragraph employs which of the following?

The statement "_____" is best described as _____.

The use of "_____" instead of "_____" accomplishes which of the following?

In line _____ the author emphasizes "_____" because _____.

The use of "_____" suggests most strongly _____.

The major purpose of the word/phrase/statement "_____" is to make clear that _____.

By "_____", the speaker means/most probably means _____.

The mention of _____ is appropriate to the development of the argument because _____.

In the sentence/paragraph/section, the speaker seeks to draw attention to _____ by stressing _____.

In the context of the passage as a whole/the _____ paragraph, the word/phrase/sentence "_____" is best interpreted to mean _____.

In relation to _____, which of the following best describes the function of the word/phrase/sentence/paragraph?

The antecedent for "_____" (pronoun) is _____.

Which of the following best describes the word/phrase/sentence _____?

Which of the following is an example of "_____" mentioned in line _____?

All of the following qualities are present in the scene EXCEPT _____.

The subject of the verb "_____" is which of the following?

Questions about Logic and Sentence Construction

For these questions, you are asked to identify how words work together in groups. You are asked to analyze syntax, identify sentence construction, analyze relationships of sentences or phrases, identify logical fallacies, or determine patterns of exposition.

These questions usually appear in the following format:

The syntax of sentence/sentences _____ serves to _____.

All of the following antitheses may be found EXCEPT _____.

The relationship between _____ and _____ is explained primarily by the use of _____.

What is the function of the two (or three) words/phrases/clauses?

The author's discussion of _____ depends on which of the following?

The type of argument employed in _____ by _____ is _____.

The speaker describes _____ in an order described as _____.

The pattern of exposition exemplified in the passage is best described as _____.

Despite its length, the _____ sentence remains coherent chiefly because of its use of _____.

Questions about Inferences

For these questions, you are asked to draw conclusions based on context clues. You are asked to determine relationships or identify references. They usually appear as follows:

It can be inferred that _____ is/are _____.

It can be inferred from the description of _____ that _____ is _____.

It can be inferred that _____ refers to _____.

Questions About General Conclusions

For these questions, you are asked to predict outcomes and make inferences. You are asked to determine what the author would think about a certain subject, what the author wants us to do, or what the author would/would not advise us. Most of the questions have the following format:

The author believes that we should _____.

According to the author, _____ should _____ because _____.

Which of the following would the author be LEAST/MOST likely to encourage?

If one were to take the author's advice, one should _____.

After you read the questions and underline or circle the most significant nouns and verbs, read the passage carefully. Pay attention to the point of view (that literary device the author uses to invoke or employ a narrator), setting, characters, conflicts, etc. Underline well-chosen words or phrases, short sentences, significant details, irony, and descriptions that seem significant.

After you read the passage, go back to the questions. Read each question entirely and carefully, including the answer choices. Go to the passage to look for the answer.

The first time you read a passage, you'll probably pick up a basic familiarity with what is being said—maybe even enough to answer some of the questions. After reading the questions, you'll probably go back and read through the passage more carefully, looking for details that will help you answer the remaining questions. You may end up reading only far enough to find the answer to a particular question. You'll probably go back and answer that question, and then return to the passage where you left off to find the answer to the next question. If this is your practice, keep in mind that some questions on overall tone may require you to read quickly through most of the passage one last time. But again, remember not to spend too much time on any one question. All questions count the same amount, so it is never to your advantage to spend so much time on a handful of questions that you end up leaving a significant number of the later questions blank!

Answering Essay Questions

The essay section of the test is composed of three topics, for which you are given 120 minutes. Don't spend more than 40 minutes on an essay (unless you qualify for extended time on the AP examination, in which case you should check with the College Board to find out exactly how long you will have on each section). Train yourself to be conscious of the time when you are reading the passage, brainstorming your ideas for an answer, and then writing your essay. You definitely don't want to run out of time while you are still writing!

The College Board will provide you with a booklet for the essay section of the test. Don't feel obliged to fill up the whole booklet. If your responses are brief or if your handwriting is very small, you may find that you have blank space left.

Throughout this chapter and during the practice tests, you should use lined 8½- by 11-inch paper with standard lines. To simulate test conditions, use only 12 pages for the essay section.

Essays on the English Language and Composition exam are scored on a scale of 0 to 9 points, with the point count and standards being tailored to suit each essay question. More than one trained reader scores each paper. If the scores of two readers differ by more than one point, a third reader is brought in. Many hours are spent training readers so that they can score different kinds of responses to the essays with great consistency. Though the essays are read quickly, they are read accurately and thoroughly!

Strategies for Answering Essay Questions

Read the question carefully before you read the passage. Know what you are looking for before you read. As you read the question, underline the directions. Make sure you understand what you are looking for as you read. In the passage underline significant details, words with connotative meaning, reasons, logical structure, notable sentence beginnings or endings, unusual sentence structures, sentences that are noticeably short or long, vivid imagery, figures of speech, and words or phrases that may indicate the author's attitude.

The English Language and Composition essay answers are graded as "first draft" papers. You are not given enough time to do prewriting, rough draft, and final copy—prewriting and one draft are really all you have time for in a 40-minute time period. Therefore, prewriting—organizing in advance of writing, in which you decide on content and order of ideas—is critical to your success. Give yourself about 5-10 minutes to read the essay question, write a working thesis sentence, and list 3-5 points in order of importance or logical development. The remaining time (15-20 minutes) should be spent writing, with 5 minutes to correct/revise and proofread.

You are pressed for time, so you should never use long introductory or long concluding remarks. Long introductions and conclusions take valuable time away from your main argument. Remember that you have only about 40 minutes to read the question, read the passage, plan your strategy, write your answer, and proofread and revise. Another argument against lengthy introduction and conclusions is that your central development will be shorter, and therefore most probably weaker in development. One or two sentences of introduction and conclusion are adequate.

Ideas should lead one to the other in a smooth, logical progression. Organization of ideas in prewriting and composing will depend on the type of essay, but organize before you write. The five-paragraph essay structure is adequate for answering many of the AP essay prompts as long as you make sure to shorten the introduction and conclusion. In particular, remember that the introduction should generally be no more than one sentence long! Further, it is often a good idea to start your essay by answering the prompt in the first sentence you write. In case you are most comfortable with the five-paragraph structure, the following chart should remind you of what its basic components require.

Paragraph Number	Type of Paragraph	What to Include
1	Thesis Paragraph	Introductory remarks, thesis
2	First Body Paragraph	Topic sentence containing first observation, then details and quotations bolstered and explained by elaboration
3	Second Body Paragraph	Development of second observation to prove thesis, same order as above
4	Third Body Paragraph	Development of third observation to prove thesis, same order as above
5	Conclusion	Summary of position in different words, observation about the topic

Although it is possible to use the five-paragraph structure effectively, it is much more important simply *to write persuasively and logically.* If you can, *you should answer the prompt in the essay directions in your first sentence*—or, at the very latest, in the second sentence. The AP graders will be reading your essays rapidly, and it is critical to show them right away that you know the answer to the question they ask. In addition, as mentioned before, the longer you spend writing an introduction, the less time you'll have to write a convincing body of the essay. Make sure you have *specific* supports, referring to the text of the essay whenever possible. General observations or vague references to the reading material will usually cause your score to be in the mediocre range at best. Your thesis sentence should be similar to or a close variation of this formula:

author's name + author's attitude/purpose + subject + devices.

Example: Hemingway's belief in the nobility of the struggle against nature in the short novel *The Old Man and The Sea* is achieved partly through the stark contrast between the single old man and the setting of the vast, unfathomable sea, where though alone, the old man nobly sets out on his quest to conquer the big fish.

Example: In "The Gettysburg Address" by Abraham Lincoln,
            [Title of work]   [author]

the ninth President uses the setting of the
                        [device]

battlefield and the special jargon of democratic
                        [device]

ideals ironically to promote a new idea of rebirth
                        [thesis]

of government in the United States.

The elements of the formula can be re-arranged in any order comfortable for you, but leaving out one of the elements is not advised unless you are an advanced writer. Beginning with this thesis makes you focus on the essential problem and gives your essay a specific direction.

In your essay answer it is useful, but not necessary, to name the specific term ("metaphor," "inverted sentence," "parallelism"). Superior essay writers will, of course, know and use the basic devices of style in a smooth, mature manner. However, remember that your essay answer must include specific examples in the form of short, direct quotations and your answer should explain.

Scoring Guidelines

Content counts much more than grammar, word choice, or spelling; however, seldom does an essay with even as few as three or four significant errors receive the top score. It is wise, therefore, to proofread and correct your writing before going on to the next topic. Recasting (rewording) some of your sentences is acceptable, but make sure your paper is easily legible. You must address the given task carefully: do not deviate from the topic or dwell too long on one point. You should attend to subtle nuances of language in your essay. The mediocre paper fails to identify and to analyze subtleties of meaning. Better quality papers recognize and respond to the emotional shadings of the topic. The scores are usually given as follows:

Scores of 9–8 These are superior essays. They have a clear statement of position, thoughtful support, convincing examples, and stylistic maturity (sentence structure, diction, organization). Although there may be a few grammar or spelling errors, the author demonstrates a superior control of language in writing the essay.

Scores of 7–6 These are excellent essays. However, they have a thesis which lacks the specific and convincing proof of the superior essays. The author's writing style is less mature and thus has occasional lapses of diction, tone, syntax, or organization. Although there may be errors of grammar and spelling, the author demonstrates an adequate control of language.

Scores of 5–4 These are mediocre, but adequate, essays. The thesis may not be quite clear, the argument not as well developed, and the organization not especially effective. There are some grammatical and spelling errors. These essays will receive a score no higher than 4 if they show *any one* of the following:
  (a) oversimplify or overgeneralize the issues;
  (b) write only in general terms, ignoring fine distinctions;
  (c) fail to discuss the issue completely satisfactorily;
  (d) mismanage the evidence;
  (e) contain insufficient details;
  (f) fail to establish the importance to the writer;
  (g) treat only one aspect of a two-sided issue;
  (h) cite examples but fail to consider the consequences;
  (i) cite stylistic techniques but fail to explain the impact;
  (j) characterize the passage without analyzing the language.

Scores of 3–2 These are weak essays. They lack clear organization and adequate support, the writing style is simplistic, and there are frequent grammar and spelling errors.
Score of 1 These are poor essays. Although they may mention the question, they lack clarity, have little or no evidence, and contain consistent grammar and spelling errors. They are badly written, unacceptably brief, or off topic.

Essay Question Types

One type of question, often used in the past but one which has not appeared since the 1989 test, directs you to write a descriptive essay which will create a feeling or atmosphere or reveal your attitude toward the subject. For this essay you will be given specific instructions to describe a person or a place, or perhaps two incidents in a person's life, or perhaps two contrasting locations. Your essay must reveal your attitude toward that place or person, or must reveal the character of the person you describe, or must create an atmosphere for a location. Sometimes an essay of definition is used instead of the descriptive essay. You will be asked to define a term, or to elaborate on the distinctions between two words which are related in meaning but differ in connotative meaning (Man–Gentleman).

The essay should be a sterling example of "show, not tell." You should, for example, show your person barely hiding a smirk at someone who has just tripped, or give a quotation in which the character says something rather rude to another person, rather than just say that the character you are describing has a strange sense of humor that sometimes hurts others. Do not oversimplify your approach. The graders are looking for mature, not simplistic, writing. Descriptive writing should be spatially organized and contain no extraneous details which might detract from a unified overall impression. Essays of definition should be organized from least important to most important, or vice versa.

Another type of essay asks you to analyze the language used in a passage and to explain how the language achieves a certain effect. Do not oversimplify the author's position or attitude. Even if the essay is satirical in tone, take care not to exaggerate the tone and classify it as "bitter" or "biting" unless you are certain this is the author's intention. However, be aware that extreme satire rarely appears on the test. Remember, the makers of the test are looking for subtle gradations of analysis in your answer, and subtlety is difficult to achieve if you are analyzing a simplistic piece of literature, one with an obvious, one-sided, or "cut-and-dried" approach or tone.

Frequently, this question takes the form of two passages on the same topic but written in different styles and with different attitudes. Again, if you are asked to discuss the differences between two passages, do not oversimplify or overexaggerate the differences.

This question expects you to analyze the style of a passage. The question directs you to read the passage carefully. Then, you are instructed to write an essay that (1) analyzes the effect of the passage on the reader; or (2) defines the author's attitude toward his or her topic (usually, the AP test question will name the topic of the passage for you); or, (3) describes the rhetorical purpose of the passage; or (4) identifies the author's purpose or views and how he or she achieves that purpose or conveys those views.

A List of Typical Instructions

Below, you will find a list of the most common directions used for writing essays. Become familiar with these directions, since they have been used frequently on past exams.

- analyze the language and rhetorical devices; consider such elements as narrative structure, selection of detail, manipulation of language, and tone;
- analyze how the author uses juxtaposition of ideas, choice of details, and other aspects of style;
- analyze stylistic, narrative, and persuasive devices;
- analyze the figures of speech and syntax;
- consider word choice, manipulation of sentences, imagery, and use of allusions;
- consider the rhetorical devices such as arguments, assumptions, attitudes, and diction.

Don't let the wording intimidate you: "rhetoric" and "rhetorical devices" refer to word choice and such things as poetic devices; "diction" refers to word choice; "syntax" refers to sentence structure and placement of words within the sentence; "juxtaposition" refers to unlike ideas or details that appear side-by-side or in close proximity to each other.

Basically, this type of question asks you to examine (with attention to nuance) these stylistic devices:

WORD CHOICE
IMAGERY
FIGURES OF SPEECH
SELECTION OF DETAIL
SENTENCE STRUCTURE
TONE

"Word choice" or "diction" refers to individual words. "Imagery" refers to vivid pictures that appeal to the senses. "Figures of speech" refers to common devices, such as simile, allusion, alliteration, etc. "Selection of detail" is not exactly the same as word choice; rather, it is a significant piece of information about the character or location. "Sentence structure" or "syntax" is the arrangement of words in the sentence; sentence structure also includes types of sentences. "Tone" is the author's attitude toward the character, or location, and the author will use all of the devices above to generate that tone or attitude.

The question may ask you to consider these items in your answer:

NARRATIVE STRUCTURE
PERSUASIVE DEVICES
RHETORICAL DEVICES

"Narrative structure" refers to plot structure, or how the details are arranged. "Persuasive devices" refers to valid arguments the author uses, or perhaps logical fallacies. "Rhetorical devices" refers to imagery, word choice, figurative language, sentence structure.

The third type of question will give a quotation from a famous person. The quotation will present an assertion or an opinion which is arguable. You are asked to present a logical argument for or against the position or to defend, challenge, or qualify the position. The directions will tell you to include evidence from your observation, experience, or reading to defend your position.

Begin your essay with a statement of the author's opinion, or one to two sentences of introduction and then the author's opinion. Then, as your thesis, state that you agree or disagree with the author's position; or state that you agree or disagree with some portion of the author's position (and give some indication of which portion you would qualify).

CHAPTER 5

AP English Language & Composition

Glossary of Literary and Rhetorical Terms

Abstract Language

Language describing ideas and qualities rather than observable or specific things, people, or places. The observable or "physical" is usually described in concrete language.

Ad hominem

Latin for "against the man." When a writer personally attacks his or her opponents instead of their arguments.

Allegory

A story, fictional or nonfictional, in which characters, things, and events represent qualities or concepts. The interaction of these characters, things, and events is meant to reveal an abstraction or a truth. The characters and other elements may be symbolic of the ideas referred to.

Alliteration

The repetition of initial identical consonant sounds. Or, vowel sounds in successive words or syllables that repeat.

Allusion

An indirect reference to something (usually a literary text) with which the reader is supposed to be familiar. Allusion is often used with humorous intent, to establish a connection between writer and reader, or to make a subtle point.

Ambiguity

An event or situation that may be interpreted in more than one way. Also, the manner of expression of such an event or situation may be ambiguous. Artful language may be ambiguous. Unintentional ambiguity is usually vagueness.

Analogy

An analogy is a comparison to a directly parallel case. When a writer uses an analogy, he or she argues that a claim reasonable for one case is reasonable for the analogous case.

Anaphora

Repetition of a word, phrase, or clause at the beginning of two or more sentences in a row. This is a deliberate form of repetition and helps make the writer's point more coherent.

Anecdote

A brief recounting of a relevant episode. Anecdotes are often inserted into fictional or nonfictional texts as a way of developing a point or injecting humor.

Annotation

Explanatory notes added to a text to explain, cite sources, or give bibliographical data.

Antithesis

A balancing of two opposite or contrasting words, phrases, or clauses.

Assonance

Repetition of a vowel sound within two or more words in close proximity.

Asyndeton

Commas used (with no conjunction) to separate a series of words. The parts are emphasized equally when the conjunction is omitted; in addition, the use of commas with no intervening conjunction speeds up the flow of the sentence. Asyndeton takes the form of X, Y, Z as opposed to X, Y, and Z.

Authority

Arguments that draw on recognized experts or persons with highly relevant experience are said to rest on authoritative backing or authority. Readers are expected to accept claims if they are in agreement with an authority's view.

Backing

Support or evidence for a claim in an argument.

Balance

Construction in which both halves of the sentence are about the same length and importance.

Begging the Question

Often called circular reasoning, begging the question occurs when the believability of the evidence depends on the believability of the claim.

Causal Relationship

In causal relationships, a writer asserts that one thing results from another. To show how one thing produces or brings about another is often relevant in establishing a logical argument.

Chiasmus

Arrangement of repeated thoughts in the pattern of X Y Y X. Chiasmus is often short and summarizes a main idea.

Common Knowledge

Shared beliefs or assumptions are often called common knowledge. A writer may argue that if something is widely believed, then readers should accept it.

Concrete Language

Language that describes specific, observable things, people or places, rather than ideas or qualities.

Connotation

Rather than the dictionary definition, the associations suggested by a word. Implied meaning rather than literal meaning or denotation.

Consonance

Repetition of a consonant sound within two or more words in close proximity.

Conventional

Following certain conventions, or traditional techniques of writing. An overreliance on conventions may result in a lack of originality. The five-paragraph theme is considered conventional.

Cumulative

Sentence which begins with the main idea and then expands on that idea with a series of details or other particulars.

Deconstruction

A critical approach that debunks single definitions of meaning based on the instability of language. The deconstructionist re-examines literary conventions in light of a belief that deconstruction "is not a dismantling of the structure of a text, but a demonstration that it has already dismantled itself."

Diction

Word choice, particularly as an element of style. Different types and arrangements of words have significant effects on meaning. An essay written in academic diction would be much less colorful, but perhaps more precise than street slang.

Didactic

A term used to describe fiction or nonfiction that teaches a specific lesson or moral or provides a model of correct behavior or thinking.

Dramatic Irony

When the reader is aware of an inconsistency between a fictional or nonfictional character's perception of a situation and the truth of that situation.

Either-Or Reasoning

When the writer reduces an argument or issue to two polar opposites and ignores any alternatives.

Elliptical

Sentence structure which leaves out something in the second half. Usually, there is a subject-verb-object combination in the first half of the sentence, and the second half of the sentence will repeat the structure but omit the verb and use a comma to indicate the elliptical material.

Emotional Appeal

When a writer appeals to readers' emotions (often through pathos) to excite and involve them in the argument.

Epigraph

A quotation or aphorism at the beginning of a literary work suggestive of theme.

Equivocation

When a writer uses the same term in two different senses in an argument.

Ethical Appeal

When a writer tries to persuade the audience to respect and believe him or her based on a presentation of image of self through the text. Reputation is sometimes a factor in ethical appeals, but in all cases the aim is to gain the audience's confidence.

Example

An individual instance taken to be representative of a general pattern. Arguing by example is considered reliable if examples are demonstrably true or factual as well as relevant.

Explication

The act of interpreting or discovering the meaning of a text. Explication usually involves close reading and special attention to figurative language.

Exposition

Background information provided by a writer to enhance a reader's understanding of the context of a fictional or nonfictional story.

False Analogy

When two cases are not sufficiently parallel to lead readers to accept a claim of connection between them.

Fiction

A product of a writer's imagination, usually made up of characters, plot, setting, point of view, and theme. Fiction is often described as lies told with the consent of the reader.

Figurative Language

A word or words that are inaccurate literally, but describe by calling to mind sensations or responses that the thing described evokes. Figurative language may be in the form of metaphors or similes, both non-literal comparison. Shakespeare's "All the world's a stage" is an example of non-literal, figurative language (metaphor, specifically).

Freight-train

Sentence consisting of three or more very short independent clauses joined by conjunctions.

Generalization

When a writer bases a claim upon an isolated example or asserts that a claim is certain rather than probable. Sweeping generalizations occur when a writer asserts that a claim applies to all instances instead of some.

Hyperbole

Conscious exaggeration used to heighten effect. Not intended literally, hyperbole is often humorous.

Image

A word or words, either figurative or literal, used to describe a sensory experience or an object perceived by the senses. An image is always a concrete representation.

Imagery

The use of images, especially in a pattern of related images, often figurative, to create a strong, unified sensory impression.

Inversion

Variation of the normal word order (subject first, then verb, then complement) which puts a modifier or the verb as first in the sentence. The element that appears first is emphasized more than the subject.

Irony

When a reader is aware of a reality that differs from a character's perception of reality (dramatic irony). The literal meaning of a writer's words may be verbal irony.

Logic

An implied comparison resulting when one thing is directly called another. To be logically acceptable, support must be appropriate to the claim, believable and consistent.

Metaphor

A comparison of two things, often unrelated. A figurative verbal equation results where both "parts" illuminate one another. I.A. Richards called the literal term in a metaphor the "tenor" and the figurative term the "vehicle."

Mood

An atmosphere created by a writer's word choice (diction) and the details selected. Syntax is also a determiner of mood because sentence strength, length, and complexity affect pacing.

Moral

The lesson drawn from a fictional or nonfictional story. A heavily didactic story.

Negative-positive

Sentence that begins by stating what is not true, then ending by stating what is true.

Non-sequitur

Latin for "it does not follow." When one statement isn't logically connected to another.

Objectivity

A writer's attempt to remove himself or herself from any subjective, personal involvement in a story. Hard news journalism is frequently prized for its objectivity, although even fictional stories can be told without a writer rendering personal judgment.

Onomatopoeia

The use of a word whose pronunciation suggests its meaning. "Buzz," "hiss," "slam," and "pop" are frequently used examples.

Oversimplification

When a writer obscures or denies the complexity of the issues in an argument.

Oxymoron

A rhetorical antithesis. Juxtaposing two contradictory terms, like "wise fool" or "eloquent silence."

Paradox

A seemingly contradictory statement which is actually true. This rhetorical device is often used for emphasis or simply to attract attention.

Parallelism

Sentence construction which places in close proximity two or more equal grammatical constructions. Parallel structure may be as simple as listing two or three modifiers in a row to describe the same noun or verb; it may take the form of two or more of the same type of phrases (prepositional, participial, gerund, appositive) that modify the same noun or verb; it may also take the form of two or more subordinate clauses that modify the same noun or verb. Or, parallel structure may be a complex blend of single-word, phrase, and clause parallelism all in the same sentence.

Parody

An exaggerated imitation of a serious work for humorous purposes. The writer of a parody uses the quirks of style of the imitated piece in extreme or ridiculous ways.

Pathos

Qualities of a fictional or nonfictional work that evoke sorrow or pity. Over-emotionalism can be the result of an excess of pathos.

Periodic

Sentence that places the main idea or central complete thought at the end of the sentence, after all introductory elements.

Persona

A writer often adopts a fictional voice (or mask) to tell a story. Persona or voice is usually determined by a combination of subject matter and audience.

Personification

Figurative language in which inanimate objects, animals, ideas, or abstractions are endowed with human traits or human form.

Point of View

The perspective from which a fictional or nonfictional story is told. First-person, third-person, or omniscient points of views are commonly used.

Polysyndeton

Sentence which uses *and* or another conjunction (with no commas) to separate the items in a series. Polysyndeton appears in the form of X and Y and Z, stressing equally each member of the series. It makes the sentence slower and the items more emphatic than in the asyndeton.

Post hoc, ergo propter hoc

Latin for "after this, therefore because of this." When a writer implies that because one thing follows another, the first caused the second. But sequence is not cause.

Red Herring

When a writer raises an irrelevant issue to draw attention away from the real issue.

Refutation

When a writer musters relevant opposing arguments.

Repetition

Word or phrase used two or more times in close proximity.

Rhetoric

The art of effective communication, especially persuasive discourse. Rhetoric focuses on the interrelationship of invention, arrangement, and style in order to create felicitous and appropriate discourse.

Satire

A work that reveals a critical attitude toward some element of human behavior by portraying it in an extreme way. Satire doesn't simply abuse (as in invective) or get personal (as in sarcasm). Satire targets groups or large concepts rather than individuals.

Sarcasm

A type of verbal irony.

Simile

A figurative comparison of two things, often dissimilar, using the connecting words "like" or "as."

Straw Man

When a writer argues against a claim that nobody actually holds or is universally considered weak. Setting up a straw man diverts attention from the real issues.

Style

The choices in diction, tone, and syntax that a writer makes. In combination they create a work's manner of expression. Style is thought to be conscious and unconscious and may be altered to suit specific occasions. Style is often habitual and evolves over time.

Symbol

A thing, event, or person that represents or stands for some idea or event. Symbols also simultaneously retain their own literal meanings.

Syntactic Fluency

Ability to create a variety of sentence structures, appropriately complex and/or simple and varied in length.

Syntactic Permutation

Sentence structures that are extraordinarily complex and involved. Often difficult for a reader to follow.

Theme

The central idea of a work of fiction or nonfiction, revealed and developed in the course of a story or explored through argument.

Tone

A writer's attitude toward his or her subject matter revealed through diction, figurative language, and organization on the sentence and global levels.

Tricolon

Sentence consisting of three parts of equal importance and length, usually three independent clauses.

Unity

A work of fiction or nonfiction is said to be unified if all the parts are related to one central idea or organizing principle. Thus, unity is dependent upon coherence.

Verbal Irony

When the reader is aware of a discrepancy between the real meaning of a situation and the literal meaning of the writer's words.

PRACTICE EXAM 1

AP English Language & Composition

PRACTICE EXAM 1

AP English Language & Composition

Section 1

TIME: 60 Minutes
60 Questions

(Answer sheets appear in the back of this book.)

DIRECTIONS: This test consists of selections from literary works and questions on their use of language. After reading each passage, choose the best answer to each question and blacken the corresponding oval on the answer sheet.

Questions 1–3 are based on the following passage. Read the passage carefully before choosing your answers.

London was the focus of all this excitement. Court, Capital and City, it was also the island's greatest port, buzzing with yarns and fables about the New World and its riches. In 1605, inspired by such dreams, two companies, chartered by rival merchants, set out from London and Plymouth. Ralegh, out of
5   favour with the new king, James I, was not involved, but there was a continuity with his earlier expedition. Richard Hakluyt was among the leading lights in the London company. And among the leaders of the Plymouth group were Ralegh Gilbert and his brother John, sons of Walter Ralegh's half-brother, Sir Humphrey Gilbert.
10   The pioneers were lucky. In 1606, the year in which Shakespeare wrote *Antony and Cleopatra,* three ships financed by the London company set sail on the southern route past the Azores and the Canary Islands. They cruised in the West Indies, and then headed north, intending to settle somewhere north of the Spanish in Florida and south of the French in Canada. In April 1607, they
15   sailed into Chesapeake Bay, then—as now—a vast, shallow tidal estuary dotted

with flat, scrubby islands, and teeming with fish, crab and oysters. After about a month they reached the James River and moored in six fathoms off a wooded island which they named after their new king—Jamestown.

This time the English language took root in the New World. Unlike the unfortunate settlers in Roanoke, the men of Jamestown survived, partly thanks to the leadership and determination of Captain John Smith, who pronounced the stark but simple truth that "He that will not work neither shall he eat." In due course—but not until only 38 of the original 105 who had landed were left—they were joined by more colonists.

The processes of language change are often mysterious, but strangely enough, there is still—here and there—some tantalizing, fragmentary evidence of the lost voices of the early Americans. In the Eastern United States today there is nowhere stranger, or more isolated, than the islands of the Chesapeake Bay, "the most valuable and vulnerable estuary in the world," according to one marine biologist. Tangier Island, one of the largest, is a short ride by ferry or light plane from mainland Crisfield, one of the centres for a local industry that supplies one-quarter of America's oysters. It is tiny and very flat: barely three miles long, one mile wide and five feet above sea level at its highest elevation. Graves have heavy lids to prevent the corpses from floating away when the island floods. It has two churches, a guest house for summer tourists, a school, a store-café called Nice's where the local teenagers play electronic games and eat soft-shell crab sandwiches. It is very quiet. The main street is a gritty gravel path, down which the Tangierines (as they are called) walk or bicycle. The island has no cars. Arrive during the morning and it can seem almost deserted. All the men are out in the Bay catching crabs.

The fishermen call themselves "watermen." The word has a chequered history. In Elizabethan times, the word mainly denoted river-borne taxi-drivers "who [ply] for hire on a river." It took root in the Chesapeake Bay, mainly because the geography demanded a lot of water-transport. The comment of a local crab captain shows a typical use of the word: "My father raised me a waterman and it's all what I know how to do…Follow the water one year same as the next. Ain't no sense in it, but I do it just the same."

The watermen have a hard life. Their day starts about three in the morning when the men start to gather in Ray's café. There they gossip, drink Coca-Cola, eat Ray's toast, and wait for each crew to assemble. It is usually still dark when they set out into the Bay, the port and starboard lights of their long white crab boats winking over the water. By the time the dawn has broken the wharves

are empty, and will remain so until the boats come back, in the early afternoon or evening, as soon as they have their quota of *jimmies* and *sooks*, mature male
55   and female crabs. Listening to the Tangier Island watermen chatting together in Ray's café or on the boats, many English listeners could imagine they were in Devon or Cornwall. Their pattern of speech has many characteristic West Country intonations. As one fisherman remarked, "Our voice, our language, hasn't changed since people first moved to Tangier Island, or so some people
60   have told us...."

The Tangierines—approximately 800 residents—say that their island was first settled in 1686 by a certain John Crockett, a Cornishman. There are no records of this, but the evidence of the Tangier Island speech is overwhelming. To English ears, they sound West Country. Most striking of all "sink" is
65   pronounced *zink*. *Mary* and *merry* have a similar pronunciation, though this is common to much of the tidewater district. "Paul" and "ball" sound like *pull* and *bull*. For "creek" they will say *crik*. And they have a special local vocabulary: *spider* for "frying-pan," bateau for "skiff" and *curtains* for "blinds."

1.   The words "this time" in paragraph three imply the English language

(A)   took root in the New World for the first time

(B)   never had been brought to the New World before

(C)   had been rejected by the New World previously

(D)   had yet to be introduced to the New World

(E)   had been introduced to the New World, accepted, and then rejected at a previous time

2.   Tangierines are those who

(A)   are infatuated with tangerines

(B)   dress solely in light orange shades

(C)   are originally from Tangiers

(D)   inhabit Tangier Island

(E)   first spoke English in the New World

3.   We know that watermen have a hard life because

(A)   they never set foot on dry land

(B)   they begin their day at about 3:00 A.M

(C)   they set out to gather crabs before dawn

(D) both (B) and (C)

(E) they are restricted to the island

Questions 4–6 are based on the following passage. Read the passage carefully before choosing your answers.

In the theatre itself—we were then located at the Maxine Elliott—the atmosphere resembled that of the actors' quarters. Its old star dressing-room, right off the stage, had become the Group office. There was hardly any privacy at all. Everyone wandered in at will. There we conducted a little business, interviewed
5   actors, chatted, carried on controversies, prepared publicity, discussed policy.

Performances were kept at a high level, however, except when Luther Adler was overcome by lassitude. On such occasions we pepped him up by inventing distinguished guests in the audience. Stella Adler was almost always at top form, owing to her craft integrity and to her unusual energy. This energy, with
10   which she jolted her brother, often shocked him into fierce resistance. They quarreled at least four times a week, and the curtain calls amused, amazed, and terrified the company because between bows they turned on each other to resume their cat-and-dog fight.

Carnovsky regarded the Adlers' conduct as undisciplined. Besides their quar-
15   rels they sometimes delayed the curtains by their tardiness in coming from their dressing-rooms. But one night Carnovsky himself failed to appear for his entrance. Luther and Stella had to ad lib. for an unconscionable time. Finally Carnovsky appeared and instead of speaking his usual line: "I am five minutes too early," he confessed: "I am five minutes late." Hilarity followed the tension
20   backstage. When I inquired into the cause of this late entrance, something almost without precedent in Carnovsky's career, someone misinformed me, with a touch of malice, that he had been reading the *Communist Manifesto* of Marx and Engels in his dressing-room and had thus forgotten his entrance cue.

For the rest, the actors, insufficiently occupied, demanded more opportu-
25   nity to work at whatever duties we could find for them. Walter Coy alternated with Bill Challee in a small part in the play, as did Grover Burgess with Russell Collins. The graduate apprentice Elia Kazan, or "Gadget," as he was called for unspecified reasons, served as an example of enterprise by painting display signs, typing and aiding our harassed, underpaid press agent, whose office was
30   a dressing-room with a privy, around which a screen had been placed, a screen that perversely fell whenever visitors appeared.

Some of the actors began to seek an outlet for their energies outside our

circle. There were, as noted, occasional performances of our experimental work at workers' clubs. But more than that, certain new groups were forming, and
35   they asked some of our actors to help them, perhaps to give talks or classes. Besides Gorelik's new Theatre Collective—which, according to him, was to be a "realistic" organization in contrast to our "romantic" Group—Charles and Adelaide Walker had spoken to me of a project on a larger, more professional basis than the modest Collective, a "proletarian theatre," which was to develop
40   into the Theatre Union, which opened on West Fourteenth Street in the spring of 1933.

    At this time the Theatre Collective and the Theatre Union were holding formative meetings for discussion, some of which I attended. I noticed the presence of a few Group Theatre actors, notably Joe Bromberg. When word
45   about these meetings was reported back to our people, a certain suspicion, even resentment, manifested themselves among some of them, because they feared that people like Bromberg would be estranged from us. Actors like Carnovsky spoke for a moment, without meaning to, as if these new organizations were upstarts, with no right to divert serious actors from their legitimate work in the
50   still struggling Group. Bromberg pointed out, quite properly, that there was not enough for him to do around the Group then. He drew himself up to his full height (unfortunately insufficient for the occasion) and announced in an almost defiant voice: "Besides, I like workers," a statement that struck everyone as a bewildering *non sequitur*.
55   Though no official policy had been announced by the Group directorate, it was now established that our actors were free to use their extra time as they would; and if some were interested in contributing to the development of new groups, amateur or professional, no one would gainsay them in any way.

4.   In the last paragraph, "gainsay" probably means

    (A) support   (D) report

    (B) ignore   (E) banish

    (C) oppose

5.   One of the reasons the actors sought a place in other groups is that they

    (A) wanted to challenge the Group

    (B) were insufficiently occupied

    (C) needed to raise capital for the Group

(D)   admired the directors of the Theatre Collective and the Theatre Union

(E)   sought to create disharmony within the Group

6.   We may infer, for the most part, that the actors enjoyed each other since

(A)   there was hardly any privacy

(B)   everyone wandered into the office at will

(C)   performances were kept at a high level most of the time

(D)   both (A) and (C)

(E)   (A), (B), and (C)

Questions 7–16 are based on the following passage. Read the passage carefully before choosing your answers.

THE Number of Souls in *Ireland* being usually reckoned one Million and a half; of these I calculate there may be about Two hundred Thousand Couple whose Wives are Breeders; from which Number I subtract thirty thousand Couples, who are able to maintain their own Children; although I apprehend
5   there cannot be so many, under *the present Distresses of the Kingdom*; but this being granted, there will remain an Hundred and Seventy Thousand Breeders. I again subtract Fifty Thousand, for those Women who miscarry, or whose Children die by Accident, or Disease, within the Year. There only remain an Hundred and Twenty Thousand Children of poor Parents, annually born:
10   The Question therefore is, How this Number shall be reared, and provided for? Which, as I have already said, under the present Situation of Affairs, is utterly impossible, by all the Methods hitherto proposed: For we can *neither employ them in Handicraft* or *Agriculture*; we neither build Houses, (I mean in the Country) nor cultivate Land: They can very seldom pick up a Livelyhood
15   by *Stealing* until they arrive at six Years old; except where they are of towardly Parts; although, I confess, they learn the Rudiments much earlier; during which Time, they can, however, be properly looked upon only as Probationers; as I have been informed by a principal Gentleman in the County of *Cavan*, who protested to me, that he never knew above one or two Instances under the
20   Age of six, even in a Part of the Kingdom *so renowned for the quickest Proficiency in that Art.*

I AM assured by our Merchants, that a Boy or a Girl before twelve Years old, is no saleable Commodity; and even when they come to this Age, they will not yield above Three Pounds, or Three Pounds and half a Crown at most, on
25   the Exchange; which cannot turn to Account either to the Parents or the

Kingdom; the Charge of Nutriment and Rags, having been at least four Times that Value.

I SHALL now therefore humbly propose my own Thoughts, which I hope will not be liable to the least Objection.

30 I HAVE been assured by a very knowing *American* of my Acquaintance in *London*; that a young healthy Child, well nursed, is, at a Year old, a most delicious, nourishing, and wholesome Food; whether *Stewed, Roasted, Baked,* or *Boiled*; and, I make no doubt, that it will equally serve in a *Fricasie,* or *Ragoust.*

35 I DO therefore humbly offer it to *publick Consideration*, that of the Hundred and Twenty Thousand Children, already computed, Twenty thousand may be reserved for Breed; whereof only one Fourth Part to be Males; which is more than we allow to *Sheep, black Cattle,* or *Swine*; and my Reason is, that these Children are seldom the Fruits of Marriage, *a Circumstance not much regarded by*

40 *our Savages*; therefore, *one Male* will be sufficient to serve *four Females.* That the remaining Hundred thousand, may, at a Year old, be offered in *Sale to the Persons of Quality* and *Fortune*, through the Kingdom; always advising the Mother to let them suck plentifully in the last Month, so as to render them plump, and fat for a good Table. A Child will make two Dishes at an Entertainment for

45 Friends; and when the Family dines alone, the fore or hind Quarter will make a reasonable Dish; and seasoned with a little Pepper or Salt, will be very good Boiled on the fourth Day, especially in *Winter.*

I HAVE reckoned upon a Medium, that a Child just born will weigh Twelve Pounds; and in a solar Year, if tolerably nursed, encreaseth to twenty

50 eight Pounds.

I GRANT this Food will be somewhat dear, and therefore *very proper for Landlords*; who, as they have already devoured most of the Parents, seem to have the best Title to the Children.

INFANTS Flesh will be in Season throughout the Year; but more plentiful

55 in *March*, and a little before and after: For we are told by a grave Author, an eminent *French* Physician, that *Fish being a prolifick Dyet*, there are more Children born in *Roman Catholick Countries* about Nine Months after Lent than at any other Season: Therefore reckoning a Year after *Lent*, the Markets will be more glutted than usual; because the Number of *Popish Infants*, is, at

60 least three to one in this Kingdom; and therefore it will have one other Collateral Advantage, by lessening the Number of *Papists* among us.

I HAVE already computed the Charge of nursing a Beggar's Child (in

which List I reckon all *Cottagers*, *Labourers*, and Four fifths of the *Farmers*) to be about two Shillings *per Annum*, Rags included; and I believe, no Gentleman
65 would repine to give Ten Shillings for the *Carcase of a good fat Child*; which, as I have said, will make four Dishes of excellent nutritive Meat, when he hath only some particular Friend, or his own Family, to dine with him. Thus the Squire will learn to be a good Landlord, and grow popular among his Tenants; the Mother will have Eight Shillings net Profit, and be fit for Work until she
70 produceth another Child.

7. The phrase "I GRANT this Food will be somewhat dear, and therefore *very proper for Landlords*; who, as they have already devoured most of the Parents, seem to have the best Title to the Children" (lines 51–53) does all of the following EXCEPT

    (A)   understate the cost of the "Food"

    (B)   reverse the metaphor which dominates the passage

    (C)   sarcastically indict the children's parents

    (D)   reveal the speaker's attitudes toward landlords and tenants in a seeming aside

    (E)   suggest persons who may play a role in giving the children better outcomes to their lives

8. Throughout the passage, poor children and their parents are metaphorically described using images of

    (A)   urban decay   (D)   scientific analysis

    (B)   animal husbandry   (E)   religious rituals

    (C)   business transactions

9. What does the word "Popish" (line 59) mean?

    (A)   Tiny   (D)   Fish Eating

    (B)   Unruly   (E)   Irish

    (C)   Roman Catholic

10. What effect does the construction of the argument in lines 1–47 have upon the reader?

    (A)   Its seemingly rational progression makes the startling proposal even more jarring.

(B) The emphasis upon "Souls" (line 1) initiates an atmosphere of religious reverence.

(C) The references to animal breeding in the first and fifth paragraphs detract from the passage's main point.

(D) The use of census-like statistics before the proposal confuses the issue and makes the reader more susceptible to persuasion.

(E) The emphatic first person opening of each paragraph except the first underscores the speaker's reasonableness.

11. The antecedent of "many" (line 5) is

(A) "Children" (line 4)   (D) "Wives" (line 3)

(B) "Number" (line 3)   (E) "Couples" (line 4)

(C) "Souls" (line 1)

12. Which of the following can be inferred to be the intent of the passage?

I. To rebuke landlords for their callousness

II. To force a reexamination of other proposals

III. To offer a measured solution to a crisis

IV. To build the speaker's reputation as a civic-minded person

(A) I only   (D) I, II, and III only

(B) I and II only   (E) I, II, III, and IV

(C) III and IV only

13. Stylistically, the passage may best be described as

(A) philosophical   (D) hortative

(B) lyrical   (E) satirical

(C) scientific

14. The speaker's use of "Breeders" (line 3) as a predicate adjective for "Wives"

(A) depersonalizes the women

(B) praises the women's fertility

(C) describes the women's occupation

(D) distinguishes the women from the men

(E) criticizes the women for having children

15. The phrase "I SHALL now therefore humbly propose my own Thoughts, which I hope will not be liable to the least Objection" (lines 28–29) is an example of

   (A) hyperbole

   (B) oxymoron

   (C) understatement

   (D) metaphor

   (E) digression

16. In the context of the passage as a whole, the references to women as "Breeders" and children as a "saleable Commodity" (line 23) serve as

   (A) digressions from the course of the argument.

   (B) statements of fact

   (C) summaries of the argument

   (D) omens of the proposal to come

   (E) objections to the proposal itself

Questions 17–22 are based on the following passage. Read the passage carefully before choosing your answers.

   UNDER the strange nebulous envelopment, wherein our Professor has now shrouded himself, no doubt but his spiritual nature is nevertheless progressive, and growing: for how can the "Son of Time," in any case, stand still? We behold him, through those dim years, in a state of crisis, of transition: his mad

5 Pilgrimings, and general solution into aimless Discontinuity, what is all this but a mad Fermentation; wherefrom, the fiercer it is, the clearer product will one day evolve itself.

   Such transitions are ever full of pain: thus the Eagle when he moults is sickly; and, to attain his new beak, must harshly dash-off the old one upon rocks. What

10 Stoicism soever our Wanderer, in his individual acts and motions, may affect, it is clear that there is a hot fever of anarchy and misery raging within; coruscations of which flash out: as, indeed, how could there be other? Have we not seen him disappointed, bemocked of Destiny, through long years? All that the young heart might desire and pray for has been denied; nay, as in the last worst instance, offered

15 and then snatched away. Ever an "excellent Passivity"; but of useful, reasonable Activity, essential to the former as Food to Hunger, nothing granted: till at length, in this wild Pilgrimage, he must forcibly seize for himself an Activity, though useless, unreasonable. Alas, his cup of bitterness, which had been filling drop by drop, ever since that first "ruddy morning" in the Hinterschlag Gymnasium, was at

20 the very lip; and then with that poison-drop, of the Towngood-and-Blumine business, it runs over, and even hisses over in a deluge of foam.

He himself says once, with more justice than originality: "Man is, properly speaking, based upon Hope, he has no other possession but Hope; this world of his is emphatically the Place of Hope." What, then, was our Professor's
25 possession? We see him, for the present, quite shut-out from Hope; looking not into the golden orient, but vaguely all round into a dim copper firmament, pregnant with earthquake and tornado.

17. All of the following name the main character of the passage EXCEPT

(A) our Wanderer

(B) the Eagle

(C) he/him

(D) our Professor

(E) the "Son of Time" (line 3)

18. Which phrase best summarizes the speaker's intent in examining this stage of the main character's life?

(A) "Such transitions are ever full of pain" (line 8)

(B) "Have we not seen him disappointed, bemocked of Destiny, through long years" (lines 12–13)

(C) "there is a hot fever of anarchy and misery raging within" (line 11)

(D) "what is all this but a mad Fermentation; wherefrom, the fiercer it is, the clearer product will one day evolve itself" (lines 5–7)

(E) "We see him, for the present, quite shut-out from Hope" (line 25)

19. The accumulative painfulness of this time for the main character is illustrated primarily by the use of

(A) metaphors

(B) digressions

(C) hyperbole

(D) oxymoron

(E) onomatopoeia

20. What is the function of the clause introduced by "nay" in line 14?

(A) It negates the clause that precedes it.

(B) It contradicts the clause that precedes it.

(C) It intensifies the clause that precedes it.

(D) It restates the clause that precedes it.

(E) It downplays the clause that precedes it.

21. It can be inferred that the speaker considers the statement "Man is, properly speaking, based upon Hope, he has no other possession but Hope; this world of his is emphatically the Place of Hope" (lines 22–24) to be

(A) a simile   (D) an epiphany

(B) a quotation   (E) a platitude

(C) a metaphor

22. "Coruscations" (line 11) can best be defined as

(A) boils   (D) blocks

(B) threads   (E) scars

(C) sparks

Questions 23-34 are based on the following passage. Read the passage carefully before you choose your answers. This passage is a portion of the National Institute of Mental Health Publication No. 01-4929, entitled "Teenage Brain: A work in progress."

New imaging studies are revealing—for the first time—patterns of brain development that extend into the teenage years. Although scientists don't know yet what accounts for the observed changes, they may parallel a pruning process that occurs early in life that appears to follow the principle of "use-it-or-lose-it:" neural connections, or synapses, that get exercised are retained, while those that don't are lost. . . . While it's known that both genes and environment play major roles in shaping early brain development, science still has much to learn about the relative influence of experience versus genes on the later maturation of the brain. . . . Nonetheless, it's tempting to interpret the new findings as empowering teens to protect and nurture their brain as a work in progress.

The newfound appreciation of the dynamic nature of the teen brain is emerging from MRI (magnetic resonance imaging) studies that scan a child's brain every two years, as he or she grows up. . . . In the first such longitudinal study of 145 children and adolescents, reported in 1999, NIMH's Dr. Judith Rapoport and colleagues were surprised to discover a second wave of overproduction of gray matter, the thinking part of the brain—neurons and their branch-like extensions—just prior to puberty.[1] Possibly related to the influence of surging sex hormones, this thickening peaks at around age 11 in girls, 12 in boys, after which the gray matter actually thins some.

---

[1] J.N. Giedd, J. Blumenthal, N.O. Jeffries, et al. "Brain Development During Childhood and Adolescence: A Longitudinal MRI Study." *Nature Neuroscience*, 1999; 2(10): 861-3.

20   Prior to this study, research had shown that the brain overproduced gray
matter for a brief period in early development—in the womb and for about the
first 18 months of life—and then underwent just one bout of pruning. Researchers are now confronted with structural changes that occur much later in
adolescence. The teen's gray matter waxes and wanes in different functional
25   brain areas at different times in development. For example, the gray matter
growth spurt just prior to puberty predominates in the frontal lobe, the seat of
"executive functions"—planning, impulse control and reasoning . . . Unlike
gray matter, the brain's white matter—wire-like fibers that establish neurons'
long-distance connections between brain regions—thickens progressively from
30   birth in humans. A layer of insulation called myelin progressively envelops
these nerve fibers, making them more efficient, just like insulation on electric
wires improves their conductivity.

Advancements in MRI image analysis are providing new insights into how
the brain develops. UCLA's Dr. Arthur Toga and colleagues turned the NIMH
35   team's MRI scan data into 4-D time-lapse animations of children's brains
morphing as they grow up—the 4th dimension being rate-of-change.[2] Researchers report a wave of white matter growth that begins at the front of the
brain in early childhood, moves rearward, and then subsides after puberty.
Striking growth spurts can be seen from ages 6 to 13 in areas connecting brain
40   regions specialized for language and understanding spatial relations, the temporal and parietal lobes. This growth drops off sharply after age 12, coinciding
with the end of a critical period for learning languages.

While this work suggests a wave of brain white matter development that
flows from front to back, . . . studies have suggested that gray matter
45   maturation flows in the opposite direction, with the frontal lobes not fully
maturing until young adulthood. . . . increased myelination in the adult
frontal cortex likely relates to the maturation of cognitive processing and
other "executive" functions. Parietal and temporal areas mediating spatial,
sensory, auditory and language functions appeared largely mature in the
50   teen brain.

Another series of MRI studies is shedding light on how teens may process
emotions differently than adults. Using functional MRI (fMRI), a team led by
Dr. Deborah Yurgelun-Todd at Harvard's McLean Hospital scanned subjects'
brain activity while they identified emotions on pictures of faces displayed on a

---

[2] P.M. Thompson, J.N. Giedd, R.P. Woods, et al. "Growth Patterns in the Developing Brain
Detected by Using Continuum Mechanical Tensor Maps." *Nature*, 2000; 404(6774): 190-3.

55 computer screen.[3] Young teens, who characteristically perform poorly on the task, activated the amygdala, a brain center that mediates fear and other "gut" reactions, more than the frontal lobe. As teens grow older, their brain activity during this task tends to shift to the frontal lobe, leading to more reasoned perceptions and improved performance. Similarly, the researchers saw a shift in
60 activation from the temporal lobe to the frontal lobe during a language skills task, as teens got older. These functional changes paralleled structural changes in temporal lobe white matter.

While these studies have shown remarkable changes that occur in the brain during the teen years, they also demonstrate what every parent can confirm:
65 the teenage brain is a very complicated and dynamic arena, one that is not easily understood.

23. Which of the following best reflects the subject of this article?

(A) Research on the changing behavior of teenagers

(B) Research on brain development during adolescence

(C) Comparison of adult brain matter and adolescent brain matter

(D) The use of MRIs in brain research

(E) Functional and structural changes in the brain throughout life

24. To which of the following does the term "pruning" refer in lines 3 and 22?

(A) The loss of unused synapses

(B) Parallel roles of genes and environment in brain development

(C) Gray matter growth spurts that occur at specific growth phases

(D) Progressive thickening of the brain's white matter

(E) The contrasting flow of gray and white matter in the brain

25. The tone of this passage can best be described as mainly

(A) humorous   (D) urbane

(B) informative   (E) candid

(C) sarcastic

---

[3] A.A. Baird, S.A. Gruber, D.A. Fein, et al. Functional Magnetic Resonance Imaging of Facial Affect Recognition in Children and Adolescents. *Journal of the American Academy of Child and Adolescent Psychiatry*, 1999; 38(2): 195-9.

26. Which of the following is an accurate reading of the first footnote?

    (A) The article *Nature Neuroscience* appeared on page 861 of "Brain Development During Childhood and Adolescence: A Longitudinal MRI Study" in 1999.

    (B) The article "Brain Development During Childhood and Adolescence: A Longitudinal MRI Study" by Giedd, Blumenthal, Jeffries and others can be found on page 10 in *Nature Neuroscience*.

    (C) The second of ten articles about brain development during childhood and adolescence was published in *Nature Neuroscience* in 1999.

    (D) An article by Giedd, Blumenthal, Jeffries and others begins on page 861 in a 1999 issue of *Nature Neuroscience*.

    (E) *Nature Neuroscience* is an article that Giedd, Blumenthal, Jeffries, and others wrote in 1999 for a longitudinal study on brain development.

27. Based on the information given in this article, what did studies by Dr. Rapoport and Dr. Toga have in common?

    (A) Both focused on involved time-lapse animations of the brains of children.

    (B) Both focused on the pruning process of the brain.

    (C) They used one another's research findings in their studies of the brain.

    (D) They focused on the differences between the brain development of females and that of males during the adolescent years.

    (E) Both involved the changes that a brain undergoes as a person grows up.

28. The last two sentences in the fourth paragraph (lines 39–42) imply that we should learn foreign languages before reaching what age?

    (A) Six years   (D) Sixteen years

    (B) Eleven years   (E) Adulthood

    (C) Twelve years

29. References to a "wave" in lines 15, 37, and 43 serve to

    (A) remind the reader that the brain contains water

    (B) highlight the steady development of the brain's gray and white matter

    (C) highlight the fact that some parts of the brain do not grow steadily and continuously

    (D) detail the size limitations of the brain's gray matter

    (E) detail the size limitations of the brain's white matter

30. The second footnote lets the reader know that

    (A) P. M. Thompson and colleagues interviewed Dr. Toga about the UCLA 4-D study

    (B) more information about the UCLA 4-D study may be available in a *Nature* article written by P. M. Thompson and colleagues

    (C) P. M. Thompson and colleagues worked with Dr. Toga and his associates on the UCLA 4-D study

    (D) Thompson, Giedd, Woods, and others wrote an article titled "Nature" for a journal that was published in 2000

    (E) an article about growth patterns in the developing brain appears on page 404 in a 2000 issue of *Nature*

31. The structure of lines 22-32 ("Researchers...conductivity") can best be described as

    (A) general statement followed by examples

    (B) general statement followed by other general statements

    (C) specific examples followed by general statement

    (D) easily understood statement followed by more technical terminology

    (E) technical terminology that an average reader probably could not understand

32. Lines 24 and 25 state, "The teen's gray matter waxes and wanes in different functional brain areas at different times in development." Which of the following is a different way to say "waxes and wanes"?

    (A) Progresses

    (B) Predominates

    (C) Becomes increasingly efficient with maturity

    (D) Is "wishy-washy"

    (E) Has growth spurts

33. In context, the word "dynamic" (line 65) is best interpreted to mean

    (A) ever-changing   (D) moving

    (B) emphatic   (E) strenuous

    (C) forceful

34. A look at the three footnotes in this article might lead one to conclude that

(A) the articles contain much more technical terminology than the passage does

(B) brain research was a popular topic of many magazines in 1999 and 2000

(C) not much brain research was conducted prior to 1999

(D) research on the brain's development occurred during 1999 and 2000

(E) J. Giedd liked to write articles in collaboration with other scientists

Questions 35–44 are based on the following passage. Read the passage carefully before choosing your answers.

The house of fiction has in short not one window, but a million—a number of possible windows not to be reckoned, rather; every one of which has been pierced, or is still pierceable, in its vast front, by the need of the individual vision and by the pressure of the individual will. These apertures, of dissimilar
5   shape and size, hang so, all together, over the human scene that we might have expected of them a greater sameness of report than we find. They are but windows at the best, mere holes in a dead wall, disconnected, perched aloft; they are not hinged doors opening straight upon life. But they have this mark of their own that at each of them stands a figure with a pair of eyes, or at least
10 with a field-glass, which forms, again and again, for observation, a unique instrument, insuring to the person making use of it an impression distinct from every other. He and his neighbours are watching the same show, but one seeing more where the other sees less, one seeing black where the other sees white, one seeing big where the other sees small, one seeing coarse where the
15 other sees fine. And so on, and so on; there is fortunately no saying on what, for the particular pair of eyes, the window may not open; "fortunately" by reason, precisely, of this incalculability of range. The spreading field, the human scene, is the "choice of subject"; the pierced aperture, either broad or balconied or slitlike and low-browed, is the "literary form"; but they are, singly
20 or together, as nothing without the posted presence of the watcher—without, in other words, the consciousness of the artist. Tell me what the artist is, and I will tell you of what he has *been* conscious. Thereby I shall express to you at once his boundless freedom and his "moral" reference.

35. The "house of fiction" (line 1) is

    (A) a symbol that represents the meeting place of authors

    (B) a conceit that unifies the passage

    (C) a metaphor that portrays the genre

    (D) a simile that describes fiction as a structure

    (E) a concrete image that names a literary dynasty

36. What is the function of the quotation marks surrounding "choice of subject" (line 18) and "literary form" (line 19)?

    (A) They indicate that the speaker is using another author's ideas.

    (B) They reveal the speaker's disgust with literary terminology.

    (C) They are the speaker's appeal to authority.

    (D) They emphasize the major points of the speaker's argument.

    (E) They set the generic critical labels apart from the more expansive field of human experience and structure the author has to choose from.

37. The phrase "they are not hinged doors opening straight upon life" (line 8) implies that

    (A) fiction does not directly mirror life

    (B) works of fiction are windows not doors

    (C) fiction presents twisted versions of life

    (D) fictional works are not easily created

    (E) each example of fiction has its own individuality

38. What is the antecedent of "they" in line 6?

    (A) Windows (line 7)

    (B) Apertures (line 4)

    (C) Holes (line 7)

    (D) Need (line 3) and pressure (line 4)

    (E) Eyes (line 9)

39. The shifts in point of view from "we" (lines 5–6) to "he" (line 12) to "I" (line 22) has which of the following effects?

    (A) The shifts indicate the speaker's distinguishing himself/herself from the critics who inhabit the house of fiction.

(B)   The shifts symbolize the speaker's alienation from the genre.

(C)   The movement from group to individual parallels the movement from the group "house of fiction" (line 1) to individual "figure with a pair of eyes" (line 9).

(D)   The movements separate the readers from the authors.

(E)   The shifts reveal the inconsistencies in the speaker's argument.

40.   Which of these phrases contains an example of antithesis?

(A)   "These apertures, of dissimilar shape and size, hang so, all together, over the human scene" (lines 4–5)

(B)   "They are but windows at the best, mere holes in a dead wall, disconnected, perched aloft; they are not hinged doors" (lines 6–8)

(C)   "...at each of them stands a figure with a pair of eyes, or at least with a field-glass" (lines 9–10)

(D)   "...one seeing more where the other sees less, one seeing black where the other sees white, one seeing big where the other sees small, one seeing coarse where the other sees fine" (lines 12–15)

(E)   "...they are, singly or together, as nothing without the posted presence of the watcher" (lines 19–20)

41.   Which of the following does the speaker consider to be the most important element in the "house of fiction"?

(A)   The "figure with a pair of eyes" (line 9)

(B)   The "apertures" (line 4)

(C)   The "hinged doors" (line 8)

(D)   The "human scene" (line 5)

(E)   The "spreading field" (line 17)

42.   It may be inferred from the connotations of windows being "pierced" in the "house of fiction" (lines 1–4) that

(A)   individual works of fiction are merely tiny components of the larger genre

(B)   the windows are merely decorative and have no practical function in the house

(C)   the literary canon resists new works of fiction

(D)   the writer needs special tools and techniques to create fiction

(E)   the writer bends fiction to his/her vision rather than bending his vision to predetermined strictures of fiction

43. The speaker apparently believes that the distinctiveness of a work of fiction

    (A) is directly correlated to the subject matter

    (B) is determined by the literary form

    (C) is dependent upon the individuality of the author

    (D) is subject to the dictates of the author's contemporaries

    (E) is immaterial to the construction of the "house of fiction"

44. The syntax of the sentence in lines 21–22 presents an example of

    (A) parallelism   (D) hyperbole

    (B) chiasmus   (E) ellipsis

    (C) alliteration

Questions 45–60 are based on the following passage. Read the passage carefully before choosing your answers.

After considering the historic page, and viewing the living world with anxious solicitude, the most melancholy emotions of sorrowful indignation have depressed my spirits, and I have sighed when obliged to confess, that either nature has made a great difference between man and man, or that the civiliza-
5 tion which has hitherto taken place in the world has been very partial. I have turned over various books written on the subject of education, and patiently observed the conduct of parents and the management of schools; but what has been the result?—a profound conviction that the neglected education of my fellow-creatures is the grand source of the misery I deplore; and that women,
10 in particular, are rendered weak and wretched by a variety of concurring causes, originating from one hasty conclusion. The conduct and manners of women, in fact, evidently prove that their minds are not in a healthy state; for, like the flowers which are planted in too rich a soil, strength and usefulness are sacrificed to beauty; and the flaunting leaves, after having pleased a fastidious
15 eye, fade, disregarded on the stalk, long before the season when they ought to have arrived at maturity.—One cause of this barren blooming I attribute to a false system of education, gathered from the books written on this subject by men who, considering females rather as women than human creatures, have been more anxious to make them alluring mistresses than affectionate wives
20 and rational mothers; and the understanding of the sex has been so bubbled by this specious homage, that the civilized women of the present century, with a

few exceptions, are only anxious to inspire love, when they ought to cherish a nobler ambition, and by their abilities and virtues exact respect.

25 In a treatise, therefore, on female rights and manners, the works which have been particularly written for their improvement must not be overlooked; especially when it is asserted, in direct terms, that the minds of women are enfeebled by false refinement; that the books of instruction, written by men of genius, have had the same tendency as more frivolous productions; and that, in the true style of Mahometanism, they are treated as a kind of subordinate 30 beings, and not as a part of the human species, when improveable reason is allowed to be the dignified distinction which raises men above the brute creation, and puts a natural sceptre in a feeble hand.

Yet, because I am a woman, I would not lead my readers to suppose that I mean violently to agitate the contested question respecting the quality or infe-35 riority of the sex; but as the subject lies in my way, and I cannot pass it over without subjecting the main tendency of my reasoning to misconstruction, I shall stop a moment to deliver, in a few words, my opinion.—In the government of the physical world it is observable that the female in point of strength is, in general, inferior to the male. This is the law of nature, and it does not 40 appear to be suspended or abrogated in favour of women. A degree of physical superiority cannot, therefore, be denied—and it is a noble prerogative! But not content with this natural pre-eminence, men endeavour to sink us still lower, merely to render us alluring objects for a moment; and women, intoxicated by the adoration which men, under the influence of their senses, pay them, do 45 not seek to obtain a durable interest in their hearts, or to become the friends of the fellow creatures who find amusement in their society.

45. The terms "the historic page" (line 1) and "the living world" (line 1) are synonymous with

   (A) fiction and reality
   (B) books and specimens
   (C) page and globe
   (D) past and present
   (E) antiques and contemporaries

46. The speaker's description of her own manner as filled with "anxious solicitude" and "the most melancholy emotions of sorrowful indignation [which] have depressed my [her] spirits" (lines 2–3) is notable for its

   (A) emphatic repetitiveness
   (B) pointed brevity
   (C) controlled wittiness
   (D) bitter irony
   (E) delicate understatement

47. Which of the following assumptions can be made about the speaker's original conclusion that "either nature has made a great difference between man and man, or that the civilization which has hitherto taken place in the world has been very partial" (lines 3–5)?

    (A) The speaker does not decide between the two propositions.

    (B) The speaker eventually concludes that nature has created man unequal.

    (C) The speaker determines that civilization has rendered man unequal.

    (D) The speaker asserts that both nature and civilization have created man unequal.

    (E) The speaker decides that neither nature nor civilization have created man unequal.

48. Rhetorically, the passage as a whole can best be described as

    (A) deliberative

    (B) judicial

    (C) panegyric

    (D) analytical

    (E) expository

49. The speaker's study of "the historic page" (line 1), "the living world" (line 1), books on education, parents, schools, and other works on women has which of the following effects?

    I.   It reveals the speaker's lack of confidence in her theories.

    II. It portrays the speaker as a rational and thorough researcher.

    III. It provides the reader with the basis of the speaker's conclusions.

    IV. It lends authority to the speaker's own work.

    (A) I only

    (B) II only

    (C) II and III only

    (D) I, II, and III only

    (E) II, III, and IV only

50. In the first paragraph the main point of the argument, the unnatural inequality of women, is introduced by

    (A) an ellipsis

    (B) a metaphor

    (C) a paradox

    (D) a rhetorical question

    (E) a proverb

51. What is the "one hasty conclusion" (line 11) which has resulted in reduced status for women?

    (A) Women have been undereducated.

    (B) The minds of women are weak.

    (C) Women inspire love rather than respect.

    (D) Women peak before they reach maturity.

    (E) Women's roles are "wife" and "mother."

52. All of the following can be inferred about the speaker's female contemporaries EXCEPT

    (A) their very actions prove that their minds' cultivation has been neglected

    (B) as women, they are other than human

    (C) their education makes them better suited as idolized lovers than effective mothers

    (D) they receive little or no respect

    (E) they have been educated primarily by males

53. The description of women's minds as "not in a healthy state" (line 12) is expanded using

    (A) a conceit   (D) a parable

    (B) a metaphor   (E) a pun

    (C) a simile

54. Which of the following phrases contains an oxymoron?

    (A) "the most melancholy emotions of sorrowful indignation have depressed my spirits" (lines 2–3)

    (B) "like the flowers which are planted in too rich a soil, strength and usefulness are sacrificed to beauty" (lines 13–14)

    (C) "One cause of this barren blooming I attribute to a false system of education" (lines 16–17)

    (D) "men who…have been more anxious to make them alluring mistresses than affectionate wives and rational mothers" (lines 18–20)

    (E) "improveable reason is allowed to be the dignified distinction which raises men above the brute creation" (lines 30–32)

55. The alliteration occurring in lines 11–16 has the effect of

    (A) linking the behavior resulting from, the cause of, and the ultimate effect of the unequal status of women

    (B) digressing from the main point of the argument

    (C) contradicting the description contained in the simile that precedes it

    (D) downplaying the role unequal treatment has forced upon women

    (E) joining the simile to the concept it seeks to describe

56. Despite its length, the sentence that makes up the second paragraph maintains coherence through

    (A) parallel syntax

    (B) compound sentence structure

    (C) repetition of key phrases

    (D) strings of prepositional phrases

    (E) complex sentence structure

57. Who has made the assertions in lines 25–32?

    (A) The authors of works "which have been particularly written for their [women's] improvement" (lines 24–25)

    (B) The speaker of the passage

    (C) Other female authors

    (D) "Men of genius" (lines 27–28)

    (E) Men who "have been more anxious to make them [women] alluring mistresses than affectionate wives and rational mothers" (lines 18–20)

58. It can be inferred that lines 33–37 function as

    I. an assuaging of the fear of radical reformation

    II. a presentation of the speaker as builder of a rational argument

    III. an example of women as other than "enfeebled by false refinement" (lines 26–27)

    IV. a disclaimer of any involvement in the struggle for the betterment of women

    (A) I only   (D) I, II, and III only

    (B) I and II only   (E) I, II, III, and IV

    (C) I and IV only

59. Whom would the speaker most probably blame for the unequal status of women?

    (A) Men

    (B) Women

    (C) Men and women

    (D) Authors of works intended for women's education

    (E) Parents

60. The overall style of the passage can best be described as

    (A) humorous and light

    (B) colloquial and unstructured

    (C) florid and pedantic

    (D) formal and complex

    (E) urbane and ironic

STOP

This is the end of Section 1.
If time still remains, you may check your work only in this section.
Do not begin Section 2 until instructed to do so.

Section 2

Question 1   (Suggested reading time—15 minutes)
(Suggested writing time—40 minutes)

Directions: The following prompt is based on the accompanying six sources.

This question requires you to synthesize a variety of sources into a coherent, well-written essay. *Refer to the sources to support your position; avoid mere paraphrase or summary. Your argument should be central; the sources should support this argument.*

Remember to attribute both direct and indirect sources.

Introduction: Throughout the history of the United States, the country's presidents have delivered speeches to Congress and to the public. These presentations reflect their concerns and beliefs as they lead the country. What have these speeches had in common? What do they reflect about the focus of this country? Do these speeches seem to indicate that any specific topics or themes have run throughout the history of America?

Assignment: Read carefully the following sources, all of which are excerpted passages taken from speeches by United States Presidents. Then, in an essay that synthesizes at least three of the sources for support, take a position that defends, challenges, or qualifies the claim that the concerns and beliefs of American Presidents have remained basically the same throughout the history of this country.

You may refer to the sources by their titles (Source A, Source B, etc.) or by the descriptions in parentheses.

> Source A (Washington)
>
> Source B (Roosevelt)
>
> Source C (Truman)
>
> Source D (Kennedy)
>
> Source E (Reagan)
>
> Source F (Clinton)

Source A

Washington, George. "First Annual Message." 8 January 1790.

. . . In resuming your consultations for the general good, you cannot but derive encouragement from the reflection that the measures of the last Session have been as satisfactory to your Constituents, as the novelty and difficulty of the work allowed you to hope. Still further to realize their expectations and to secure the blessings which a Gracious Providence has placed within our reach, will in the course of the present important Session, call for the cool and deliberate exertion of your patriotism, firmness and wisdom.

Among the many interesting objects, which will engage your attention, that of providing for the common defence will merit particular regard. To be prepared for War is one of the most effectual means of preserving peace.

A free people ought not only to be armed but disciplined; to which end a uniform and well digested plan is requisite: And their safety and interest require, that they should promote such manufactories, as tend to render them independent on others for essential, particularly for military supplies. . . .

The interests of the United States requires that our intercourse with other nations should be facilitated, by such provisions as will enable me to fulfill my duty in that respect, in the manner which circumstances may render most conducive to the public good. . . .

. . . I cannot forbear intimating to you the expediency of giving effectual encouragement as well to the introduction of new and useful inventions from abroad, as to the exertions of skill and genius in producing them at home; and of facilitating the intercourse between the distant parts of our Country by a due attention to the Post-Office and Post-Roads.

Nor am I less persuaded, that you will agree with me in opinion, that there is nothing which can better deserve your patronage than the promotion of Science and Literature. Knowledge is in every country the surest basis of public happiness. In one in which the measures of Government receive their impression so immediately from the sense of the Community as in ours it is proportionably essential. . . .

Source B

Roosevelt, Theodore. "Inaugural Address." 4 March 1905.

My fellow-citizens,

No people on earth have more cause to be thankful than ours, and this is said reverently, in no spirit of boastfulness in our own strength, but with gratitude to the Giver of Good who has blessed us with the conditions which have enabled us to achieve so large a measure of well-being and of happiness. . . .

Much has been given us, and much will rightfully be expected from us. We have duties to others and duties to ourselves; and we can shirk neither. We have become a great nation, forced by the fact of its greatness into relations with the other nations of the earth, and we must behave as beseems a people with such responsibilities. Toward all other nations, large and small, our attitude must be one of cordial and sincere friendship. We must show not only in our words, but in our deeds, that we are earnestly desirous of securing their good will by acting toward them in a spirit of just and generous recognition of all their rights. . . .

Our relations with the other powers of the world are important; but still more important are our relations among ourselves. Such growth in wealth, in population, and in power as this nation has seen during the century and a quarter of its national life is inevitably accompanied by a like growth in the problems which are ever before every nation that rises to greatness. Power invariably means both responsibility and danger. . . .

Source C

Truman, Harry S. "Inaugural Address." 20 January 1949.

. . . In performing the duties of my office, I need the help and prayers of every one of you. I ask for your encouragement and your support. The tasks we face are difficult, and we can accomplish them only if we work together. . . .

It may be our lot to experience, and in large measure to bring about, a major turning point in the long history of the human race. The first half of this century has been marked by unprecedented and brutal attacks on the rights of man, and by the two most frightful wars in history. The supreme need of our time is for men to learn to live together in peace and harmony.

The peoples of the earth face the future with grave uncertainty, composed almost equally of great hopes and great fears. In this time of doubt, they look to the United States as never before for good will, strength, and wise leadership. . . .

We are moving on with other nations to build an even stronger structure of international order and justice. We shall have as our partners countries which, no longer solely concerned with the problem of national survival, are now working to improve the standards of living of all their people. We are ready to undertake new projects to strengthen the free world. . . .

The United States is pre-eminent among nations in the development of industrial and scientific techniques. The material resources which we can afford to use for the assistance of other peoples are limited. But our imponderable resources in technical knowledge are constantly growing and are inexhaustible. . . .

Greater production is the key to prosperity and peace. And the key to greater production is a wider and more vigorous application of modern scientific and technical knowledge. . . .

Steadfast in our faith in the Almighty, we will advance toward a world where man's freedom is secure.

To that end we will devote our strength, our resources, and our firmness of resolve. With God's help, the future of mankind will be assured in a world of justice, harmony, and peace.

Source D

Kennedy, John F. "Inaugural Address." 20 January 1961.

. . . I have sworn before you and Almighty God the same solemn oath our fore-bears prescribed nearly a century and three quarters ago.

The world is very different now. For man holds in his mortal hands the power to abolish all forms of human poverty and all forms of human life. And yet the same revolutionary beliefs for which our forebears fought are still at issue around the globe-the belief that the rights of man come not from the generosity of the state but from the hand of God . . . .

Let every nation know, whether it wishes us well or ill, that we shall pay any price, bear any burden, meet any hardship, support any friend, oppose any foe to assure the survival and the success of liberty . . . .

To those old allies whose cultural and spiritual origins we share, we pledge the loyalty of faithful friends. United, there is little we cannot do in a host of cooperative ventures. Divided, there is little we can do—for we dare not meet a powerful challenge at odds and split asunder.

To those new states whom we welcome to the ranks of the free, we pledge our word that one form of colonial control shall not have passed away merely to be replaced by a far more iron tyranny. . . .

Finally, to those nations who would make themselves our adversary, we offer not a pledge but a request: that both sides begin anew the quest for peace, before the dark powers of destruction unleashed by science engulf all humanity in planned or accidental . . .

Let both sides seek to invoke the wonders of science instead of its terrors. Together let us explore the stars, conquer the deserts, eradicate disease, tap the ocean depths and encourage the arts and commerce . . . .

Now the trumpet summons us again-not as a call to bear arms, though arms we need—not as a call to battle, though embattled we are—but a call to bear the burden of a long twilight struggle, year in and year out, "rejoicing in hope, patient in tribulation"—a struggle against the common enemies of man: tyranny, poverty, disease and war itself.

And so, my fellow Americans: ask not what your country can do for you—ask what you can do for your country.

My fellow citizens of the world: ask not what America will do for you, but what together we can do for the freedom of man.

Finally, whether you are citizens of America or citizens of the world, ask of us here the same high standards of strength and sacrifice which we ask of you. With a good conscience our only sure reward, with history the final judge of our deeds, let us go forth to lead the land we love, asking His blessing and His help, but knowing that here on earth God's work must truly be our own.

> **Source E**
>
> Reagan, Ronald. "First Inaugural Address." 20 January 1981.

. . . To those neighbors and allies who share our freedom, we will strengthen our historic ties and assure them of our support and firm commitment. We will match loyalty with loyalty. We will strive for mutually beneficial relations. We will not use our friendship to impose on their sovereignty, for our own sovereignty is not for sale.

As for the enemies of freedom, those who are potential adversaries, they will be reminded that peace is the highest aspiration of the American people. We will negotiate for it, sacrifice for it; we will not surrender for it, now or ever. . . .

Above all, we must realize that no arsenal or no weapon in the arsenals of the world is so formidable as the will and moral courage of free men and women. It is a weapon our adversaries in today's world do not have. It is a weapon that we as Americans do have. Let that be understood by those who practice terrorism and prey upon their neighbors.

I'm told that tens of thousands of prayer meetings are being held on this day, and for that I'm deeply grateful. We are a nation under God, and I believe God intended for us to be free. It would be fitting and good, I think, if on each Inaugural Day in future years it should be declared a day of prayer.

The crisis we are facing today . . . does require, however, our best effort and our willingness to believe in ourselves and to believe in our capacity to perform great deeds, to believe that together with God's help we can and will resolve the problems which now confront us. . . .

Source F

Clinton, William J. "Inaugural Address." 20 January 1997.

. . . Each and every one of us, in our own way, must assume personal responsibility not only for ourselves and our families but for our neighbors and our Nation. Our greatest responsibility is to embrace a new spirit of community for a new century. For any one of us to succeed, we must succeed as one America. The challenge of our past remains the challenge of our future: Will we be one Nation, one people, with one common destiny, or not? Will we all come together, or come apart?

. . . now we are building bonds with nations that once were our adversaries. Growing connections of commerce and culture give us a chance to lift the fortunes and spirits of people the world over. And for the very first time in all of history, more people on this planet live under democracy than dictatorship. . . .

The promise we sought in a new land, we will find again in a land of new promise. In this new land, education will be every citizen's most prized possession. Our schools will have the highest standards in the world, igniting the spark of possibility in the eyes of every girl and every boy. And the doors of higher education will be open to all. The knowledge and power of the information age will be within reach not just of the few but of every classroom, every library, every child. Parents and children will have time not only to work but to read and play together. And the plans they make at their kitchen table will be those of a better home, a better job, the certain chance to go to college. . . .

We will stand mighty for peace and freedom and maintain a strong defense against terror and destruction. Our children will sleep free from the threat of nuclear, chemical, or biological weapons. Ports and airports, farms and factories will thrive with trade and innovation and ideas. And the world's greatest democracy will lead a whole world of democracies.

Our land of new promise will be a nation that meets its obligations, a nation that balances its budget but never loses the balance of its values, a nation where our grandparents have secure retirement and health care and their grandchildren know we have made the reforms necessary to sustain those benefits for their time, a nation that fortifies the world's most productive economy even as it protects the great natural bounty of our water, air, and majestic land. And in this land of new promise, we will have reformed our politics so that the voice of the people will always speak louder than the din of narrow interests, regaining the participation and deserving the trust of all Americans. . . .

From the height of this place and the summit of this century, let us go forth. May God strengthen our hands for the good work ahead, and always, always bless our America.

CONTINUE TO QUESTION 2

Question 2 (Suggested time—40 minutes.) This question is worth one-third of the total essay score.

The passages below represent early and later drafts of a poem. Write a well-organized essay in which you discuss the probable reasons for the writer's additions and deletions and the ways in which those revisions change the effect of the poem.

Early Draft

My hope was one, from cities far
Nursed on a lonesome heath:
Her lips were red as roses are,
Her hair a woodbine wreath.

She lived among the untrodden ways
Besides the springs of Dove,
A maid whom there were none to praise,
And very few to love;

A violet by a mossy stone
Half-hidden from the eye!
Fair as a star when only one
Is shining in the sky!

And she was graceful as the broom
That flowers by Carron's side;
But slow distemper checked her bloom,
And on the Heath she died.

Long time before her head lay low
Dead to the world was she:
But now she's in her grave, and Oh!
The difference to me!

Later Draft

She dwelt among th' untrodden ways
Beside the springs of Dove,
A Maid whom there were none to praise
And very few to love.
A Violet by a mossy stone
Half-hidden from the Eye!

—Fair, as a star when only one
Is shining in the sky!

She *liv'd* unknown, and few could know
When Lucy ceas'd to be;
But she is in her Grave, and Oh!
The difference to me.

CONTINUE TO QUESTION 3 ▷

Question 3 (Suggested time—40 minutes.) This question is worth one-third of the total essay score.

Our use of language differs depending upon the manner or conditions in which it is used. Our language may differ in use of syntax, inflection, vocabulary and pronunciation, dependent on circumstances.

Write an essay describing the differences in the language you would use in two different circumstances—a conversation with a friend versus the dialogue in a job interview, for example. Your essay should indicate what purposes the differences in your use of language serve.

END OF EXAM

PRACTICE EXAM 1

AP English Language & Composition

Answer Key

Section 1

1.	(A)	21.	(E)	41.	(A)
2.	(D)	22.	(C)	42.	(E)
3.	(D)	23.	(B)	43.	(C)
4.	(C)	24.	(A)	44.	(B)
5.	(B)	25.	(B)	45.	(D)
6.	(E)	26.	(D)	46.	(A)
7.	(C)	27.	(E)	47.	(C)
8.	(B)	28.	(C)	48.	(A)
9.	(C)	29.	(C)	49.	(E)
10.	(A)	30.	(B)	50.	(D)
11.	(E)	31.	(A)	51.	(B)
12.	(B)	32.	(E)	52.	(B)
13.	(E)	33.	(A)	53.	(C)
14.	(A)	34.	(D)	54.	(C)
15.	(C)	35.	(B)	55.	(A)
16.	(D)	36.	(E)	56.	(A)
17.	(B)	37.	(A)	57.	(B)
18.	(D)	38.	(B)	58.	(D)
19.	(A)	39.	(C)	59.	(C)
20.	(C)	40.	(D)	60.	(D)

PRACTICE EXAM 1

AP English Language & Composition

Detailed Explanations of Answers

Section 1

1. **(A)** (A) is the correct answer since (B) and (D) suggest this was the first time English had been introduced to the New World, which is incorrect according to the first paragraph that tells of the Englishman Ralegh's earlier forays into the New World. (C) and (E) are also incorrect since each would need the word "at" before the phrase to indicate that past attempts to introduce English to the New World had been rejected by current inhabitants.

2. **(D)** By re-reading paragraph four, we see that (D) is the correct answer. (A) and (B) are not mentioned and so are incorrect. (C) sounds plausible, but a re-reading informs us it is an incorrect answer. (E) is also incorrect since the previous paragraph informs us Jamestown is where the English language took root in the New World.

3. **(D)** (A) and (E) are both incorrect since neither is mentioned, nor implied, in the passage. (B) and (C) are both true, but each is incorrect because it refers to only one part of a two part answer. (D) is the correct answer due to each of its parts being stated in the passage.

4. **(C)** (C) is the correct answer because although it was established that the actors' free time spent with other groups may have been problematic previously, this would now be permitted under the Group's unofficial policy. (A) is incorrect due to the fact that the Group had been worried about—rather than encouraging—their actors being involved with other acting groups. (B) is also incorrect since it had been the mention of actors involved in other acting groups prior to this unofficial policy which prompted the policy. (D) is incorrect because it is specifically mentioned in the passage that involvement in other acting groups could be noted but not held against the members of the Group. Lastly, (E) is also incorrect because it is stated "our actors were free to use their extra time as they would."

5. **(B)** Since (B) is clearly stated in paragraph four, this is the correct answer. There is no mention of (A), (C), (D), or (E) in the passage, despite each sounding as if it were plausible.

6. **(E)** (E) is the correct answer since each choice is stated within the first two paragraphs and are all positive aspects of the Group's members. While (A), (B), and (C) are each true, each is only one aspect of the inference, thereby making each incorrect. (D) contains two of the three aspects of the correct answer but omits the third which causes it to be incorrect also.

7. **(C)** (A) is correct because the invaluable life of a child is understatedly appraised as "somewhat dear" (line 51). (B) is also correct because the passage's dominant metaphor is that of parents raising their infants as food for the wealthy: here the parents are being "devoured" (line 52). (D) and (E) are correct, and (C) is incorrect because the landlords are sarcastically indicted. They have financially "eaten up" the parents and can be held responsible for the ends of their children.

8. **(B)** While the monetary mechanics of buying and selling a child for food (C) are mentioned and scientific jargon briefly used (D), "animal husbandry," (B), is the best answer. The wives/mothers are referred to as "Breeders" and the children as "a most delicious, nourishing and wholesome Food" (lines 31–32) when cooked in ways associated with cuts of animal meats (lines 32–34). Lines 35–40 compare ratios of human males and females to those found among domesticated animal herds. Children are described as if they were holiday turkeys, with instructions for fattening them and calculating the number of persons they will serve. Images of a dying, unstable city [urban decay, (A)], or religious rivals (E) are not found in the passage.

9. **(C)** (C) is correct because "Popish" is a disparaging term used to describe someone or something as being of the Roman Catholic church. Although "Fish Eating" (D) and the "Irish" (E) are mentioned in the passage, they are unrelated to the term "Popish," as are "Tiny" (A) and "Unruly" (B).

10. **(A)** The argument in these lines moves from a statement of a problem to a refutation of previously suggested solutions. Evidence to support a new remedy (the shocking revelation of the "American") is followed by this new proposal. The juxtaposition of such a frightening suggestion with such logical order shows the proposal in heightened horrific relief; therefore, (A) is correct. "Souls" [line 1, (B)] is simply a synonym for "persons"; moreover, no other religious sentiments or principles follow. (D) is incorrect because the author is using statistics to introduce and clarify his idea, not to befuddle his reader. References to animal breeding (C) and first person openings (E) occur but do not have the effects given.

11. **(E)** The speaker is calculating the number of fertile "Couples" and subtracts 30,000 who can afford the upkeep of their children (although there cannot be "so many" because of the economic situation). The "couples" are numbered, not the "children" (A). "Number" (B) is incorrect because its own antecedent is "200,000 Couple" (line 2). "Souls" (C) is equal to the total number of persons in Ireland and not the subtracted "many." "Wives" (D) is incorrect because it is only a component of the "many" couples.

12. **(B)** III and IV may appear correct: the author creates a satiric speaker who leads the reader to expect a plausible solution suggested by a rational, concerned citizen. The terrifying and definitively unmeasured proposal shatters these initial illusions. The author's actual appraisal of the landlords as uncaring (I), and even responsible for much of the problem of poverty, is revealed in lines 51–53 (they financially "devoured" parents and are best suited nonmetaphorically to consume their children), lines 62–63 (cottagers and farmers have beggars' status), and lines 68–69 (the landlord will learn that being good to his tenants means giving them financial assistance). The previous proposals (lines 12–14) have seemed impossible; juxtaposed with such an improbable idea as raising children for food, they accrue new reasonableness and possibility (II).

13. **(E)** Stylistically the passage is neither philosophical (A); lyrical [(B), expressing the writer's thoughts and sentiments, usually poetically]; scientific (C); nor hortative [(D), earnestly urging a specific course of action]. It is satirical [(E), sarcastically and ironically exposing vice or folly].

14. **(A)** The best answer is (A); the animalistic connotations of "Breeders" dehumanizes the women. The speaker is so removed from these persons that no emotions toward them, such as those in choices (B) and (E) are present. The women are not given any special status over that of the men (C); they are simply singled out as the actual producers of children. The speaker does not blame or chastise the women for bearing children, (D) but the landlords for impoverishing these children.

15. **(C)** The proposal which follows these lines is likely to cause explosive reactions far beyond the understated "least Objection" (line 29). It does not contain exaggeration (A), seemingly opposite but apt terms (B), or an implied comparison (D). The phrase signals the coming of the main point of the argument rather than a distraction from it (E).

16. **(D)** Under an argument whose logical progression seems to suggest the coming of a rational proposal, these references are warning flags. While couched in nonemotional language, they imply that people can be bought and sold as animals. The "knowing American" (line 30) adds the concept of children as food. If the reader has missed this direction so far, letting the argument's rational layout sweep over him/her, the speaker "humbly" hammers it home. (A) and (E) are incorrect because the references are key elements of the argument, not digressions from or objections to it. Children as food of breeder mothers are not actual occurrences (B) but the speaker's "invention." The argument has not been fully introduced; therefore, these terms cannot be summarizing it (C).

17. **(B)** The main character is named "our Professor" (line 1), "the Son of Time" (line 3), and "our Wanderer" (line 10). Choice (B), "the Eagle" (line 8), is incorrect because it is the subject of a metaphor that describes the transitional state the main character is in, not the character himself. The main character is also called "he/him" [choice (C)]. (B) is therefore the proper choice, since it is the only incorrect answer.

18. **(D)**   The speaker intends to show that this turbulent time is necessary for the formation of the main character's self; the more chaotic it is, the more composed the person who emerges from it. Choices (A), (B), (C), and (E) are incorrect because each describes this period of the main character's life but does not indicate why the speaker considers it worth examining.

19. **(A)**   The subject's life thus far is extensively compared to a cup overflowing with bitterness (lines 18–21). (B) is incorrect because the subject's pain is the focal point, not an aside from another topic. There is no overstatement of the pain [(C), hyperbole] or description using seemingly contradictory terms [(D), oxymoron]. There are no descriptive words which imitate sounds [(E), onomatopoeia].

20. **(C)**   This clause offers the more intense "last worst instance" (line 14) of having one's desires denied. (C) is the best choice because the "nay" clause relates and emphasizes its predecessor. (A) and (B) misinterpret "nay" as a strict negative rather than as a corrective pause before a restatement. (D) merely restates without emphasizing. (E) is incorrect because it lists the opposite effect.

21. **(E)**   The speaker qualifies this statement as having "more justice than originality" (line 22), implying that while solemnly delivered and true it is still a common observation (E), "platitude." (A) and (C) are incorrect because there is no comparison being made in the statement. The statement is not attributed to another person and therefore cannot be considered a quotation (B). The statement is commonplace and thus cannot have come as a sudden revelation [(D), epiphany].

22. **(C)**   Contextually, coruscations "flash" out, making "sparks" (C) the best definition. "Boils" (A) and "scars" (E) may seem to be consequences of an illness ("fever," line 11), but they would form over time and not flash out suddenly. "Threads" (B) and "blocks" (D) are not supported by contextual evidence.

23. **(B)**   The article mentions (A) the changing behavior of teenagers, (C) adolescent brain matter, (D) the use of MRIs in brain research, and (E) functional and structural changes in the brain throughout life. However, none of the topics is the main subject of the article. The main subject of the entire article is (B) research on brain development during adolescence.

24. **(A)**   The answer (A) is correct because the first paragraph states "a pruning process that occurs early in life that appears to follow the principle of 'use-it-or-lose-it:' neural connections, or synapses, that get exercised are retained, while those that don't are lost." Choices (B), (C), (D), and (E) are all part of the brain development that the passage describes, but they do not refer specifically to the "pruning" that lines 3 and 20 address.

25. **(B)**   The author is presenting the facts and implications of studies on the brain's development primarily during the teen years. The author's tone is (B) informative.

Nothing in the passage is (A) humorous, (C) sarcastic, or (D) urbane. And although the author does not appear to be concealing information, the tone is more informative than (E) candid: a candid tone would be more blunt and outspoken.

26. **(D)** In answering this question, you must know the different parts of a footnote, regardless of the format used. In the first footnote, Giedd, Blumenthal, Jeffries and others (indicated by "et al") are the authors. "Brain Development During Childhood and Adolescence: A Longitudinal MRI Study" is the title of the article. Depending on the format used, an article title may or may not be placed in quotation marks. Following the article title is the name of the magazine or journal, which may be italicized or underlined. Here, the journal is *Nature Neuroscience*. The volume number and the issue number come next: here, the article appears in the tenth issue of the second volume. The last part of the footnote is the page number or numbers. This particular article appears on pages 861 to 863. (D) is the only one that correctly describes the parts of the first footnote. *Nature Neuroscience* is the journal title, not the article title; the article title is "Brain Development During Childhood and Adolescence: A Longitudinal Study." Therefore, (A) and (E) are incorrect. The article appears on pages 861–863, instead of page 10; the number 10 refers to the issue number. So (B) is wrong. Nothing in the footnote indicates that the article is one of several articles; instead, the number 2 refers to the volume number, and the number 10 refers to the issue number. Therefore, choice (C) is incorrect.

27. **(E)** (E) is the only choice that correctly indicates the similarity between the two researchers' studies. The article says that Dr. Toga and colleagues used "4-D time-lapse animations of children's brains morphing as they grow up," but nothing indicates that Dr. Rapoport's study used such animations. Therefore, (A) is incorrect. (B) is wrong because nothing specifically says that the two researchers focused on the pruning process mentioned elsewhere in the paragraph, although one might infer that the concepts are related. Although Dr. Toga did use Dr. Rapoport's data, we do not know if Dr. Rapoport used the findings of Dr. Toga; thus, (C) is not correct. And nothing in the article indicates that either of them studied the differences between the brains of males and females; therefore, (D) is incorrect.

28. **(C)** Lines 39–44 refer to "striking growth spurts...from ages 6 to 13 in areas connecting brain regions specialized for language . . . ," which stop "sharply after age 12, coinciding with the end of a critical period for learning languages." Thus, (C) is the correct answer.

29. **(C)** The author refers to "waves" of growth to emphasize that parts of the brain grow more rapidly at some stages of development than at others. Lines 15–17 mention "a second wave of overproduction of gray matter . . . just prior to puberty." Lines 37–38 reveal "a wave of white matter growth that begins at the front of the brain in early childhood . . . then subsides after puberty." And lines 43–44 address "a wave of brain white matter development that flows from front to back." The article does not indicate that (A) the brain contains water, (B) the brain's gray matter and white matter develop steadily, or the size of the brain's (D) gray matter or (E) white matter is limited.

30. **(B)** The purpose of a footnote is to let the reader know the original source of the information; usually, this source contains additional information about the footnoted topic. In this article, the footnote is used to indicate the source where the author found information about the UCLA 4-D study conducted by Dr. Toga and his colleagues. It is reasonable to assume that additional information is available in this source, which is an article written by Thompson, Giedd, Woods, and others. Therefore, (B) is correct. We have no way of knowing if Thompson (A) interviewed Dr. Toga or (C) worked with him. *Nature* is the title of the journal, not (D) the title of the article. And the article appeared on pages 190–3; the volume number—not the page number—is (E) 404.

31. **(A)** (A) is the best description of lines 22–32, since the statement "Researchers are not confronted with structural changes that occur much later in adolescence" is a general statement. The sentences that finish the paragraph give specific examples of those structural changes. This passage does not contain (B) a general statement followed by more general statements. It does not (C) start with specific examples that are followed by a general statement. And it does not contain technical terminology; so (D) and (E) are not correct.

32. **(E)** The author clarifies the phrase "waxes and wanes" in the following sentences, indicating that the gray matter has growth spurts in different areas of the brain at different stages of development. So (E) is the correct answer. (A) is incorrect because the term "progress" implies steady, continuous growth or development. If you chose (C), you may have read the passage too quickly: the sentence immediately following the quoted sentence indicates that the gray matter growth spurt in the frontal lobe—not the gray matter itself—predominates at a certain point in development. Although the last sentence of the paragraph indicates that the brain's white matter become more efficient, (C) the phrase "becomes increasingly efficient" is not an accurate substitution for the phrase "waxes and wanes" in reference to gray matter in the quoted sentence. Likewise, (D) "wishy-washy"—meaning "ineffectual or weak"—is an inappropriate description of the brain's gray matter and has nothing to do with the phrase "waxes and wanes."

33. **(A)** While all of the choices are synonyms that you might find in a dictionary or thesaurus if you looked up "dynamic," the only one that fits in this context is (A) "ever-changing."

34. **(D)** The three articles cited in this passage were published in 1999 or 2000. The titles of all three articles indicate that the topics are scientific studies, and the article itself indicates that they all focus on brain development. Therefore, (D) is an appropriate conclusion. (A) is incorrect because the footnotes tell us nothing about how the technical level of the language in the articles. (B) is not correct since we know only that the three cited journals contain articles about brain research, and we do not know how popular the topic was during that time. And (C) is incorrect, since the footnotes tell us nothing about how much brain research was conducted prior to 1999, although the third paragraph of the passage does indicate that research had

been conducted prior to the 1999 NIMH study. And although Giedd was one of the writers of two of the articles, we have no way of knowing if he liked writing those articles with the other writers, and the footnotes do not tell us if any of the writers were scientists. Therefore, (E) is not correct.

35. **(B)**   (B) is a better answer than (C) because the metaphor of fiction as a house is extended and expanded throughout the passage (conceit). Authors who write fiction are figuratively gathered in the "house of fiction," but they do not literally meet in an actual place (A). (D) is incorrect because there is no comparison using "like" or "as." The image is concrete, but it does not pertain to any particular group of authors (E).

36. **(E)**   The quotation marks indicate that the framed terms are not the speaker's own: the speaker prefers "the spreading field, the human scene" (lines 17–18) to the narrow "choice of subject" and the multifaceted "pierced aperture" (line 18) to "literary form" (E). (A) is incorrect because the speaker applies these labels to his/her own terminology but does not attribute them to a specific author. The speaker may prefer his/her own terminology, but there is no negative emotion toward the labels (B). The quotation marks do not give authoritative weight to the labels (C). (D) is incorrect because the terms in quotation marks are not the speaker's but generic labels he expands upon.

37. **(A)**   A door that would open "straight upon life" would directly reveal life: fictional works are not such doors and do not strictly imitate life (A). (A) is a better answer than (B) because (B) interprets the phrase literally, not as the metaphor it is. (C) is incorrect because it relies upon a misinterpretation of "not...opening straight." There are no contextual references to the making of fiction (D). (E) is incorrect because it refers to the sentence which follows this phrase and introduces additional information.

38. **(B)**   "Apertures" (openings) precedes "they" and is synonymous with its predicate "windows" (B). (A) and (C) are incorrect because they follow "they" and are its predicates. "Need" and "pressure" (D) describe the formation of the windows, not the windows themselves. "Eyes" (E) follows "they" and cannot be its antecedent.

39. **(C)**   The shifts in point of view from "we" to "I" mimic the description of fiction that moves from building/genre housing all authors to each watcher at a window with an individual perspective (C). (A) is incorrect because the "house of fiction" contains authors, not their critics. The speaker neither affirms nor denies that he/she is a writer of fiction, making (B) incorrect. The use of "we" draws readers in and allies them with, rather than alienating them from, the speaker's perspective (D). The argument moves logically from house to windows to individual perspective, making (E) incorrect.

40. **(D)**   (D), with its parallel pairs of contrasting words, exemplifies antithesis. There are no such contrasts in the other four choices. Shape and size (A), windows and doors (B), eyes and field-glass (C), and singly and together (E) are not opposites.

41. **(A)**   The speaker states that human scene/choice of subject and window/literary form are nothing without the "consciousness of the artist" (line 21). (B) and

(D) are consequently incorrect. (E) is incorrect because it is synonymous with (D). Hinged doors (C) are dismissed because they do not have the same function as the windows.

42. **(E)** "Piercing" connotes forceful action, force that an author directs toward the "house of fiction" to make his work part of it (E). (A) and (B) are incorrect because they misinterpret piercing as making holes for jewelry, and contradict the speaker's emphasis upon the importance of windows and the "watcher" behind them. There is no evidence that established authors reject or fight new works (C). The windows are created by "the need of the individual vision and by the pressure of the individual will" (lines 3–4), not by any special implements (D).

43. **(C)** The speaker states "tell me what the artist is, and I will tell you of what he has been conscious" (lines 21–22), implying that the individuality of the work comes from its author's own distinct character (C). The subject and form [(A) and (B)] cannot give the work its individuality without the author's "posted presence" (line 20). (D) is incorrect because there is no mention of an author's contemporaries in the passage. The passage details the shaping of fiction by the individual author and his work and thus affirms their importance; (E) is consequently incorrect.

44. **(B)** The sentence contains a chiasmus (B), a reversal of grammatical structures:

> "[you] tell me
> I will tell you."

(A) is incorrect because there is no repetition of similarly constructed clauses. "Alliteration" (C), the repetition of initial consonants, is not present. There is no exaggeration [hyperbole, (D)] or omission of easily understood words [ellipsis, (E)].

45. **(D)** The conclusion the speaker makes from reviewing these items, nature has created men unequal or civilization "which has hitherto taken place" (lines 4–5), indicates that they are the past and the present. (A), (B), and (C) rely upon misinterpretations of "page," each assuming that this page is literally part of a book. (D) misreads "historic" as "old" and "aged."

46. **(A)** The speaker emphasizes the depths of her concern by stacking words with the same meanings, such as "anxious" with "solicitude" (meaning "anxiety") and "melancholy" (meaning "sadness") with "sorrowful" and "depressed." The description is neither short (B) nor lessened (E). (C) is incorrect because the speaker is not attempting to be cleverly amusing. The rest of the paragraph makes it clear that the speaker is not mockingly describing her feelings with their opposites [irony, (D)].

47. **(C)** The speaker's subsequent affirmation that "the neglected education of my fellow creatures is the grand source of the misery I deplore" (lines 8–9) makes it clear that she believes that civilization (C), not nature (B), is responsible for man's inequality. (A), (D), and (E) are consequently incorrect.

48. **(A)** The passage is "deliberative" because the speaker seeks to persuade the reader of the injustice of the inequality of women. It is not "judicial" (B) because it is neither accusing nor defending. "Panegyric" (C) is incorrect because the passage does not praise or blame. (D) and (E) are incorrect because the passage's rhetorical purpose is not analyzing or explaining.

49. **(E)** (I) is incorrect [and thus (A) and (D)] because the speaker strongly states that it is her "profound conviction" (line 8) that education creates inequality among men. The speaker's study indicates the sources for her ideas (III) and extensive research (II), both of which give greater weight to her own conclusions (IV); (E) (II, III, and IV only) is thus the correct answer.

50. **(D)** The speaker's main point, that lack of education leads to inequality, particularly of women, is the speaker's answer to the question "what has been the result" (lines 7–8). "Ellipsis" (A) is incorrect because no words are omitted in the introduction. There is no comparison being made (B). "A paradox" (C) would involve a seemingly contradictory yet true statement. The sentences which precede this point do not contain "a proverb" (E), a statement of a general truth.

51. **(B)** Mention of the "one hasty conclusion" is followed by the admission that the behavior of women would prove that their minds are unhealthy. (A) is subsequently explained as a cause of the behavior that indicates a weakened mind. (C) and (D) are given as results of women's undereducation rather than the cause of their inequality. (E) is incorrect because these are the roles the speaker would have for women if their status were not reduced and their roles prescribed as "alluring mistresses" (line 19).

52. **(B)** (A), (C), (D), and (E) are listed in lines 9–23 as consequences and examples of women's undereducation. (B), women are less than human (see lines 29–32), is the speaker's summary of this treatment women receive rather than their natural state.

53. **(C)** Using "like," women are compared to flowers, fragile and short-lived (C), "simile." "Metaphor" (B) is incorrect because the comparison is explicit. "Conceit" (A) and "parable" (D) are both extended forms of metaphor. There is no play on words, making "pun" (E) incorrect.

54. **(C)** "Barren blooming" (C) is an oxymoron combining the seemingly contradictory terms of sterility and fertility. (A) is incorrect because sorrow and indignation are not opposites. (B), (D), and (E) also lack a pairing of apparent opposites.

55. **(A)** The alliterated *f*'s join the "flaunting leaves" (line 14) of female coquettishness, the "fastidious eye" (lines 14–15) of male admiration, and the subsequent "fade" (line 15) of the only skill woman has been led to cultivate. (B), (C), and (E) are incorrect because the alliterative phrase is part of the simile that expands upon the speaker's description of the origin of the inequality of women. The phrase draws attention to, rather than downplays, the unequal treatment of women, making (D) incorrect.

56. **(A)**   An independent clause ["In a treatise...must not be overlooked" (lines 24–25)] is followed by two parallel dependent clauses, each beginning with "when" ["when it is asserted..." (line 26) and "when improveable reason is allowed..." (lines 30–31), (A)]. In addition, the first adverbial clause contains three parallel clauses introduced by "that." (B) is incorrect because the sentence does not contain more than one independent clause. Each of the dependent clauses makes a new point without repetition (C). While there are a number of prepositional phrases, they are not strung directly together (D) but interspersed throughout the passage. The sentence is complex (E), containing one independent and a number of dependent clauses, but (A) is a better answer because it specifically describes the type of complex structure.

57. **(B)**   All three of these points assert the inequality of women, the main point of the speaker. (A), (D), and (E) are incorrect because all three groups are described as contributing to this inequality rather than countering it. There is no reference to other female authors (C) in the passage.

58. **(D)**   The speaker asserts that she will not "violently...agitate" (line 34) for women's equality (I) but will face the issue to prevent her argument from being misunderstood (line 36, II). A woman who could argue so calmly and logically would obviously counteract her contemporaries' decorative education (III). (IV) misreads "I would not lead my reader to suppose that I mean violently to agitate the contested question" (lines 33–34): the speaker does not deny agitation itself, only violent agitation.

59. **(C)**   Each of these persons has a contributory role in the unequal status of women—men, parents, and authors as miseducators and women as so flattered by admiration that they prefer to receive love rather than respect (lines 21–23). (C) is the best answer because it is the most inclusive.

60. **(D)**   (D) is correct because the passage's diction is formal and its syntax complex. The passage takes its subject very seriously, making (A) incorrect. (B) is incorrect because the passage is just the opposite of colloquial (common speech) and unstructured. The speaker is not blatantly parading book learning (C) nor sarcastically adopting a stance in order to ridicule it (E).

Model Student Response to Essay Question 1:

The United States of America has a firm foundation, based on the standards established by the U.S. Constitution. Since the beginning of the Presidency, it has been the responsibility of our leaders to uphold certain principles. Our Presidents' beliefs and concerns have focused on those issues, as their speeches to Congress and to the public reveal.

Faith in God, on which our nation was founded, has remained important to our Presidents. Therefore, they often thanked God for America's good fortune or prayed for God's blessing and help. Our first President, George Washington, referred to "the blessings which a Gracious Providence has placed within our reach." Roosevelt expressed "gratitude to the Giver of Good." Truman requested the prayers of his audience, and implied the importance of "faith in the Almighty" and "God's help." Likewise, Kennedy mentioned "Almighty God" as he acknowledged that his predecessors had taken the same oath. And, like the other Presidents, he asked for God's blessing and help, indicating that "here on earth God's work must truly be our own." Because Reagan believed in God's desire that Americans be free, he wanted Inaugural Day to be a day devoted to prayer. And, like those who had led America before him, President Clinton sought God's blessing as he asked for strength.

Clearly, American Presidents have understood the importance of the country's military forces and readiness for war, as well as efforts to maintain peace. None have been eager to fight, but all have been willing to defend our freedom. "To be prepared for War is one of the most effectual means of preserving peace" (Washington). Referring to the wars in which the United States had been involved, Truman emphasized that we must "live together in peace and harmony." Other Presidents have stressed the need to stand up to any enemy (Kennedy), make sacrifices to maintain peace (Reagan), and defend our country against all types of weapons and potential destruction (Clinton).

Closely related to these concerns is America's establishment of foreign relations. George Washington believed in facilitating the country's "intercourse with other nations. . . . for the public good." And as it has progressed into perhaps the greatest nation on earth, our country has needed to establish positive relationships with nations around on earth, our country has needed to establish positive relationships with nations around the world (Roosevelt). Harry Truman was aware that other nations regarded the United States as a leader who was working to achieve "international order and justice." The Presidents have realized the endless potential in our country's united efforts with other nations (Kennedy), recognized the benefits of cooperation among nations (Reagan), and understood the importance of joint cultural and commercial efforts (Clinton).

Also, the Presidents have consistently promoted education. Washington, Truman, and Kennedy all stressed the importance of scientific knowledge. Washington encouraged Americans to come up with new inventions, and believed knowledge results in happiness. Truman also promoted the acquisition and application of our technical knowledge. President Clinton regarded education as "every citizen's most prized possession," and believed that all Americans should have access to knowledge and education.

A look at these six Presidents' speeches tells us that the beliefs and concerns of our nation's leaders have not changed much throughout history. They have focused on the importance of faith in God, strength in the military forces and defense, relations with foreign countries, and promotion of education. These principles have been part of the foundation of the United States throughout history.

Analysis of Student Response to Essay Question 1:

The student's response has addressed the main challenge of the question (synthesize at least three of the sources for support, and take a position that defends, challenges, or qualifies the claim that the concerns and beliefs of American Presidents have remained basically the same throughout the history of this country). The first paragraph introduces the general topic of the foundation of the U.S., gradually narrowing to the specific idea of the essay. The writer has analyzed the six excerpts from Presidential speeches, selecting four beliefs or concerns that appear in at least three of those speeches. One paragraph is devoted to each belief or concern. Each paragraph contains direct references to the sources. Sometimes the writer directly quotes a portion of the essay; for example, the second paragraph says, "Our first President, George Washington, referred to 'the blessings which a Gracious Providence has placed within our reach.'" At other times, the writer paraphrases the ideas in the Presidents' speeches; an example in the second paragraph is "Because Reagan believed in God's desire that Americans be free, he wanted Inaugural Day to be a day devoted to prayer." The conclusion echoes the main ideas of the essay's body. Each source is clearly attributed. The language and development of the essay are effective, and the writer's position is supported with appropriate examples. Overall, the essay is an effective response to the prompt.

Model Student Response to Essay Question 2:

Through stringent use of deletion, the poet turns a somewhat rambling, unfocused poem into a tightly-knit, moving memorial to a lost love. The later draft is superior because it lacks the physical descriptions of the subject that the earlier draft gives us, creating a mystical aura around the subject.

The first and fourth stanzas that were deleted in the later draft of the poem paint a vivid picture of the nameless dead woman. We learn that her hair was a "woodbine wreath," her lips were "red as roses are," and that she was "graceful." This description happens even though the narrator of the poem states that she was a "maid whom there were none to praise" (line 7). If there were none to praise her, who is it that is doing this praising? The writer must have realized this contradiction, solving the problem by deleting the descriptive passages.

The later draft veils the subject in mystery, so that it does indeed seem that there were none to praise her. All that we learn of the subject is that she was "Fair." It becomes impossible for the reader to create a mental image of the subject, making it apparent that her existence was a solitary one. To avoid the possibility that the reader might not feel sympathy for the "she" of the early draft, the poet makes up for the lack of physical description by giving the subject a name, "Lucy." This use of the proper noun allows the reader to believe that the subject of the poem was a real, living person, since we all identify ourselves and others by our names. Since the "she" now has a name, "Lucy," we can identify her in this way, without needing the contradictory physical description provided in the early draft.

In the early draft, we learn how the subject died, "slow distemper checked her bloom" (15). This is an unnecessary detail, and in the later draft, all that we know is that Lucy "ceas'd to be" (10). This lack of detail as to her means of death adds to the mysterious quality of the hardly known Lucy. The shorter length of the later draft shows that even the narrator of the poem did not have much to say about Lucy's physical being. This allows for her to be portrayed as otherworldly, like an angel.

In addition to the deletions, the poet changes some of the wording of the poem. In the first stanza of the later draft, "dwelt" replaces "lived" from the earlier draft.

"Liv'd" is then inserted in the final stanza to emphasize (note the italics) that the important thing about Lucy's life was not where she lived, but that she lived "unknown." This leads to the final idea that this poem is giving her something that she did not have when alive. In death she is now known, because of this poem eulogizing her. Another small change that the poet made is the capitalization of the word "Eye" in the later version. This shows that Lucy was hidden not only from the eye of one person, but from a universal "Eye," maybe even the "Eye" of God. The poet calls Lucy a "Maid" and a "Violet" in both drafts, but it is only in the final draft that these words are capitalized. This capitalization serves to portray Lucy as the perfect embodiment of all "Maids" and "Violets" by turning the nouns of the early draft into proper nouns that could only be describing Lucy.

The later draft of this poem is superior to the earlier draft because all extraneous detail has been removed, resulting in a concise poem that gives Lucy an ethereal quality. Since the reader cannot know who Lucy is, the final couplet has a much stronger dramatic effect in the later version. The narrator says that now that Lucy is no longer living, "Oh!/The difference to me" (11-12). The speaker of the poem is the only one who really knew Lucy, and the reader can sense the feeling of aloneness that the speaker is left with upon the death of his solitary love.

Analysis of Student Response to Essay Question 2:

This essay provides a strong and clear thesis that addresses all parts of the question. It persuasively argues that the poet's deletions serve to create a more concise, moving poem. In addition, the essay discusses some of the more subtle, less obvious changes that the author made in the passages, revealing a strong understanding of the finer points of the language.

The thesis is persuasively developed in the second, third, and fourth paragraphs of this essay. These paragraphs show why the lack of descriptive language in the final draft of the poem make it a stronger poem. The second paragraph illustrates that by removing physical description from the poem, the poet is following the internal logic of what he has written.

The third paragraph of the essay shows the importance of the introduction of a proper noun in the later draft by showing an awareness that a name can function as a non-physical way to show identity. The fourth paragraph further strengthens the central thesis by revealing that the shorter length of the final draft better serves the purpose of portraying the subject of the poem as ethereal and mysterious.

The essay is presented in a well-organized manner. The fifth paragraph addresses some of the small differences between the two passages, logically drawing on arguments made earlier in the essay, concerning proper nouns, to further solidify an already strong argument.

The final paragraph returns to the central thesis. This paragraph clearly illustrates the importance that the removal of all "extraneous detail" plays in making the later draft stronger than the earlier draft. The final paragraph also shows that the final couplet of the revised poem creates a stronger dramatic effect, by clearly showing that the poet's anguish over Lucy's death is a solitary anguish.

Model Student Response to Essay Question 3:

The language I would use in talking to a friend would certainly be different than the language I would use during a job interview. My purposes in both cases would contrast a great deal, and this would be reflected in the ways I spoke. In talking with a friend, I would be informal and not very concerned with such things as showing off my vocabulary or using correct grammar, and I would be more inclined to use slang terms.

My pronunciation and inflection would reflect the common ways that my friends and I speak, reflecting my desire to be casual and "cool." During a job interview I would speak in a more formal vein, to show my potential employer that I am mature and have a firm grasp of the English language.

In talking with a friend, I would be more prone to use phrases drawn from popular culture that we are both aware of. For example, I might say "That's cool," or "That sucks," to make a reference to a popular show on MTV, instead of using such stock phrases as "I like that" or "I'm not fond of that." I would know that my friends and I are members of a group by using such language, since we all know the jokes. I would never use such language during a job interview. Instead I would speak in the clearest language possible in an attempt to show my potential employer that I am intelligent. If s/he were to ask me what I think of school, I wouldn't chuckle and say dismissively, "Sometimes it's cool and sometimes it sucks." I would reflect for a few seconds, and then reply in full sentences, pointing out both the positive and negative aspects of my school—"I enjoy Shakespeare immensely, especially 'Macbeth,' but I find chemistry quite challenging sometimes."

In talking with friends I would be more prone to use certain words and phrases, such as "hey," "like," and "you know," in ways that are both unconventional and grammatically incorrect. Upon greeting a friend I would probably address him or her by saying, "Hey man, what's up?" The use of "hey" implies a certain amount of casualness and familiarity, as it is a short monosyllable that rolls off the tongue effortlessly. I would say "man" regardless of the sex of the addressee since among my friends we all understand "man" is an informal way of saying "friend." The final part of my phrase of greeting would be pronounced as one word "whazup." Furthermore my inflection would not rise at the end of this phrase, it would be more of a statement than a question.

In talking with my friends I would pepper my vocabulary with words that have no set meaning on their own, such as "like." "Like" functions as an intensifier, "He was, like, so gone," with emphasis on "like," would imply that the person of whom I was speaking was very, very drunk. I would consciously resist such usage of "like" during a job interview since it is not grammatically correct and it would also show a lack of respect if I were to address my potential employer as if he were one of my peers.

When greeting my interviewer, I would clearly say, in an even tone, "Hello, it's nice to meet you." I would follow this by questioning "How are you?" with a rise in my voice to show that I really want to know how this person is doing. I would continue throughout the interview in this way, being sure that I used my vocabulary in a conventional, intelligent way. I would also make certain that I employed proper grammar during my interview to show my potential employer that I am both respectful and smart.

My use of language among friends would be casual, informal and idiosyncratic, reflecting these same qualities in our relationships. I would speak properly and formally during a job interview to make a positive impression on the interviewer, to show him or her that I am an intelligent human being who is capable of communicating clearly and effectively with all people.

Analysis of Student Response to Essay Question 3:

This well-written essay expertly contrasts the different ways in which one might use language, dependent on circumstances. The opening paragraph clearly states the different purposes that language would serve during a job interview and during a conversation with a friend.

The essay goes on to describe how a conversation with a friend would draw from the vernacular of popular culture. The essay gives concrete examples of such phrases, as well as pointing out that the purpose of using them is to form a group identity in which friends feel at ease with each other.

The essay proceeds in a logical way to describe why such language would not be proper during a job interview. The writer of this essay would want to be seen as intelligent during a job interview. The essay states that the way to do this is through the use of full sentences, conventional vocabulary, and correct grammar, of which examples are then given.

The third, fourth, and fifth paragraphs of this essay contrast the use of pronunciation and inflection under the different circumstances. The essay cites many idiosyncrasies that would be used in talking with friends, and explains how pronouncing such phrases as "whazup" imply a certain amount of casualness and informality. The essay contrasts this by saying that it would be proper to use common pronunciation and inflection during a job interview, and provides examples of such pronunciation and inflection, as well as describing why it would be employed.

The final paragraph of this essay returns to its central thesis, clearly stating the reasons why one would use language in different ways in different circumstances, casual and informal when talking with friends to reflect a laid-back attitude, but formal and conventional during a job interview to express intelligence and respect.

PRACTICE EXAM 2

AP English Language & Composition

PRACTICE EXAM 2
AP English Language & Composition

Section 1

TIME: 60 Minutes
60 Questions

(Answer sheets appear in the back of this book.)

DIRECTIONS: This test consists of selections from literary works and questions on their use of language. After reading each passage, choose the best answer to each question and blacken the corresponding oval on the answer sheet.

Questions 1–5 are based on the following passage. Read the passage carefully before choosing your answers.

Sawyer shouted at her when she entered the kitchen, but she just turned her back and reached for her apron. There was no entry now. No crack or crevice available. She had taken pains to keep them out, but knew full well that at any moment they could rock her, rip her from her moorings, send the birds twittering back into her hair. Drain her mother's milk, they had already done. Divided her back into plant life—that too. Driven her fat-bellied into the woods—they had done that. All news of them was rot. They buttered Halle's face; gave Paul D iron to eat; crisped Sixo; hanged her own mother. She didn't want any more news about whitefolks; didn't want to know what Ella knew and John and Stamp Paid, about the world done up the way whitefolks loved it. All news of them should have stopped with the birds in her hair.

Once, long ago, she was soft, trusting. She trusted Mrs. Garner and her husband too. She knotted the earrings into her underskirt to take along, not so much to wear but to hold. Earrings that made her believe she could discriminate among them. That for every schoolteacher there would be an Amy; that

for every pupil there was a Garner, or Bodwin, or even a sheriff, whose touch at her elbow was gentle and who looked away when she nursed. But she had come to believe every one of Baby Suggs' last words and buried all recollection of them and luck. Paul D dug it up, gave her back her body, kissed her divided
20 back, stirred her memory and brought her more news: of clabber, of iron, of roosters' smiling, but when he heard *her* news, he counted her feet and didn't even say goodbye.

"Don't talk to me, Mr. Sawyer. Don't say nothing to me this morning."

"What? What? What? You talking back to me?"

25 "I'm telling you don't say nothing to me."

"You better get them pies made."

Sethe touched the fruit and picked up the paring knife.

When pie juice hit the bottom of the oven and hissed, Sethe was well into the potato salad. Sawyer came in and said, "Not too sweet. You make it too
30 sweet they don't eat it."

"Make it the way I always did."

"Yeah. Too sweet."

None of the sausages came back. The cook had a way with them and Sawyer's Restaurant never had leftover sausage. If Sethe wanted any, she put
35 them aside soon as they were ready. But there was some passable stew. Problem was, all her pies were sold too. Only rice pudding left and half a pan of gingerbread that didn't come out right. Had she been paying attention instead of daydreaming all morning, she wouldn't be picking around looking for her dinner like a crab. She couldn't read clock time very well, but she knew when
40 the hands were closed in prayer at the top of the face she was through for the day. She got a metal-top jar, filled it with stew and wrapped the gingerbread in butcher paper. These she dropped in her outer skirt pockets and began washing up. None of it was anything like what the cook and the two waiters walked off with. Mr. Sawyer included midday dinner in the terms of the job—along
45 with $3.40 a week—and she made him understand from the beginning she would take her dinner home. But matches, sometimes a bit of kerosene, a little salt, butter too—these things she took also, once in a while, and felt ashamed because she could afford to buy them; she just didn't want the embarrassment of waiting out back of Phelps' store with the others till every white in Ohio
50 was served before the keeper turned to the cluster of Negro faces looking through a hole in his back door. She was ashamed, too, because it was stealing and Sixo's argument on the subject amused her but didn't change the way she felt; just as it didn't change schoolteacher's mind.

1. In lines 4–5, the words "send the birds twittering back into her hair" provide an example of

    (A) alliteration   (D) metaphor

    (B) simile   (E) hyperbole

    (C) onomatopoeia

2. The passage suggests

    (A) Sawyer is Sethe's husband

    (B) the Garners stole Sethe's earrings

    (C) Sethe was not intelligent

    (D) the others waiting at the back of Phelps' store were whites

    (E) Sethe has a sense of pride

3. To which of the following people does "she" refer in the sentence, "Once, long ago, she was soft, trusting?"

    (A) Mrs. Garner   (D) Ella

    (B) Mrs. Sawyer   (E) Bodwin

    (C) Sethe

4. What might be the purpose of the author's first paragraph?

    (A) To show how whites mistreated Sethe

    (B) To list the atrocities committed upon her friends

    (C) To create sympathy for Sethe

    (D) To demonstrate her fragile state of mind at this point

    (E) To reinforce Seethe's lack of memory

5. "Clabber" (paragraph 2) probably means

    (A) speak incessantly

    (B) positive emotional experiences

    (C) engage in love making

    (D) thickened or curdled sour milk

    (E) beat in a brawl

Questions 6–10 are based on the following passage. Read the passage carefully before choosing your answers.

'Are you ill, Edward?' she said, rising immediately.

'I felt some uneasiness in a reclining posture. I will sit here for a time.' She threw wood on the fire, wrapped herself up, and said, 'You would like me to read to you?'

5 'You would oblige me greatly by doing so, Dorothea,' said Mr Casaubon, with a shade more meekness than usual in his polite manner. 'I am wakeful: my mind is remarkably lucid.'

'I fear that the excitement may be too great for you,' said Dorothea, remembering Lydgate's cautions.

10 'No, I am not conscious of undue excitement. Thought is easy.' Dorothea dared not insist, and she read for an hour or more on the same plan as she had done in the evening, but getting over the pages with more quickness. Mr Casaubon's mind was more alert, and he seemed to anticipate what was coming after a very slight verbal indication, saying, 'That will do—mark that'

15 or 'Pass on to the next head—I omit the second excursus on Crete.' Dorothea was amazed to think of the bird-like speed with which his mind was surveying the ground where it had been creeping for years. At last he said—

'Close the book now, my dear. We will resume our work to-morrow. I have deferred it too long, and would gladly see it completed. But you observe that

20 the principle on which my selection is made, is to give adequate, and not disproportionate illustration to each of the theses enumerated in my introduction, as at present sketched. You have perceived that distinctly, Dorothea?'

'Yes,' said Dorothea, rather tremulously. She felt sick at heart.

'And now I think that I can take some repose,' said Mr Casaubon. He lay

25 down again and begged her to put out the lights. When she had lain down too, and there was a darkness only broken by a dull glow on the hearth, he said—

'Before I sleep, I have a request to make, Dorothea.'

What is it?' said Dorothea, with a dread in her mind.

'It is that you will let me know, deliberately, whether, in case of my death,

30 you will carry out my wishes: whether you will avoid doing what I should deprecate, and apply yourself to do what I should desire.'

Dorothea was not taken by surprise: many incidents had been leading her to the conjecture of some intention on her husband's part which might make a new yoke for her. She did not answer immediately.

35 'You refuse?' said Mr Casaubon, with more edge in his tone.

'No, I do not yet refuse,' said Dorothea, in a clear voice, the need of freedom asserting itself within her, 'but it is too solemn—I think it is not right—to make a promise when I am ignorant what it will bind me to. Whatever affection prompted I would do without promising.'

40 'But you would use your own judgment: I ask you to obey mine; you refuse.'

'No, dear, no!' said Dorothea, beseechingly, crushed by opposing fears. 'But may I wait and reflect a little while? I desire with my whole soul to do what will comfort you; but I cannot give any pledge suddenly—still less a pledge to

45 do I know not what.'

'You cannot then confide in the nature of my wishes?'

'Grant me till to-morrow,' said Dorothea beseechingly.

'Till to-morrow then,' said Mr Casaubon.

6. "Excursus" in the fifth paragraph probably means

   (A) excuses

   (B) appendix or germane digression

   (C) illustration

   (D) map

   (E) allusion

7. In paragraph six, the author is inferring

   (A) Mr Casaubon doubted Dorothea's ability to finish the work

   (B) Dorothea had already expressed no desire to help him

   (C) Mr Casaubon feared he would not be able to complete his work alone

   (D) Dorothea was Mr Casaubon's teacher

   (E) Mr Casaubon and Dorothea were partners in this scholarly work

8. Mr Casaubon's statement, "Before I sleep, I have a request to make, Dorothea," is an example of

   (A) double entendre   (D) figure of speech

   (B) metaphor   (E) elegy

   (C) simile

9.   Mr Casaubon's question to Dorothea, "You cannot then confide in the nature of my wishes?" implies

   (A)   he thinks her a liar

   (B)   he feels trapped

   (C)   he wants her to promise blindly

   (D)   he has had past experience with disobedience

   (E)   Dorothea has always questioned his orders

10.   By writing "Dorothea was not taken by surprise…," the author is telling us

   (A)   she was unaware that she would be expected to make this promise

   (B)   she knew Mr Casaubon well

   (C)   she had not had to take orders from him before

   (D)   she was unintelligent

   (E)   she didn't understand her role in this relationship

Questions 11–15 are based on the following passage. Read the passage carefully before choosing your answers.

   I looked at the sea of yellow faces above the garish clothes—faces all happy and excited over this bit of fun, all certain that the elephant was going to be shot. They were watching me as they would watch a conjuror about to perform a trick. They did not like me, but with the magical rifle in my hands, I
5 was momentarily worth watching. And suddenly I realized that I would have to shoot the elephant after all. The people expected it of me and I had got to do it; I could feel their two thousand wills pressing me forward, irresistibly. And it was at this moment, as I stood there with the rifle in my hands, that I first grasped the hollowness, the futility of the white man's dominion in the
10 East. Here was I, the white man with his gun, standing in front of an unarmed native crowd — seemingly the leading actor of the piece; but in reality I was only an absurd puppet pushed to and fro by the will of those yellow faces behind. I perceived in this moment that when the white man turns tyrant it is his own freedom he destroys. He becomes a sort of hollow posing dummy,
15 the conventionalized figure of a sahib. For it is the condition of his rule that he shall spend his life in trying to impress the "natives," and so in every crisis he has got to do what the "natives" expect of him.

11. The controlling metaphor of the piece involves

   (A)   the stage and acting

   (B)   magic and mystery

   (C)   the thrill of the hunt

   (D)   the crowd's will

   (E)   the ventriloquist's dummy

12. The narrator must shoot the elephant for the following reasons EXCEPT

   (A)   he is willed by the crowd

   (B)   his role of sahib demands it

   (C)   he must impress the natives

   (D)   his role of policeman demands it

   (E)   the people expect it

13. The resolution to kill the elephant symbolizes the

   (A)   power yet stupidity of the white man in the East

   (B)   domination of the white man in the East

   (C)   prejudice the white man has toward the natives

   (D)   emptiness of the role the white man plays in the East

   (E)   role of the sahib as clown

14. The narrator uses the personal pronoun frequently and the term "white man" to show his

   (A)   scorn of the rabble

   (B)   distancing himself from the situation

   (C)   realization that he stands for many

   (D)   fear of the rabble

   (E)   awareness that he stands alone

15. Which word best describes the tone of the passage?

   (A)   Furious

   (B)   Philosophic

   (C)   Amused

   (D)   Sardonic

   (E)   Disillusioned

Questions 16–32 are based on the following passage. Read the passage carefully before choosing your answers.

A   "Is this the end?

B   O Life, as futile, then, as frail!

C   What hope of answer or redress?"

A cloudy day: do you know what that is in a town of iron-works? The sky sank down before dawn, muddy, flat, immoveable. The air is thick, clammy with the breath of crowded human beings. It stifles me. I open the window, and, looking out, can scarcely see through the rain the grocer's shop opposite,
5   where a crowd of drunken Irishmen are puffing Lynchburg tobacco in their pipes. I can detect the scent through all the foul smells ranging loose in the air.

The idiosyncrasy of this town is smoke. It rolls sullenly in slow folds from the great chimneys of the iron-foundries, and settles down in black, slimy pools on the muddy streets. Smoke on the wharves, smoke on the dingy boats,
10   on the yellow river,—clinging in a coating of greasy soot to the house-front, the two faded poplars, the faces of the passersby. The long train of mules, dragging masses of pig-iron through the narrow street, have a foul vapor hanging to their reeking sides. Here, inside, is a little broken figure of an angel pointing upward from the mantel-shelf; but even its wings are covered with
15   smoke, clotted and black. Smoke everywhere! A dirty canary chirps desolately in a cage beside me. Its dream of green fields and sunshine is a very old dream,—almost worn out, I think.

From the back-window I can see a narrow brick-yard sloping down to the river-side, strewed with rain-butts and tubs. The river, dull and tawny-colored,
20   (*la belle rivière*!) drags itself sluggishly along, tired of the heavy weight of boats and coal-barges. What wonder? When I was a child, I used to fancy a look of weary, dumb appeal upon the face of the negro-like river slavishly bearing its burden day after day. Something of the same idle notion comes to me to-day, when from the street-window I look on the slow stream of human life creeping
25   past, night and morning, to the great mills. Masses of men, with dull, besotted faces bent to the ground, sharpened here and there by pain or cunning; skin and muscle and flesh begrimed with smoke and ashes; stooping all night over boiling caldrons of metal, laired by day in dens of drunkenness and infamy;

breathing from infancy to death an air saturated with fog and grease and soot, vileness for soul and body. What do you make of a case like that, amateur psychologist? You call it an altogether serious thing to be alive: to these men it is a drunken jest, a joke,—horrible to angels perhaps, to them commonplace enough. My fancy about the river was an idle one: it is no type of such a life. What if it be stagnant and slimy here? It knows that beyond there waits for it odorous sunlight,—quaint old gardens, dusky with soft, green foliage of apple-trees, and flushing crimson with roses,—air, and fields, and mountains. The future of the Welsh puddler passing just now is not so pleasant. To be stowed away, after his grimy work is done, in a hole in the muddy graveyard, and after that,—*not* air, nor green fields, nor curious roses.

Can you see how foggy the day is? As I stand here, idly tapping the window-pane, and looking out through the rain at the dirty back-yard and the coalboats below, fragments of an old story float up before me,—a story of this old house into which I happened to come to-day. You may think it is a tiresome story enough, as foggy as the day, sharpened by no sudden flashes of pain or plea-sure.—I know: only the outline of a dull life, that long since, with thousands of dull lives like its own, was vainly lived and lost: thousands of them,—massed, vile, slimy lives, like those of the torpid lizards in yonder stagnant water-butt.— Lost? There is a curious point for you to settle, my friend, who study psychology in a lazy, *dilettante* way. Stop a moment. I am going to be honest. This is what I want you to do. I want you to hide your disgust, take no heed to your clean clothes, and come right down with me,—here, into the thickest of the fog and mud and foul effluvia. I want you to hear this story. There is a secret down here, in this nightmare fog, that has lain dumb for centuries: I want to make it a real thing to you. You, Egoist, Pantheist, or Arminian, busy in making straight paths for your feet on the hills, do not see it clearly,—this terrible question which men here have gone mad and died trying to answer. I dare not put this secret into words. I told you it was dumb. These men, going by with drunken faces and brains full of unawakened power, do not ask it of Society or of God. Their lives ask it; their deaths ask it. There is no reply. I will tell you plainly that I have a great hope; and I bring it to you to be tested. It is this: that this terrible dumb question is its own reply; that it is not the sentence of death we think it, but, from the very extremity of its darkness, the most solemn prophecy which the world has known of the Hope to come. I dare make my meaning no clearer, but will only tell my story. It will, perhaps, seem to you as foul and dark as this thick vapor about us, and as pregnant with death; but if your eyes are free as mine are to look deeper, no perfume-tinted dawn will be so fair with promise of the day that shall surely come.

16. What is the function of the epigraph that opens the passage?

    (A) It makes it clear that the passage which follows is a retrospective of the speaker's life.

    (B) It establishes a mood of despair and hopelessness.

    (C) It lends authority to the speaker's work by quoting another writer.

    (D) It sets the scene as that of a preapocalyptic society.

    (E) It comments critically upon the speaker's work.

17. The opening sentence of the passage (line 1) does all of the following EXCEPT

    (A) draw the reader into the passage

    (B) directly address the reader

    (C) challenge the reader's knowledge and experience

    (D) reveal to the reader the speaker's lack of knowledge about her subject matter

    (E) imply that the reader belongs to a different world than that being described here

18. It can be inferred that "Lynchburg tobacco" (line 5) is

    (A) the preferred brand of Irishmen

    (B) detrimental to its smokers' health

    (C) a particularly inferior brand

    (D) obtainable at the "grocer's shop" (line 4)

    (E) a scent pleasing to the speaker

19. The sentence "Smoke…passersby" (lines 9–11) contains which of the following?

    (A) An ellipsis   (D) Alliteration

    (B) A metaphor   (E) Abstract imagery

    (C) Metonymy

20. Which of the following best describes what the "little broken figure of an angel" (line 13) represents?

    (A) The poverty that extends even into the homes of the inhabitants of the ironworks town

    (B) The irreverence that prevails in the speaker's home

    (C) The smoke that invades every aspect of ironworks town life

    (D) The grime of ironworks town life that weighs down even dreams of an afterlife

    (E) The sincere piety of the speaker

21. The aside "(*la belle rivière*)" (line 20) can best be interpreted as

    (A) an ironical description

    (B) a nostalgic memory

    (C) a pedantic display of the speaker's education

    (D) a humorous comment

    (E) a redundant characterization

22. A "dirty canary" (line 15) with its "dream of green fields and sunshine" (line 16) and the river that "drags itself sluggishly along, tired of the heavy weight of boats and coal-barges" (lines 20–21) are examples of

    (A) metaphor   (D) hyperbole

    (B) personification   (E) assonance

    (C) oxymoron

23. The expository technique of the third paragraph (lines 18–39) is best described as

    (A) cause and effect   (D) question and answer

    (B) chronological order   (E) comparison/contrast

    (C) classification

24. The relationship between the rivers and men (paragraph 3)

    I.   crosses the characteristics of water and humans

    II.   comparatively implies that the town's workers are slaves

    III. gives superior status to the river

    IV.   dehumanizes the worker

(A)   I only

(D)   II, III, and IV only

(B)   II and III only

(E)   I, II, III, and IV

(C)   III only

25.   The speaker assumes that the reader's attitude toward the ironworks laborer is one of

(A)   sympathy

(D)   antipathy

(B)   defensiveness

(E)   ignorance

(C)   clinical observation

26.   A "Welsh puddler" (line 37) is most probably

(A)   a grave digger

(D)   a street cleaner

(B)   an ironworks employee

(E)   a bartender

(C)   a hand on a coal barge

27.   In line 36, the phrase "air, and fields, and mountains" parallels yet contrasts with

(A)   "fog and grease and soot" (line 29)

(B)   "skin and muscle and flesh" (lines 26–27)

(C)   "soul and body" (line 30)

(D)   "*not* air, nor green fields, nor curious roses" (line 39)

(E)   "quaint old gardens, dusky with soft, green foliage of apple-trees, and flushing crimson with roses" (lines 35–36)

28.   The antecedent of "it" (line 53) is

(A)   "this nightmare fog" (line 53)

(B)   "this story" (line 52)

(C)   the "foul effluvia" (line 52)

(D)   the "secret down here" (line 52)

(E)   "this terrible question" (line 55)

29.   Considering the passage as a whole, the "terrible question which men here have gone mad and died trying to answer" (lines 55–56) can best be identified as:

(A)   How can the life of the ironworks town laborer be bettered?

(B)   What is the meaning of life?

(C)   How can the pollution from the ironworks be lessened?

(D)   What is the responsibility of the upper to the lower classes?

(E)   Why are the workers Western Europeans?

30.   The speaker's characterization of the reader as "Egoist, Pantheist, or Arminian, busy in making straight paths for [his/her] feet on the hills, [does] not see it clearly" (lines 54–55) implies that

(A)   the reader, absorbed in ordering his/her own life according to various doctrines, cannot fully comprehend the struggle for meaning in life

(B)   the reader is a landowner making civic improvements without regard to the concerns of ironworks town inhabitants

(C)   the reader seeks meaning in a materialistic existence

(D)   the reader, relying on psychology and its terminology, would scientifically order life

(E)   as a foreigner, the reader is only briefly and dispassionately trekking through the ironworks town

31.   It can be inferred that the speaker believes that

(A)   human existence is pointless

(B)   social reform is imminent

(C)   afterlife is the ultimate hope

(D)   men live more desperate lives than women

(E)   educated persons experience life differently than factory workers

32.   The speaker's story is most probably

(A)   a bitter life lived without redress

(B)   an example of a terrible life ending with an anticipated unearthly reward

(C)   a retelling of his/her own life in the ironworks town

(D)   a futuristic tale of life to come in the ironworks town

(E)   a fantasy transporting the pampered reader into the ironworks employee's role

Questions 33–45 are based on the following passage. Read the passage carefully before choosing your answers.

I then inquired for the person that belonged to the petticoat; and, to my great surprise, was directed to a very beautiful young damsel, with so pretty a face and shape, that I bid her come out of the crowd, and seated her upon a little crock at my left hand. "My pretty maid," said I, "do you own yourself to have been the inhabitant of the garment before us?" The girl I found had good sense, and told me with a smile, "That notwithstanding it was her own petticoat, she should be very glad to see an example made of it; and that she wore it for no other reason, but that she had a mind to look as big and burly as other persons of her quality; that she had kept out of it as long as she could, and till she began to appear little in the eyes of all her acquaintance; that if she laid it aside, people would think she was not made like other women." I always give great allowances to the fair sex upon account of the fashion, and therefore was not displeased with the defense of the pretty criminal. I then ordered the vest, which stood before us to be drawn up by a pulley to the top of my great hall, and afterwards to be spread open by the engine it was placed upon, in such a manner, that it formed a very splendid and ample canopy over our heads, and covered the whole court of judicature with a kind of silken rotunda, in its form not unlike the cupola of St. Paul's. I entered upon the whole cause with great satisfaction, as I sat under the shadow of it.

The counsel for the petticoat was now called in, and ordered to produce what they had to say against the popular cry which was raised against it. They answered the objections with great strength and solidity of argument, and expatiated in very florid harangues, which they did not fail to set off and furbelow (if I may be allowed the metaphor) with many periodical sentences and turns of oratory. The chief arguments for their client were taken, first, from the great benefit that might arise to our woolen manufactory from this invention, which was calculated as follows: the common petticoat has not above four yards in the circumference; whereas this over our heads had more in the semidiameter; so that by allowing it twenty-four yards in the circumference, the five millions of woolen petticoats, which (according to Sir William Petty) supposing what ought to be supposed in a well-governed state, that all petticoats are make of that stuff, would amount to thirty millions of those of the ancient mode. A prodigious improvement of the woolen trade! and what could not fail to sink the power of France in a few years.

To introduce the second argument, they begged leave to read a petition of

the rope-makers, wherein it was represented, that the demand for cords, and the price of them, were much risen since this fashion came up. At this, all the company who were present lifted up their eyes into the vault; and I must confess, we did discover many traces of cordage which were interwoven in the
40 stiffening of the drapery.

A third argument was rounded upon a petition of the Greenland trade, which likewise represented the great consumption of whalebone which would be occasioned by the present fashion, and the benefit which would thereby accrue to that branch of the British trade.

45 To conclude, they gently touched upon the weight and unwieldiness of the garment, which they insinuated might be of great use to preserve the honor of families.

These arguments would have wrought very much upon me (as I then told the company in a long and elaborate discourse), had I not considered the great
50 and additional expense which such fashions would bring upon fathers and husbands; and therefore by no means to be thought of till some years after a peace. I further urged, that it would be a prejudice to the ladies themselves, who could never expect to have any money in the pocket, if they laid out so much on the petticoat. To this I added, the great temptation it might give to
55 virgins, of acting in security like married women, and by that means give a check to matrimony, an institution always encouraged by wise societies.

33. The argument takes the form of

   (A) a question and answer session

   (B) a trial

   (C) a confession

   (D) a sermon

   (E) a debate

34. The girl "began to appear little in the eyes of all her acquaintance" (line 10)

   (A) in girth and social standing

   (B) in size and wealth

   (C) in body and mind

   (D) in waist and undergarment

   (E) in weight and education

35. The girl's statement in lines 6–11 can best be interpreted as

    (A) the actions of a slave to fashion

    (B) the scheme of a social climber

    (C) the tricks of an underweight woman

    (D) the response of a sensible woman pressured by social dictates

    (E) the rantings of a condemned woman

36. The "vest" of line 13 is

    (A) a garment   (D) a jacket

    (B) a petticoat   (E) a robe

    (C) an umbrella

37. All of the following are present in the sentence in lines 13–18 EXCEPT

    (A) hyperbole   (D) metaphor

    (B) simile   (E) humor

    (C) oxymoron

38. The description of the argument of the counsel for the petticoat (lines 21–25) parallels

    (A) the petticoat itself

    (B) the formality of the inquiry

    (C) the complexity of the woolen industry

    (D) the "power of France" (line 34)

    (E) the good sense of the owner of the petticoat

39. The observation that the production of large petticoats "could not fail to sink the power of France in a few years" (line 34) is

    (A) an understatement of the might of fashion

    (B) a hyperbolic statement

    (C) a declaration of war

    (D) an economic statistic

    (E) an egotistical boast

40. The "petition of the Greenland trade" (line 41) was most likely issued from

    (A)   petticoat makers   (D)   whalers

    (B)   carvers   (E)   shipowners

    (C)   merchants

41. Why would petticoats, such as the one being examined in the passage, "be of great use to preserve the honor of families" (lines 46–47)?

    (A)   Ladies would be able to dress as fashion demands women of their station should.

    (B)   Families would exhibit their wealth through their clothing.

    (C)   A bulky petticoat could not be easily removed during illicit love affairs.

    (D)   The size of the petticoat would prevent young ladies from being kid-napped.

    (E)   Demeaning small places could not be entered by ladies wearing large petticoats.

42. The final point of the speaker's judgment against the petticoat (lines 54–56)

    (A)   assents to the concluding point of the counsel's argument

    (B)   turns the concluding point of the counsel's argument against itself

    (C)   opposes the concluding point of the counsel's argument

    (D)   is not linked to the concluding point of the counsel's argument

    (E)   is weakened by the concluding point of the counsel's argument

43. Who/what can best be identified as the passage's criminal?

    (A)   The girl who owned the petticoat

    (B)   Society

    (C)   Fashion

    (D)   "Persons of her quality" (line 9)

    (E)   The petticoat

44. Both the defense of the petticoat and the speaker's reply are primarily structured as

    (A)   appeals to authority   (D)   patriotic arguments

    (B)   appeals to emotio   (E)   ethical appeals

    (C)   economic appeals

45.   The style of the passage taken as a whole can best be described as

(A)   gently satiric   (D)   colloquially informal

(B)   bitterly ironic   (E)   pedantically formal

(C)   wryly humorous

Questions 46–51 are based on the following passage. Read the passage carefully before choosing your answers.

We laymen have always been intensely curious to know—like the cardinal who put a similar question to Ariosto—from what sources that strange being, the creative writer, draws his material, and how he manages to make such an impression on us with it and to arouse in us emotions of which, perhaps, we
5   had not even thought ourselves capable. Our interest is only heightened the more by the fact that, if we ask him, the writer himself gives us no explanation, or none that is satisfactory; and it is not at all weakened by our knowledge that not even the clearest insight into the determinants of his choice of material and into the nature of the art of creating imaginative form will ever help to make
10   creative writers of *us*.

If we could at least discover in ourselves or in people like ourselves an activity which was in some way akin to creative writing! An examination of it would then give us a hope of obtaining the beginnings of an explanation of the creative work of writers. And, indeed, there is some prospect of this being
15   possible. After all, creative writers themselves like to lessen the distance be-tween their kind and the common run of humanity; they so often assure us that every man is a poet at heart and that the last poet will not perish till the last man does.

Should we not look for the first traces of imaginative activity as early as in
20   childhood? The child's best-loved and most intense occupation is with his play or games. Might we not say that every child at play behaves like a creative writer, in that he creates a world of his own, or, rather, rearranges the things of his world in a new way which pleases him? It would be wrong to think he does not take that world seriously; on the contrary, he takes play
25   very seriously and he expends large amounts of emotion on it. The opposite of play is not what is serious but what is real. In spite of all the emotion with which he cathects his world of play, the child distinguishes it quite well from reality; and he likes to link his imagined objects and situations to the tan-gible and visible things of the real world. This linking is all that differentiates
30   the child's "play" from "fantasying."

46. What is the effect of the speaker's use of "we"?

    (A)   It separates the speaker and his/her colleagues from the reader.

    (B)   It involves the reader in the search for, yet distinguishes him/her from, the creative writer.

    (C)   It creates a royal and authoritative persona for the speaker.

    (D)   It makes the speaker the stand-in for all men.

    (E)   It unites speaker, reader, and creative writer.

47. What is the antecedent of "it" (line 7)?

    (A)   "explanation" (line 6)   (D)   "impression" (line 4)

    (B)   "fact" (line 6)   (E)   "insight" (line 8)

    (C)   "interest" (line 5)

48. Which of the following statements would the speaker be most likely to DISAGREE with?

    (A)   A layperson cannot become a creative writer by studying the writer's methods.

    (B)   All men are writers at heart.

    (C)   Creative writers are fundamentally different from nonwriters.

    (D)   Children understand the distinction between imagination and reality.

    (E)   The creative writer at work mirrors the child in play.

49. "Cathects" (line 27) can best be defined as

    (A)   constructs

    (B)   distances

    (C)   fantasizes

    (D)   discourages

    (E)   destroys

50. The structure of the passage can best be described as

    (A)   an initial paragraph that introduces an idea and two paragraphs that digress from that idea

    (B)   a series of paragraphs that answer the questions with which they begin

    (C)   a series of questions ascending in their inability to be answered

    (D)   paragraphs whose length or brevity parallel their depth or narrowness of inquiry

    (E)   sentences that grow in structural complexity

51.   It can be inferred that the speaker believes that creative writing is

    (A)   an opposite of childhood play

    (B)   unrelated to childhood play

    (C)   a continuation of childhood play

    (D)   the destiny of every man due to his play as a child

    (E)   similar to the fantasizing of childhood play

Questions 52–60 are based on the following passage. Read the passage carefully before you choose your answers. This passage is a portion of "On the Importance of Being Ernst Mayr: 'Darwin's apostle' died at the age of 100" by Axel Meyer. This tribute appeared in the PLoS Biology journal on April 5, 2006.

Born on July 5, 1904, in Kempten in southern Germany, Ernst Mayr passed away peacefully at the Methuselah-like age of 100 on February 3, 2005, in Bedford near Cambridge, Massachusetts. Mayr was, by the accounts of his Harvard colleagues the late Stephen Jay Gould and Edward O. Wilson, not
5   only the greatest evolutionary biologist of the 20th century, but even its greatest biologist overall. . . . Ernst Mayr has been called "Darwin's apostle" or the "Darwin of the 20th century" for promoting and dispersing Darwin's hypotheses throughout the past century. . . .

Ernst Mayr had many fundamental insights into evolutionary biology,
10   and almost every topic of importance in evolution was advanced by his ideas. Perhaps his most widely known contribution is to the current notion of what constitutes a species. Darwin did not think that species were real in the philosophical sense, but rather that they were the result of the human predilection to perceive discontinuity among continuously varying individuals. Most biolo-
15   gists nowadays disagree with Darwin's view of species, largely because of Mayr's "biological species concept." Together with [population geneticist] Dobzhansky, Mayr developed this definition of species "as groups of interbreeding populations in nature, unable to exchange genes with other such groups living in the same area."[1,2] Barriers to gene flow between species—termed reproductive

---

[1] T. Dobzhansky, *Genetics and the Origin of Species* (New York: Columbia University Press, 1937), p. 364.

[2] E. Mayr, *Systematics and the Origin of Species* (New York: Columbia University Press, 1942) p. 334.

isolating mechanisms—keep biological species distinct through processes such as species-specific mate choice and hybrid sterility. Although there are theoretical and operational problems with the biological species concept (e.g., it does not apply to asexually reproducing organisms such as bacteria), it is still, by far, the most widely used species concept among the 20 or so competing definitions that have been proposed in the past several decades. Students of biology all over the world have memorized Mayr's definition of species for more than half a century.

. . . Mayr's understanding of the biogeographic distributions of bird species, overlaid with extensive knowledge about variation in morphology, led him to develop concepts about the geographic mechanisms of speciation—cornerstones for those studying speciation today. The geographic separation of populations, such as by rivers or valleys, he argued, prohibits homogenizing gene flow between them. If such isolated (termed allopatric) populations accumulate mutations over time, this might lead to the divergence of such populations from each other, and reproductive isolation might arise as a simple byproduct of these separate evolutionary histories. Mayr staunchly defended this idea during sometimes heated debates and further developed it and other hypotheses regarding geographic mechanisms of speciation over many decades (outlined in depth in the 797 pages of *Animal Species and Evolution*[3]) . . . .

Clearly, Ernst Mayr felt very strongly that he had something of importance to say to the world. . . . Although Ernst Mayr lived only about a tenth of the 969 years that Methuselah is purported to have lived, he still accomplished much more than one might expect to get done, even in 100 years. . . . On the occasion of his 100th birthday Mayr published an article in Science[4] looking back over eight decades of research in evolution that he closed with the following words: "The new research has one most encouraging message for the active evolutionist: it is that evolutionary biology is an endless frontier and there is still plenty to be discovered. I only regret that I won't be present to enjoy these future developments."

[3] E. Mayr, *Animal Species and Evolution*. (Cambridge, Massachusetts: Belknap Press, 1963), 797 p.

[4] E. Mayr, "Happy Birthday: 80 Years of Watching the Evolutionary Scenery." *Science* 305: 46–47 (2004).

52. The purpose of footnotes 1 and 2 is to inform the reader that the quotation in lines 16–19

    (A) was Mayr's own original creation, copied by Dobzhansky

    (B) was used by both Mayr and Dobzhansky in their books on the origin of species

    (C) Mayr needed Dobzhansky's help in developing this definition

    (D) was Dobzhansky's own original creation, copied by Mayr

    (E) was the definition that students memorized for many years

53. In line 33, the pronoun "them" refers to

    (A) gene flow   (D) mutations

    (B) rivers or valleys   (E) populations

    (C) separation

54. Based on the information in line 39 and footnote 3, which of the following statements is accurate?

    (A) Mayr's explanation of animal species and evolution appears on page 797 of his book.

    (B) The author of the book *Animal Species and Evolution* quotes Mayr on page 797.

    (C) An outline of Mayr's hypotheses appears in the book *Animal Species and Evolution*.

    (D) Mayr wrote a 797-page book titled *Animal Species and Evolution*.

    (E) In 1942, the Columbia University Press wrote a book about Mayr's theories on animal species and evolution.

55. Which of the following accurately describes the author's tone as he describes Mayr and his work?

    (A) Envy   (D) Disgust

    (B) Gratitude   (E) Cynicism

    (C) Admiration

56. This article compares Mayr to

    (A) Darwin and Dobzhansky   (D) Wilson and Gould

    (B) Darwin and Methuselah   (E) Wilson and Darwin

    (C) Dobzhansky and Methuselah

57.   The structure of lines 11–16 can best be described as

   (A)   moving from general to specific

   (B)   moving from specific to general

   (C)   moving from general to general

   (D)   moving from specific to specific

   (E)   a presentation of conflicting ideas

58.   A look at the footnotes tells the reader that

   (A)   both Dobzhansky and Mayr wrote about Mayr's life

   (B)   Dobzhansky had a longer writing career than Mayr did

   (C)   Dobzhansky relied heavily on the works of Mayr regarding evolutionary biology

   (D)   Mayr's writing career lasted at least sixty years

   (E)   Mayr often liked to write about himself

59.   The passage's purpose can be characterized as

   (A)   expository   (D)   judicial

   (B)   analytical   (E)   exhortative

   (C)   eulogistic

60.   The quote taken from Mayr's *Science* article (lines 46–49) implies that

   (A)   Mayr believed evolutionary biology had unveiled many intriguing mysteries

   (B)   Mayr believed that evolutionary biologists will continue making new discoveries

   (C)   advances in evolutionary biology were likely to end with Mayr's death

   (D)   Mayr was worried that he would die soon

   (E)   Mayr had made tremendous contributions to the field of evolutionary biology

STOP

This is the end of Section 1.
If time still remains, you may check your work only in this section.
Do not begin Section 2 until instructed to do so.

Section 2

TIME: 2 Hours
        3 Essay Questions

Question 1 (Suggested time—40 minutes.) This question is worth one-third of the total essay score.

Our perceptions of the world around us are influenced by our feelings and conditions in life. Imagine that you are looking out of a window. Describe the view from this window at two different times, employing vivid descriptive detail to make clear the differences in your states of mind.

CONTINUE TO QUESTION 2 >

Question 2 (Suggested time—40 minutes.) This question is worth one-third of the total essay score.

The naturalist and explorer John Muir has left us a journal of his life and thoughts that is brimming with insight and brilliance. Analyze the following passage for its diction, tone, and syntax. How are these elements well suited to the theme of this passage?

There is love of wild nature in everybody, an ancient mother-love ever showing itself whether recognized or no, and however covered by cares and duties.

In God's wildness lies the hope of the world—the great fresh unblighted, unredeemed wilderness. The galling harness of civilization drops off, and the wounds heal ere we are aware.

I am often asked if I am not lonesome on my solitary excursions. It seems so self-evident that one cannot be lonesome where everything is wild and beautiful and busy and steeped with God that the question is hard to answer—seems silly.

In the mountains, free, unimpeded, the imagination feeds on objects immense and eternal.

To the Indian mind all nature was instinct with deity. A spirit was embodied in every mountain, stream, and waterfall.

—From *John of the Mountains: The Unpublished Journals of John Muir.* Ed. Linnie Marsh Wolfe.

CONTINUE TO QUESTION 3

Question 3   (Suggested reading time—15 minutes)
        (Suggested writing time—40 minutes)

Directions: The following prompt is based on the accompanying six sources.

This question requires you to synthesize a variety of sources into a coherent, well-written essay. *Refer to the sources to support your position; avoid mere paraphrase or summary. Your argument should be central; the sources should support this argument.*

Remember to attribute both direct and indirect sources.

Introduction: As technology has advanced, the curricula in American schools have changed. Schools are increasingly using technology as a means of educating students today. Not only are schools teaching computer skills, but also class work includes the use of such technology as video games and iPod. What is the effect of this changing approach to education? Is it an improvement over traditional education, or is it a compromise?

Assignment: Read the following sources (including any introductory information) carefully. Then, in an essay that synthesizes at least three of the sources for support, take a position that defends, challenges, or qualifies the claim that schools that are embracing the new technological approach to education are effectively teaching students the skills they need in today's world.

You may refer to the sources by their titles (Source A, Source B, etc.) or by the descriptions in parentheses.

Source A (Elmasry)

Source B (Beardsley)

Source C (Zeeble)

Source D (U. S. Department of Education)

Source E (Johnson)

Source F (National Aeronautics and Space Administration or NASA)

Source A

Elmasry, Faiza. "Children Can Learn From Video Games." *Voice of America,* May 2, 2006.
Available at http://www.voanews.com/english/archive/2006-05/2006-05-02-voa80.cfm.

The following passage is excerpted from an article that presents the conflicting viewpoints of Marc Prensky, author of the book <u>Don't Bother Me Mom, I'm Learning</u>, and Mitch Resnick, director of the Lifelong Kindergarten Group at the Massachusetts Institute of Technology.

Young Americans, age 8 to 18, are packing more than 8 hours' worth of media exposure into each day, listening to iTunes, instant messaging their friends and playing a computer or video game . . . all at the same time. That media multi-tasking doesn't concern some experts. In fact, they see video games as tools for acquiring the multi-tasking skills kids will need to succeed in tomorrow's workplace. But others worry that kids don't have enough time for the hands-on activities that develop and refine their creativity and other skills that are just as important. . . .

"Most games today are networked," [Marc Prensky] says. "So people play them with others. Working effectively with others, cooperating, collaborating, working in teams and doing it remotely is certainly part of a great skill that will be useful for the 21st century."

And, he says, some of today's video games encourage the development of physical skills. "Games like Dance, Dance Revolution, where you have to do complicated dance steps to a rhythm on the dance pad, and you have to get the rhythm exactly right. . . . There are more games where you involve your arms, the rest of the torso and we are seeing more and more of this. In fact in many times, it's being adopted by schools."

. . . "Kids are clearly learning *how* to do certain kinds of things, whether that's run around, whether that's actually play the game," he says. "They are learning *what* to do. Because rules are not given to them, they have to intuit them. They are learning *why* to do certain things, which is the strategic part of the game. They are learning a lot about *where*, which is the context of the game. Games are typically about something—it could be an alien civilization, it could be winning a race. And most important, they're learning *whether* to do something or not. So that just because you can hit somebody over his head with a baseball bat in the game, the question is, should you?"

. . . "Video games are all about becoming a character," he says. "In almost all of the games, you get to customize the character, the character's look, the character's behavior and traits. In other words, it's all about creativity and imagination."

But director of the Lifelong Kindergarten Group at the Massachusetts Institute of Technology, Mitch Resnick, disagrees. ". . . When kids play a videogame, which is interactive in some way, it's still largely a very passive type of interaction. What we found in our research is that children's best learning experiences come when they are actively engaged in designing things, creating things, inventing things."

Resnick says that requires a real-world hands-on approach. "If you go into a kindergarten, you'll see children building towers or bridges out of blocks," he says. "In the process they learn about structures, what makes things stand up or fall down. They make paintings with finger paints. In the process, they learn about how colors mix together . . . ."

"It's not that I think it's harmful or bad for children to spend part of their time playing video games," he says. "But I do get concerned if children get so absorbed and focus so much of their attention and energy that it takes away from other, more creative and imaginative activities."

New technologies will be an integral part of life and work in the 21st century. Resnick says he hopes more companies will begin producing new kinds of software to help kids use those technologies to create their own games.

Source B

Beardsley, Nancy. "Arizona High School Chooses Laptops Over Textbooks." *Voice of America*, October 20, 2005. Available at http://www.voanews.com/english/archive/2005-10/2005-10-20-voa65.cfm.

The following passage is excerpted from an article about a new educational approach adopted by Empire High School in Vail, Arizona.

A new high school opened in Vail, Arizona, this past July with all the resources you would expect to find in classrooms these days—except textbooks. Instead, every student received an Apple laptop computer . . . making Empire High School a pioneer in the growing use of technology in American education.

. . . a committee visited classrooms that were making partial use of laptops, and came away with two distinct impressions. "One was that students in schools where laptops were being used were clearly more engaged," Mr. Baker says. "And the other impression was that we felt we could do more with laptops. Because we had the opportunity here of opening a new school, we could make them an integral part of what we do, and actually change the way we do things. And we sort of forced that issue by not buying any textbooks."

Teachers helped plan the school's wireless curriculum, often experimenting with different ideas in classrooms where they taught before. . . .

Michael Frank teaches a first year biology course, where students use their laptops to access instructions for their lab work, organize data, and graph the results. . . . "[Students] will be putting together all the results from this experiment in a Power Point presentation for the class later. . . . And I know I can just give them an address for a web site that has information and they can go look at it there. A lot of times with science, we use it because you can get immediate access to the most recent information. You don't have to wait 5 or 6 years for it to get into a textbook. So there's much more access to just a huge amount of data about things."

. . . There was a surprise once classes got underway as well. . . . "We thought the kids would be better at computing than they actually are. Being able to drive your X-box or your I-pod is not the same thing as being able to take a computer, use it, create a document, save it with a file name, put it in a particular location and retrieve it. And that has been a real challenge."

But administrators say the system is working well overall, and students seem to agree. . . .

Calvin Baker also stresses that he is not trying to make Empire High a technology school. And he says quality education still has to be about things like hard work, self-discipline and outstanding teaching—with laptops becoming a natural part of the classroom, just as they have become a natural part of workplaces across America.

Source C

Zeeble, Bill. "U.S. Colleges Turn Portable Music Players Into Educational Devices." *Voice of America,* March 23, 2005. Available at http://www.voanews.com/english/archive/2006-03/2006-03-23-voa31.cfm.

The following passage is excerpted from an article about colleges and universities that are using mp3 players as an alternative educational tool.

Digital mp3 players like Apple's iPod can download and play hours of music and thousands of images. It's not surprising that they are among the nation's most popular entertainment devices. Now, a handful of U.S. colleges and universities are using them as education devices.

When El Centro Community College in Dallas, Texas, introduced iPods to its classrooms in January of this year, instructor Cathy Carolan wasn't excited. But she dutifully recorded her lectures and diagrams for downloading to computers and iPods. And she went along with the plan that made her students long-distance learners—meaning they rarely had to show up in class for lessons.

"I was the biggest cynic going," she admits. "I didn't trust it. Because I [wondered], what about the connection with the students? I like to see the whites of their eyes. I want to see them understand it." So in a small panic early on in the download experiment, she called the students back to the downtown campus.

She recalls the meeting vividly. "I said 'Ok, you haven't sent me e-mails of questions, whatever. I don't care, I want to see you, come up to class.' I sat with them and in the end I said, 'So you're fine?' They said, 'Yes, we're fine.' And I said 'So you're really just here because I had separation anxiety?' They said 'Yes, Miss Carolan. Can we go now?'"

The students in Carolan's yearlong, intensive medical technology training program are not the typical undergrads. Many are professional nurses and work full-time. They're usually older, and have families, homes, and other responsibilities. Sharla Scovel, 52, who lives nearly an hour away from the downtown campus, explains that the iPod lets her listen to lectures in the grocery store line, or study diagrams while commuting to work. "I watch them as I travel by train. This morning I drove, but I was able to listen to the lecture that I had previously watched. I was able to review it as I'm driving. It was great because we have such a volume of material that we have to learn, that one pass doesn't do it. This gives us the opportunity to review without having to sit down in front of a computer tied to a desk."

That chance to listen as many times as necessary makes a difference, according to Cathy Carolan. "Back in the dark days, when students came to class, they got one shot. They hear what I say, rely on their notes that they take, and then it's one shot." With the lectures on iPods and on-line discussion forums when requested by students, Carolan says her pupils grasp the material more quickly.

And there may be additional benefits for shy students. "They actually begin to shine in an on-line environment, where the fear of raising their hand and perhaps the ability to come up with an answer on the fly is just too daunting," according to Jan Poston-Day. . . . "In the on-line world," she says, "they're able to compose thoughts, write them down, spell-check them, and post them to class where they can be a full participant. . . . They really need to focus on the student experience and make the entire teaching experience not about the professor giving their lectures. It's about how can we reach out to the students in a way that meets their needs, because so many of today's students are not the so-called traditional learners."

That philosophy seemed to drive the iPod experiment at Philadelphia's Drexel University. Instead of downloading and replaying classroom lectures, Education Department chair Bill Lynch says iPods are used to encourage creativity. . . . He calls it "a catalytic technology, one we can use to think with, to think about what educational problems might we find solutions, or at least partial solutions, for. And to get the students used to the idea that they're responsible for creating knowledge as well, not just being a consumer of knowledge. . . ."

Source D

U. S. Department of Education. "Educational Technology Fact Sheet." Available at http://www.ed.gov/about/offices/list/os/technology/facts.html.

The following information is excerpted from the Department of Education's "Educational Fact Sheet" regarding the availability of technology to students in the United States. Today's technology allows distance learning courses; in these courses, students work on their own from home or another off-site location, communicating with teachers and other students by using such technology as e-mail, videoconferencing, and instant messaging.

Statistics:
- In 2003, the ratio of students to computers in all public schools was 4.4 to 1.
- 48 states included technology standards for students in 2004-2005.
- In 2003, 8 percent of public schools lent laptop computers to students. . . .
- Schools in rural areas (12 percent) were more likely than city schools (5 percent) and urban fringe schools (7 percent) to lend laptops.
- In 2003, 10 percent of public schools provided a handheld computer to students or teachers.
- 16 states had at least one cyber charter school operating in 2004–2005.
- 22 states had established virtual schools in 2004–2005.
- 56 percent of 2- and 4-year degree-granting institutions offer distance education courses, with 90 percent of public institutions offering distance education courses. . . .

Distance Learning
- 36% of school districts and 9% of all public schools have students enrolled in distance education courses.
- There were an estimated 328,000 enrollments in distance education courses by K12 students during the 2001-2002 school year.
- 68% of the enrollments were in high school with an additional 29% in combined or ungraded schools.
- 45,300 enrollments in distance education were Advanced Placement or college-level courses.
- A greater proportion of rural area districts had students enrolled in distance education courses than did urban and suburban districts.
- 42% of districts that have students enrolled in distance education courses are high poverty districts.
- When small districts offer distance learning, they are more likely to involve a greater proportion of schools.
- 80% of public school districts offering online courses said that offering courses not available at their schools is one of the most important reasons for having distance education.

- 50% of public school districts offering online courses cited distance learning as very important in making Advanced Placement or college-level courses available to all students.
- 92% of districts enrolled in online distance education courses had students access online courses from school.
- 24% of districts with students accessing online courses from home provided or paid for a computer for all students, while an additional 8% did so for some students.

Friendship Through Education
- Using the Internet to connect students in the U.S. and Arab nations to develop mutual understandings of one another's cultures.

Source E

Johnson, Doug. "A Vision for the Net Generation Media Center." *Learning and Leading With Technology,* October 205. pp. 25–26. ERIC EJ719951.

This passage is excerpted from an article by Doug Johnson, who has been director of media and technology for the Mankato (Minnesota) Public Schools since 1991.

. . . kids expect fast communication responses, tune out when things aren't interesting, and may be more visually than verbally literate. For them, technology is a tool for learning on any topic they choose. (Are you reading anything you don't already know from the media or from personal observation?)

. . . Our current crop of students believes "teachers are vital," "computers can't replace humans," and motivation is critical in learning. They like group activities, believing building social skills is a part of schooling. They identify with their parents' values. And they are achievement oriented, feeling it is "cool to be smart." And although they are fascinated with new technologies, their knowledge of them is often "shallow." (Who actually maintains the computers in your home or school?)

Finally, the studies point to how this generation learns—or likes to learn. Our current crop of students with their hypertext minds like inductive discovery rather than being told what they should know. In other words, they want to learn by doing rather than simply listening or reading. They enjoy working in teams, on "things that matter," often informally, and not just during school hours. And given their quick response requirements, they need to be encouraged to reflect.

It is my firm belief that schools will be more productive if educators acknowledge the unique attributes and preferences of the Net Generation and adapt educational environments to suit students instead of trying to change their basic natures. So what are some implications for NG (Net Generation) library media centers?

To a large degree, media centers may be the most NG-oriented places in schools. . . . Given their preference to work in groups, the NG media center should provide spaces for collaboration on school projects and socialization. It should contain the tools necessary for the production of information, not just its consumption—computers with the processing power and software to edit digital movies and photographs, scanners, and high-quality printers and projection devices—and, of course, assistance in the use of these tools.

. . . It should have comfy chairs, and be a friendly atmosphere, low-stress, safe, and forgiving—and yes, in high schools, an in-house coffee shop. Spaces for story times, puppetry, plays, and games along with computer stations with age-appropriate software and Web sites are just as important in elementary schools. If the "room" is not a wonderful place to be, students and teachers will stay on the Internet or in the classroom. Period. (And given the rise in online schools, is there a lesson here for classrooms as well?)

Source F

National Aeronautics and Space Administration. "NASA Learning Technologies: Advanced Technology Applications for Education Benchmark Study." May 1, 2001. Available at http://learn.arc.nasa.gov/benchmark/0.0.html.

The following passage has been excerpted from an article in which NASA discusses the educational use of video games.

. . . Educational video games have been described as the next "Killer App" in educational technology.

For this potential to be realized, the design and execution of educational videogames must be a well-thought-out balance of educational content, teacher input, student engagement, and student learning. For completeness, an evaluation component must be a component. The research and development of educational videogames are already well on their way.

. . . Games2train stands out in the world of learning and training for its Game-Based Learning approach—the ability to marry the fun of playing a videogame or computer game together with all the information needed to accomplish learning or training objectives. . . .

. . . At MIT's Education Arcade Program, videogames have been developed that teach high school (HS) Social Studies, HS AP Physics, and HS AP Environmental Science. Also, as part of the Games-to-Teach Project of MIT's Comparative Media Studies Program, innovative, next-generation educational videogames are being developed that teach engineering, environmental investigation with handheld PCs, physics, electromagnetism, life sciences, American history, psychology, and cultural anthropology.

END OF EXAM

PRACTICE EXAM 2

AP English Language & Composition

Answer Key

Section 1

1. **(D)**	21. **(A)**	41. **(C)**
2. **(E)**	22. **(B)**	42. **(B)**
3. **(C)**	23. **(E)**	43. **(E)**
4. **(D)**	24. **(E)**	44. **(C)**
5. **(D)**	25. **(C)**	45. **(A)**
6. **(B)**	26. **(B)**	46. **(B)**
7. **(C)**	27. **(D)**	47. **(C)**
8. **(A)**	28. **(D)**	48. **(B)**
9. **(C)**	29. **(B)**	49. **(A)**
10. **(B)**	30. **(A)**	50. **(B)**
11. **(A)**	31. **(C)**	51. **(C)**
12. **(D)**	32. **(B)**	52. **(B)**
13. **(D)**	33. **(B)**	53. **(E)**
14. **(C)**	34. **(A)**	54. **(D)**
15. **(E)**	35. **(D)**	55. **(C)**
16. **(B)**	36. **(B)**	56. **(B)**
17. **(D)**	37. **(C)**	57. **(A)**
18. **(C)**	38. **(A)**	58. **(D)**
19. **(A)**	39. **(B)**	59. **(C)**
20. **(D)**	40. **(D)**	60. **(B)**

PRACTICE EXAM 2

AP English Language & Composition

Detailed Explanations of Answers

Section 1

1. **(D)** (D) is the correct answer since this figure of speech is applied to the idea that others could make Sethe become mentally unstable, the birds representing other people and their twittering representing her mental unease from what others have done to her. (A) is incorrect since the initial sounds of most of the words are not the same. Nor is (B) the answer because no two things are being compared in the phrase. Likewise, (C) is wrong due to the lack of the words' pronunciation contributing in any way to their meaning. Finally, (E) is not acceptable; there is no exaggeration nor extravagance in the phrase.

2. **(E)** (E) is the correct answer; in paragraph 11, we read, "…she just didn't want the embarrassment of waiting out back of Phelps' store with the others till every white in Ohio was served before the keeper turned to the cluster of Negro faces looking through a hole in his back door." (A) cannot be correct; Sawyer is not Sethe's husband, but her employer, as is made clear when we read, "Mr. Sawyer included midday dinner in the terms of the job…." Since Sethe remembers the Garners among those who treated her well, "…whose touch at her elbow was gentle and who looked away when she nursed," rather than poorly as in stealing from her, (B) is incorrect. (C) is also not the answer since Sethe could figure out what time it was without being able to read the clock. We already know that those waiting at the back of Phelps' store are not white—but Negro,—so (D) is not true, either.

3. **(C)** (A) and (E) are both incorrect since each was included among the people being trusted rather than being the one who was doing the trusting as explained in (B) of Item No. 2. (B) is incorrect because it is "Mr.," not "Mrs.," Sawyer who is mentioned. (D) is another incorrect answer since Ella is only mentioned in passing. Therefore, (C) is the correct answer by a process of elimination.

4. **(D)** While Sethe's mistreatment by whites is included in the passage, it is as part of a list of people who were mistreated, so both (A) which refers to only Sethe

and (B) which refers only to her friends are incorrect. (C) may have worked, except for the unemotional statements of these facts; sympathy is an emotional reaction. The passage is a string of Sethe's memories, which makes (E) an incorrect answer. (D) is the correct answer since the metaphors refer to Sethe's mind being carefully held together despite her past experience.

5. **(D)** (A) and (E) are incorrect since the word "clabber" comes after the preposition "of ." This means the following word is a noun (the object of the preposition), not the verbs offered in these two choices. Both (B) and (C) are incorrect since each is considered a positive act which does not belong in a negative paragraph such as this one. Therefore, (D) is the correct answer.

6. **(B)** While (A) is grammatically correct, logically it makes no sense. (C), (D), and (E) may be rejected on grammatical terms; the word "on" after "excursus" would have to be "of " for (C) and (D) and "to" for (E) in order for these nouns to be used. Therefore, (B) is the correct answer.

7. **(C)** The correct answer is (C) since Dorothea begins the passage inquiring about Mr Casaubon's health, he acknowledges not feeling well, and she wonders if the excitement of her reading to him would be too exciting for him. In addition, Dorothea wonders at the rush in completing the work she has been helping him with, as well as his clarifying for her just what it is they are doing. These same facts point out that (A), (B), (D), and (E) are not true.

8. **(A)** Since (B) and (C) are comparisons and none is made in this statement, neither is the correct answer. (D) is used to produce mental images not ordinarily thought of when reading the word and also is incorrect. (E) is employed after someone has died. Therefore, (A) is the correct answer; "sleep" is meant both as a night's rest and death.

9. **(C)** (C) is the correct answer since he will not tell her specifically what it is he wants her to promise. (A), (B), (D), and (E) may be true somewhere else in their relationship, but cannot be validated from the passage; therefore, they are all incorrect answers.

10. **(B)** The key word is "not;" therefore (A), (C), and (E) are all incorrect since they imply a lack of knowledge about Mr Casaubon on Dorothea's part. (D) is also incorrect since her reading to him and his request that she work to help him quickly complete the project demonstrates her intelligence. The correct answer is (B).

11. **(A)** Although magic and mystery (B) are mentioned, as is the will of the crowd (D), the controlling metaphor hinges on the stage and acting (A) when the audience wills the leading actor of the piece. There is no mention of the hunt (C) itself nor a ventriloquist's dummy (E), simply an absurd puppet and a dummy, not necessarily a ventriloquist's.

12. **(D)**   Nowhere in this excerpt is the writer referred to as a policeman (D). You may know this from your reading but do not let knowledge outside the passage sway you. All the other reasons are clearly expressed in the passage.

13. **(D)**   The whole meaning of the piece suggests that the white man must not make a fool of himself in front of the crowd. He does not see the stupidity in his role but the emptiness of it (D). The tone of the piece here does not suggest a wish to play the fool nor any prejudice toward the natives.

14. **(C)**   There is no scorn for the rabble but a personal analysis of what must be done. Hence, the "I" pronoun. But at the same time the narrator realizes he is engaged in a much larger situation, that he represents "the white man," one of many in the colonial set-up (C). He stands alone in the sense that he must kill the animal alone but the killing represents something much bigger than just one man versus an animal. The personal pronoun use is not a distancing device but a personal involvement.

15. **(E)**   The tone of the passage involves elements of anger but "furious" (A) is too strong. There is no amusement (C) in the serious tone. There is a certain sad sarcasm in the passage, but again "sardonic" (D) is too strong, and although the narrator is expressing a philosophy of sorts, "philosophic" (B) suggests a depth that is not present. The best word is one that shows he has faced an awakening here and all illusions of his role disappear (E).

16. **(B)**   The epigraph describes life as "futile" and "frail" and altogether hopeless, creating an aura of despair (B). (A) is incorrect because it misreads "end" (line A) as "death" rather than the highest attainable standard of living. Because the source of the quoted epigraph is unclear, it carries no particular weight (C). (D) would also misread "end" as "the end of the world"; furthermore, there is no indication in the passage which follows that this society is awaiting annihilation. Taking the passage as a whole, it is clear that the despairing statement of the epigraph is in agreement with, rather than contrary to (E), the speaker's attitudes.

17. **(D)**   The speaker brings the reader into the passage (A) by directly asking him/her "do you know…"(B), and by immediately providing the answer makes it clear that the reader could not possibly have firsthand knowledge [(C) and (E)] of life in an ironworks. (D) is incorrect because it misinterprets the intent of the question; the speaker's swift and detailed response indicates that information is not actually sought from the audience.

18. **(C)**   The speaker implies that Lynchburg tobacco is inferior (C) by having it smoked by men who are loitering, drunken, and, as a result of these states, assumably poor. The smoking of this tobacco by this group does not imply that all Irishmen smoke it or even that these particular men prefer it to other brands (A). There is no suggestion of tobacco's effect upon its smokers (B). One cannot assume that the smokers bought their tobacco at the grocer's shop simply because they are loitering outside it (D). Rather than being pleasing, the scent of the tobacco must be particu-

larly noxious to be distinguishable "through all the foul smells ranging loose in the air" (line 6) (E).

19. **(A)** The sentence omits several easily understood words (A), such as a verb in the main clause ("smoke [lies] on the...") and the preposition "to" (preceding "the two faded poplars" and "the faces"). There is no comparison being implied (B) or descriptive substitution of a part for a whole [(C), metonymy]. Alliteration (D) is incorrect because there is no repetition of initial consonants. The imagery of this sentence is decidedly concrete, making (E) incorrect.

20. **(D)** "Pointing upward" (line 14), the angel symbolizes heavenly afterlife; such hope, however, is "broken" and dirtied by the ironworks soot (D). Although the angel is broken, it does not indicate that its owner lives a life of deprivation (A). The soot that covers the angel is atmospheric rather than an intentional dishonoring (B); the statue's spot on the mantle may even be a place of honor. The smoke (C) does not need to be symbolically portrayed—it is literally described as omnipresent. Display of an angel figurine is not an indication of religious fervor (E). In addition, it is unclear if the house and its contents are the speaker's own.

21. **(A)** The "dull and tawny-colored" (line 19) river is mockingly described as its opposite, a beautiful river (A). The beautiful river cannot possibly be a wistful, yearning memory (B) since the speaker later describes the river of her childhood as tired and overburdened (line 20). Neither here, nor elsewhere in the passage, is the speaker seeking arrogantly to display "book learning" (C); in fact, the speaker is sharing knowledge from life experience. The comment is not amusing (D)—it is bitterly mocking. The river is first described as dirty and slow; a second depiction of it as beautiful cannot possibly be repetitious (E).

22. **(B)** Both descriptions attribute human characteristics, dreaming and weariness, to an animal or inanimate object [(B), personification]. "Metaphor" (A) is incorrect because there is no comparison being made in these specific phrases. There is no joining of seemingly opposite terms, making "oxymoron" (C) incorrect. Neither phrase is overly exaggerated [(D), hyperbole]. "Assonance" (E), repetition of vowel sounds in words with differing initial consonants, is not present here.

23. **(E)** This paragraph compares and contrasts (E) the river and the ironworks laborer, both "working" slavishly, but one bearing hope of a better future. The paragraph does not present a series of actions or occurrences and their consequences (A). The narration is not chronological (B) because the speaker moves from present to past to present to future. There is no ordering of terms or things by groups or classes (C). (D) misinterprets the questions in lines 30–31 and 34: they are rhetorical, and the speaker expects no answers.

24. **(E)** The river is given the human sensation of weariness (line 20), and man is dehumanized by being given the river's status of "stream...creeping past" (lines

24–25) (I, II). The speaker implies that the workers are slaves (III) by describing the river as "negro-like…slavishly bearing its burden day after day" (lines 22–23) and subsequently noting that "something of the same idle notion comes to [him/her] today" when viewing the routine of the worker. The river ultimately has the higher status (IV) because it will pass on to a better "life," whereas the laborer will simply go slavishly on until his death (lines 37–39).

25. **(C)**   The speaker anticipates the reader's reaction to be what an "altogether serious thing to be alive" (line 31), a coldly detached remark (C). This projected response is not one of shared feelings (A) or contempt (D). There is no sign that the speaker considers the reader to be fending off an anticipated attack (B). The reader seems to have some understanding of the seriousness of the laborer's situation, making (E) incorrect.

26. **(B)**   By analogy, "Welsh puddler" is one out of the "masses of men" who labor in the ironworks (line 25). The river is compared to the human masses, then it is contrasted with an individual member. (A) relies upon a misreading of lines 36–39; the grave is the puddler's end, not his place of occupation. (C), (D), and (E) all misinterpret puddler as having to do with liquid.

27. **(D)**   The phrases in line 36 and in (D) are parallel in structure, being set off by dashes and organized as a series of three; the former phrase, however, is an expected destination while the latter is the opposite of an ultimate end point. Although they are tripartite in structure, (A) and (B) are not contextually related to the phrase in line 36. (C) and (E) do not have the tripartite structure necessary for parallelism.

28. **(D)**   The antecedent of "it" can be found by dropping the descriptive subordinate clauses and joining the independent clauses in lines 52–54: "there is a secret down here… I want to make it a real thing to you." The "nightmare fog" (A) is part of a prepositional phrase that describes the secret's location and not the thing that is to be made real. This "story" (B) reveals the secret. While the reader may not have yet experienced it firsthand, "foul effluvia" (C) is already a real thing. The "terrible question" (E) is the secret, but it follows "it" and thus cannot be its antecedent.

29. **(B)**   The very lives and deaths of the workers (lines 57–59) are lives so terrible and hopeless and deaths so unremarkable that they ask, "What is the point of existence?" (B). In order for (A) to be correct there would have to be suggestions for concrete reform, rather than abstract promises "of the day that shall surely come" (lines 66–67). Pollution (C) is indeed a problem, but it is a backdrop to the problems of the workers. While it is implied that the reader is of higher socioeconomic status than the worker, there is no blame given or responsibility attributed for the condition of the workers (D). The workers are variously described as Irish and Welsh, but the question of their ethnicity is irrelevant (E).

30. **(A)**   Egoism, Pantheism, and Arminianism are respectively self-worship, nature worship, and a theology opposed to predestination. They are all systems of belief,

and by using such a system the reader seeks to make his/her own way through life without seeing "it" (the "secret"/"question," inferentially the meaning of life) (A). (B) mistakenly takes the concept of making paths literally. (C) is incorrect because there is no indication that the reader considers physical possessions to be the key to life. Harkening back to the speaker's comment of "amateur psychologist" (lines 30–31), (D) misinterprets "Egoism" as the scientific jargon of Freudianism. (E) confuses "Arminian" with Armenian and also interprets "paths" as literal places for walks.

31. **(C)** The speaker states that the question answers itself and is "the most solemn prophecy…of the Hope to come" (lines 62–63); in addition, the story to be told "will be so fair with promise of the day that shall surely come" (lines 66–67). These phrases indicate that there is a reason for human life [ruling out (A)], and their religious connotations imply that this reason is a "life" after human toil (C). The predicted relief is described in vague and religious terms, not in socioeconomic language (B). Although only the terrible lives of men are described, the omission of women does not imply that they fare better (D). The reader, inferentially more educated than the worker, is "busy in making straight paths for his/her feet" (lines 54–55): he/she too is looking for a rationale for life, and by projecting [his/her] interest in the story about to be told, the speaker implies that afterlife will fulfill this goal (E).

32. **(B)** The speaker describes the projected story as "the outline of a dull life, that long since…vainly lived and lost" (lines 45–46); its conclusion in the past ruling out (C), (D), and (E). (A) is incorrect because a hard life without remedy holds none of the hope the speaker foretells. Lines 64–68 imply that the story will be dark but will end with promise of otherworldly redress (B).

33. **(B)** The argument is structured as "a trial" (B), with a defendant (the girl/petticoat) seated at a judge's left hand and counselors presenting arguments and petitions. While questions are asked and answered (A), the aforementioned persons and activities make "trial" a better answer. There is no admission of sin or error, making "confession" (C) incorrect. The argument is not a discourse on a religious or moral topic [sermon (D)]. Although the argument in front of the judge can be described as debating, the official term is a "trial." Therefore, (E) is incorrect.

34. **(A)** Without the voluminous petticoat mandated by fashion, the girl would not be physically "big and burly as other persons of her quality" (lines 8–9) or, by implication, as "large" in social standing. (B), (C), and (E) are partially correct because they name the first element of physical size. Their second elements, however, are incorrect: the girl's "quality" (line 9) depends more on social than monetary status (B), and her mental abilities [(C) and (E)] would not be indicated by her underwear. (D) takes up only the literal interpretation of "little," making the girl small because she lacks the proper underwear.

35. **(D)** The young lady dislikes the petticoat and had put off wearing one until pressured by her slipping social reputation to don one (D). Her reluctance to im-

mediately wear the garment indicates that she is not a slave to fashion (A). A social climber (B) would be so concerned about her reputation that she would quickly do what the ladies of quality do. (C) takes "little" (line 10) literally, assuming that the girl is actually physically undersized. The girl has yet to be blamed [versus being condemned, (E)], and in fact the judge seems pleased by her defense.

36. **(B)** A "vest" is "a garment" (A); "petticoat" (B) is a better answer, however, as it is the item being discussed, and its "big and burly" size matches the canopy-like description. There is no mention of any other article of clothing [(D) and (E)]. The vest is opened like "an umbrella" (C), but the displayed article is the focus of the passage and thus the petticoat.

37. **(C)** "Oxymoron" (C) is not present because this description of the petticoat does not contain a pairing of seemingly contradictory terms. The description of the petticoat is exaggerated (A) as forming a canopy over a "great hall" (line 14). Through a "simile" (B), its form is "not unlike [equaling 'like'] the cupola of St. Paul's" (line 18). Metaphorically (D), it is called a "canopy" and a "silken rotunda" (line 17). It is amusing (E) to think of a woman wearing an undergarment big enough to overspread a large room.

38. **(A)** The argument is described as great, solid, and heavily ornamented ["furbelowed...with many periodical sentences and turns of oratory," (lines 24–25)] like the petticoat (A) that spreads over the room. The argument is elaborate and decorated, but the ridiculous subject matter destroys any formality (B). The woolen industry would grow larger, but not necessarily more elaborate (C), with the production of such large petticoats. The "power of France" (D) would lessen, not grow and become more detailed. The statement which characterizes the girl's good sense (lines 5–11) is straightforward and plain, lacking elaborate devices or syntax (E).

39. **(B)** This remark grossly overstates (B) the effect that large petticoats would have on a rival economy. It exaggerates rather than understates (A) the impact of fashion upon the larger world. While the downfall of France is predicted as a side effect, the passage is concerned with the defense of the petticoat and not a direct economic attack (D). The statement may be a boast, but it is not self-aggrandizing (E) its speaker, the counselor.

40. **(D)** The "Greenland trade" supports large petticoats because of the great amount of whalebone used therein; consequently, the members of this trade must be "whalers" (D). "Petticoat makers" (A) would use whalebone but would be more concerned with consumption of their garments than the materials for making them. "Carvers" (B), "merchants" (C), and "shipowners" (E) could deal in whalebone (or other goods). (D) is the best answer because whalers would be specifically and directly affected by the use of whalebone.

41. **(C)** The counsel can only insinuate (line 47) and not directly describe how the family's honor may be sullied; the petticoat must, consequently, prevent some

extremely delicate matter, such as an adulterous or premarital affair (C). Dressing fashionably (A) and expensively (B) may preserve a family's social status, but not their honor. There is no information in the passage to suggest that dishonor results from being kidnapped (D) or from entering small rooms (E).

42. **(B)** The speaker's final point is linked to the counsel's [making (D) incorrect]: it asserts that the petticoat would remove any fear that a woman would be molested. The counsel would use this assertion in favor of wearing the petticoat, the speaker against (being secure from male assault makes seeking marriage for security unlikely). The speaker's point both assents to (A) and opposes (C) the counsel's; (B) is a better answer, however, because the speaker uses this point to make the opposite conclusion. The speaker's point is strengthened [rather than weakened, (E)] by being able to use the counsel's own ammunition against it.

43. **(E)** Although the speaker refers to the girl (A) as the "pretty criminal" (line 13), "the petticoat" (E) is the best choice for the criminal because it is the object whose merits are being debated. "Society" (B), "fashion" (C), and "persons of her quality" (D) are not being indicted; in fact, the speaker gives "great allowances to the fair sex upon account of the fashion" (line 12) and by inference the persons who dictate the styles.

44. **(C)** Both counsel and speaker concentrate on the large petticoat's effect upon the economy (C): boosting industry with increased consumption of raw materials or draining family fortunes. The counsel's argument seems logical (A), yet it ignores the expense and impracticality of the huge petticoat and raises it from mere underwear to economic savior. Neither argument appeals primarily to emotions (B) such as fear, love, or anger. An appeal to patriotism (D) occurs in the counsel's arguments but not in the speaker's. There is no appeal to moral duty (E) in either argument.

45. **(A)** Without rancor, the speaker is mildly ridiculing (A) the folly of sacrificing money and comfort for fashionably huge petticoats. The passage clearly and directly condemns such petticoats through the conclusions of the speaker/judge: it does not reach this judgment through irony's expression of meaning through an opposite point of view (B). The passage itself is funny with its underwear trial (C); "satiric" remains the better stylistic description, however, because the passage is poking fun at the petticoat and intending to "reform" this fashion. The passage is not informal (D) because of its trial format and courtroom language, yet it is not replete with self-aggrandizing language (E).

46. **(B)** The speaker uses "we" to include the reader in the quest for understanding the creative writer (B). (A) is incorrect because the group that is "We laymen" (line 1) includes all persons but the creative writers. (C) incorrectly assumes that the speaker refers to him/herself with the royal "we" disregarding "laymen" (line 1), which defines "we" as plural. The speaker's "we" is not all-inclusive (D): it excludes the creative writer from the united speaker and reader.

47. **(C)** The antecedent is revealed by the sentence's parallel structure: the subject and verb of the second clause, "it is not at all weakened" (line 7), mirror that of the first, "our interest is only heightened" (line 5). "Explanation" (A) is incorrect because it is part of the dependent clause beginning with "that" (line 6). "Fact" (B) is the object of the preposition "by" (line 6). "Impression" [line 4, (D)] is too far removed from "it" to be its antecedent. "Insight" (E) follows, rather than precedes "it."

48. **(B)** The idea that "every man is a poet at heart" (line 17) clearly belongs to creative writers themselves: the speaker claims that comprehending the writer's methods of discovering and shaping his/her work will not enable a nonwriter to become a writer [(A), see paragraph one]. In lines 16–19 the speaker delineates a difference between writer and nonwriter by describing the writers' attempt to bring ordinary man closer (C). According to the speaker, "[in] spite of all the emotion with which he cathects his world of play, the child distinguishes it quite well from reality" [lines 26–28, (D)]. If "every child at play behaves like a creative writer" (lines 21–22), it follows that the business of creative writing parallels the play of childhood (E).

49. **(A)** The child concentrates and invests emotions in the creation of a "world of play" [line 27, (A)]. "Distances" (B) cannot define "cathects" because "in spite of" (line 26) taking such action upon his play world, the child distances ("distinguishes it quite well," line 27) from reality. The child seeks to link the occurrences of his/her created world with his/her real world; it consequently is not fantasized (C). The child's created world is his/her "most intense occupation" (line 20), and would thus not wish to discourage (D) or destroy (E) it.

50. **(B)** Each paragraph begins with a question and progresses to its answer (B): in one, how does the creative writer fashion a moving work? We cannot really understand or ourselves obtain this power; two, can we find in ourselves an activity similar to creative writing? This is possible. And three, is there creative activity in childhood? Yes, play is similar to creative writing. (A) is incorrect because paragraphs two and three continue the search for understanding of the process of creative writing begun in paragraph one. An answer to the third paragraph's question is given: none is offered to paragraph one's question, making (C) incorrect. Paragraphs one and three are relatively close in length; three, however, provides a detailed and longer answer to its question [discrediting (D)]. (E) is incorrect because paragraph three, which should have the most complex sentences (containing independent and dependent clauses), mainly contains simple, one subject/verb sentences.

51. **(C)** If a "child at play behaves like a creative writer" (lines 21–22), it follows that the writer behaves like a child at play; creative writing can consequently be considered to extend and expand the processes of childhood play (C). Paragraph three's establishment of the similarity of childhood and creative writing discredits (A) and (B). Although all men were once children at play, all men do not become creative writers (D); the speaker speaks for the nonwriting layman. (E) is incorrect because the speaker "differentiates the child's 'play' from 'fantasying'" (lines 29–30).

52. **(B)** The fact that both sources are cited tells you that this quote appears in both sources. One source is by Dobzhansky and one is by Mayr; each has the words "the origin of species" in the title. Therefore, (B) is the correct answer. The passage specifically says "together with Dobzhansky, Mayr developed this definition"; it does not say that the definition was (A) Mayr's or (D) Dobzhansky's own creation. And although it does say that the two men developed the definition together, nowhere does it say that (C) Mayr needed Dobzhansky's help. If you chose (E), you probably didn't read the question as carefully as you should have. The question specifically asks you about the purpose of footnotes 1 and 2. These footnotes have nothing to do with the fact that "students of biology . . . memorized Mayr's definition of species for more than half a century," which appears at the end of the paragraph.

53. **(E)** This question requires you to read the sentence in lines 31–33 carefully. If you are confused about the antecedent of the pronoun "them," you should try to replace the pronoun with each answer choice and determine which one makes the most sense. (E) is the only logical choice: geographic separation prohibits gene flow between populations—not through (B) rivers or valleys or through (D) mutations. It does not make sense to say "gene flow through (A) gene flow" or "through (C) separation."

54. **(D)** Even if you are not familiar with the footnote style used in this paper, line 39 refers to "the 797 pages of *Animal Species and Evolution*"; therefore, (D) is correct. Another clue that you may want to keep in mind is that in a footnote, a number followed by the abbreviation "p." indicates how many pages are in the source. In contrast, the abbreviation "p." or "pp." followed by a number indicates the page(s) on which the cited information appears in the source. Here, "797 p." indicates that the book contains 797 pages. It does not indicate (A) where Mayr's explanation of animal species and evolution appears. Actually, the entire book is about animal species and evolution, as the title indicates. (B) makes little sense, because Mayr is the author of the book. If you chose (C), you probably didn't read as carefully as you should have. The passage does use the word "outlined" in referring to the book; however, the phrase "outlined in depth" means that the principles of Mayr's ideas were explained in detail. And Mayr—not (E) the Columbia University Press—is the author of the book. The Columbia University Press is the publishing company.

55. **(C)** References to Mayr as "the greatest evolutionary biologist of the 20th century," "greatest biologist overall," "Darwin's apostle," and "Darwin of the 20th century" all convey the author's admiration. So does the comment "he accomplished much more than one might expect to get done, even in 100 years." The passage contains no evidence that the author feels (A) envy, (B) gratitude, (D) disgust, or (E) cynicism toward Mayr.

56. **(B)** The first paragraph states, "Ernst Mayr has been called 'Darwin's apostle' or the 'Darwin of the 20th century'" because of his work in evolutionary biology. And lines 2 and 42 compare Mayr to Methuselah because of his longevity (long life). So (B) is the correct choice. The article does not compare Mayr to Dobzhansky; there-

fore, (A) and (C) are incorrect. It does not compare him to Wilson or Gould; these two men were his colleagues who praised him; thus, (D) and (E) are wrong.

57. **(A)** The sentence that starts with line 9 offers the general idea that "Mayr had many fundamental insights in to evolutionary biology." The next sentence becomes a little more specific, presenting "his most widely known contribution." The next sentence is more specific, explaining the specific "notion" mentioned in the preceding statement. Therefore, the structure can be described as (A) moving from general to specific. It does not move (B) from specific to general, (C) from general to general, or (D) from specific to specific. And it is not (E) a presentation of conflicting ideas.

58. **(D)** Three of the sources cited in the footnotes are by Mayr. The earliest was published in 1942, and the latest was published in 2004—a span of 62 years. So without any information other than these three footnotes, it is reasonable to assume that Mayr's writing career lasted at least sixty years. Only the first footnote cites a work by Dobzhansky, and nothing implies that this work discussed Mayr's life. Likewise, the second and third footnotes do not cite works that appear to be about Mayr's life; thus, (A) is not a reasonable choice. A look at the footnotes tells us only that Dobzhansky wrote one book—not how long his writing career was; so (B) is incorrect. And although footnote 1 tells us that Dobzhansky wrote about the origin of the species, just as Mayr did, it does not tell us whether or not (C) he relied on Mayr's works. Footnote 4 reveals that Mayr wrote at least one article about himself, but we have no way of knowing if (E) he often wrote about himself or if he liked doing so.

59. **(C)** The passage is (C) eulogistic, praising a man who recently died. It is not (A) expository, since it does not set forth a meaning or purpose. It is not (B) analytical, since it does not break down and discuss component parts. It is not (D) judicial, since it does not argue a case. And it is not (E) exhortative, since it does not try to persuade the reader to act.

60. **(B)** The passage quotes Mayr as referring to evolutionary biology as "an endless frontier" with "still plenty to be discovered," implying that he (B) believed that evolutionary biologists would continue making new discoveries. If you chose (A) or (E), you probably did not read the question closely enough. Note that the question focuses specifically on Mayr's comments quoted in lines 46–49. Although Mayr may have believed evolutionary biology had unveiled many intriguing mysteries, nothing in the quote indicated this belief; thus, (A) is incorrect. Likewise, although Mayr did make tremendous contributions to the field of evolutionary biology, nothing in lines 46–49 relates to that fact; thus, (E) is not the correct choice. Mayr was 100 years old when he made these comments. And although Mayr expressed his regret that he would not be present to enjoy the future accomplishments of active evolutionists, nothing in his statement implies that (D) he was worried that he would die soon.

Model Student Response to Essay Question 1:

I am looking out at the world from my second floor bedroom window. I should not be sitting here wasting my time, not doing all of the things I should be. I can allow myself a short break from my obligations, though. The view from my window is beautiful. Directly across the street is a tree-filled park where children play on the swings and see-saws. The happy sounds of these children playing float across the street and reach my ears. I have so much to do now, but I am enjoying looking out my window. Some little kids are playing happily in the sandbox and on the slides with no other cares in the world.

There is a road between my window and the park. An old, blue Cadillac drives by with music blaring from its speakers, momentarily silencing the playing children. Many people are walking along the sidewalk, a mother pushing a baby carriage, a young couple holding hands, a man walking a small, black dog, my friends on their skateboards. I wonder why my friends are out hanging around when they should be home studying for final exams or the SAT I should be busy at work instead of sitting here looking out the window.

In addition to the park across the street I can see the front yard of my house. There is a large maple tree on my lawn. I can see a squirrel running around on the branches of this tree. The squirrel's nest is also visible from my room. As I watch, I notice that the squirrel is carrying twigs up to its nest. The squirrel is building its nest and preparing for the future. There is also a flower garden on my lawn that I can see. Purple crocuses and tulips are blooming in the garden. They are beautiful to look at. These flowers bloom every spring. Their sweet scent drifts up to my nose on a cool spring breeze. The sun is shining brightly in the cloudless sky. It is a lovely spring day and I am filled with hope, but I must get back to my work.

I am staring through my ice covered window at the cruel world outside. I have been sitting here for hours, just watching the emptiness outside. Across the street is a park. It is the middle of winter and the park is virtually empty. A cruel wind is blowing the swings around, as if to mock the children who play during the summer. Some pigeons hop around on the frozen ground, searching for a morsel of food. There is no one in the park today to feed them.

Between my window and the park there is a road. The road has been icy and treacherous all winter. Hardly a car drives by, except for the sand truck. I can hear it approaching now. The truck comes slowly up the street, dropping sand on the ice in the hopes of melting it, but the road will freeze up again overnight. The truck is gray, the same gray as the dark, unchanging sky that I see from my window. The sidewalk is as empty as the park. The only person who passes by is the homeless man who lives in the park. He carefully pushes his shopping cart along the sidewalk. He is bundled in layer upon layer of filthy brown clothes. I wonder how he survives in this cold harsh weather.

I can also see my front lawn from my window. A huge, leafless maple tree appears to be dead. During the summer, the tree seems full of life, sprouting green leaves and with squirrels running to and fro. But now the tree is stagnant, except for the thinner branches which are swaying violently in the wind. I can see the patch of dirt where the garden grows when it is warm outside. It is only a brown plot now, with a few dead stalks being the only reminder of life. I wish that I had something to do besides sit here and stare at this bleak empty, landscape. I am very bored though, so I think I will sit here for a few more hours.

Analysis of Response to Essay Question 1:

This essay displays a strong grasp of the ways in which language can be used to reveal different situations and circumstances. The essay employs vivid descriptive detail to portray two vastly different states of mind.

Both halves of the essay describe the same scene: a park across the street from the window, and the front lawn of the observer's house. The first half of the essay uses the beauty of early spring to vividly describe a hopeful outlook, while the second half expertly employs the cold dreariness of winter to portray an attitude of hopelessness.

The first section of the essay employs metaphors and descriptive language that clearly illustrate feelings of hope and joy. It is apparent through the details noted, the young couple holding hands, the squirrel building its nest, the blooming flowers, that the observer is identifying with these images metaphorically. S/he is looking forward to realizing some future potential.

In addition, the overall upbeat tone of the first part of the essay reflects the positive attitude and circumstances of the student looking out the window, as s/he busily prepares for the future.

The second part of this essay describing the same scene, but at a different time, uses stark, dreary imagery to illustrate a mood of despair. The view from the window is described as empty and frozen, perfectly reflecting the observer's mood. The gray mood portrayed in this part of the essay exemplifies that the writer is filled with dashed hopes; it is clear that s/he identifies with the starving pigeons and the freezing homeless man. The writer obviously knows how to use language, metaphor, and detail to describe circumstances and states of mind.

Finally, the stark contrast between the two descriptive passages in this essay shows that the writer has a firm grasp of how to use language to expertly reflect disparate circumstances and situations.

Model Student Response to Essay Question 2:

This passage reveals that John Muir believed that all of nature was embodied with a wildness of spirit, and that mankind loves this wildness and should respect it—as Muir felt the "Indians" did, and as he felt "everybody" certainly would, because it is an "ancient mother-love," older than the "civilization" that inhibits our celebration of it ("galling harness of civilization drops off").

The selection is remarkable for its tone of freedom and expansiveness which is supported by the author's diction (the use, choice, and arrangement of words). In a little over 125 words, Muir has used words that are directly evocative of freedom nine times ("wild, wildness, unblighted, wilderness, solitary, free, unimpeded, immense, eternal"), as well as phrases and images that are traditionally associated with expansiveness ("galling harness...drops off, busy and steeped with God, mountain, stream, waterfall").

God and nature ("ancient mother-love") are synonymous in this passage, and are placed at some distance from those—such as the "Indians"—who had known this truth and had respected it. Muir portrays himself as one of the formerly "civilized" folk who had shaken off its destructive and jading influences and could now see as the "Indians" had—and as, he believes, "everybody" can once they realize that the "wilderness" is itself a liberating force which at the same time provides a rich diet ("feeds on") for the human imagination.

Thus, the theme of liberation is supported by appropriate diction, and is re-inforced by the repetition of evocative words and phrases. The transcendence that Muir describes is further made attainable and placed within reasonable reach by his description of this element of Indian culture, and by his testimony that he himself has made the transition from stifling "civilization" to a reunion with his "ancient mother-love"—nature in its "unblighted…wilderness."

Analysis of Response to Essay Question 2:

The response has properly analyzed the Muir passage for diction, style, and syntax, and has provided details from the text that reinforce assertions. The responder has first identified the theme, then set forth a syntactic description of the passage, and concludes with a synthesis of how these elements are well suited to the theme of the passage. The key word here, which the responder recognizes as such, is "expansive-ness," for this is the essence both of the language of the passage as well as the power of the promise of Muir's vision for "everybody" now under the "galling harness of civilization."

Model Student Response to Essay Question 3:

Technology has become an important part of our lives in today's world. One can hardly get through a day without encountering computers, video games, cell phones, iPods, and many other forms of technology. So it is not surprising that such technol-ogy can be found in our schools as they seek to prepare students for today's world.

Giving up traditional forms of education in order to use technology in the classrooms may be a mistake. School is a place where students should develop their imagination, and it is possible that depending too much on computers and other technology may stifle creativity. As Mitch Resnick points out, children use their imagination and learn as they create things with blocks and make pictures with finger paints (Source A). There is more to life than manipulating a mouse and a keyboard. And at the college level, using an iPod to listen to a lecture may be convenient, but it cheats the student out of face-to-face interactions with the professor and with fellow students. The conveniences that Source C praises—such as being able to listen to a lecture while driving or standing in a grocery line, and not having to raise one's hand to ask or answer a question in class—can also be detrimental. An important part of education is seeing and interacting with the in-structor and overcoming the fear of participating in class. And although Source D may encourage friendships via the Internet, one can learn so much more with face-to-face friendships. As Source E points out, humans and social skills are important and necessary in our schools; they are also important at work (Source A).

Clearly, technology should not replace human interaction at school or anywhere else. However, it definitely has a place in today's education. The possibilities are limitless. NASA, a leader in the technological world, praises video games as a means of educating students in various academic subjects (Source F). Empire High School in Arizona successfully uses computers instead of textbooks in every classroom and every subject (Source B). Because of technological advances, education is no longer physically confined to a classroom or even a building. The many students who are enrolled in distance learning courses (Source D) and in such iPod-based courses as those offered at El Centro Community College (Source C) may complete courses without ever actually meeting their instructors or classmates.

Schools are responsible for preparing students for the world of work, and it is difficult to be a productive worker today without possessing certain skills. Not only must we be technologically savvy, but we must also possess the ability to network. Video games are a fun way to learn technological skills, and Marc Prensky defends them as a means of teaching people to work cooperatively and collaboratively (Source A). Also, an inviting school media center that offers adequate technology can encourage teamwork among students (Source E). As Source B points out, computers are becoming just as important in the classroom as they are in the workplace.

Careful examination of the issue reveals that technology in the schools can be both detrimental and beneficial. Computers, iPods, and video games as educational tools may encourage the individual to become isolated from others. However, these devices obviously have entered the educational world and the workplace, and they are not likely to go away. So it is the responsibility of the individual—young or old—not to use technology as a substitute for interaction with teachers and peers. And it is the school's responsibility to allow time and activities to encourage students to develop their imagination and creativity, to make sure students develop adequate technology skills, and to focus on enhancing students' learning experiences and preparation for work and for life in the 21st century.

Analysis of Student Response to Essay Question 3:

The student's response effectively addresses the challenge of the question (synthesize at least three of the sources for support and take a position that defends, challenges, or qualifies the claim that schools who are embracing the new technological approach to education are effectively teaching students the skills they need in today's world). The first paragraph introduces the general topic of technology in today's world, gradually narrowing to the specific idea of the essay. In this essay, the writer has chosen to show both positive and negative effects of the use of technology in schools. The writer synthesizes—combines the sources with an opinion to form a cohesive argument—rather than simply paraphrasing or quoting the sources. Each source is clearly attributed. The second paragraph focuses on the negative aspects of schools' use of technology as an educational tool, citing specific examples from the sources. For example, the writer cites: "As Mitch Resnick points out, children use their imagination and learn as they create things with blocks and make pictures with finger paints (Source A)." The next two paragraphs cite sources to help support the positive aspects of technology in the classroom—for example, "NASA, a leader in the technological world, praises video games as a means of educating students in various academic subjects (Source F)." The conclusion echoes the main ideas of the essay's body. The essay's language and development are effective, and the writer's position is supported with well-chosen examples. Overall, this is an effective response to the prompt.

PRACTICE EXAM 3

AP English Language & Composition

PR 3

TIME: 60 Mi
60 Qu

(Answer sheets appear in the back of this book.)

DIRECTIONS: This section of the test consists of selections from literary works and questions on their use of language. After reading each passage, choose the best answer to each question and blacken the corresponding oval on the answer sheet.

Questions 1–5 are based on the following passage. Read the passage carefully before choosing your answers.

We arrived on the afternoon of the day on which we had been summoned, and found her still free from delirium: indeed, the cheery way in which she received us made it difficult to think she could be in danger. She at once explained her wishes, which had reference, as I expected, to her nephew, and
5   repeated the substance of what I have already referred to as her main source of uneasiness concerning him. Then she begged me by our long and close intimacy, by the suddenness of the danger that had fallen on her and her powerlessness to avert it, to undertake what she said she well knew, if she died, would be an unpleasant and invidious trust.

10   She wanted to leave the bulk of her money ostensibly to me, but in reality to her nephew, so that I should hold it in trust for him till he was twenty-eight years old, but neither he nor anyone else, except her lawyer and myself, was to know anything about it. She would leave £5000 in other legacies, and £15,000 to Ernest—which by the time he was twenty-eight would have accumulated to,
15   say, £30,000. "Sell out the debentures," she said, "where the money now is— and put it into Midland Ordinary.

"Let him make his mistakes," she said, "upon the money his grandfather left him. I am no prophet, but even I can see that it will take that boy many years to see things as his neighbors see them. He will get no help from his father and
20   mother, who would never forgive him for his good luck if I left him the money outright; I daresay I am wrong, but I think he will have to lose the greater part or all of what he has, before he will know how to keep what he will get from me."

Supposing he went bankrupt before he was twenty-eight years old, the
25   money was to be mine absolutely, but she could trust me, she said, to hand it over to Ernest in due time.

"If," she continued, "I am mistaken, the worst that can happen is that he will come into a larger sum at twenty-eight instead of a smaller sum at, say, twenty-three, for I would never trust him with it earlier, and if he knows
30   nothing about it he will not be unhappy for the want of it."

She begged me to take £2000 in return for the trouble I should have in taking charge of the boy's estate, and as a sign of the testatrix's hope that I would now and again look after him while he was still young. The remaining £3000 I was to pay in legacies and annuities to friends and servants.

35   In vain both her lawyer and myself remonstrated with her on the unusual and hazardous nature of this arrangement. We told her that sensible people will not take a more sanguine view concerning human nature than the Courts of Chancery do. We said, in fact, everything that anyone else would say. She admitted everything, but urged that her time was short, that nothing would
40   induce her to leave her money to her nephew in the usual way. "It is an un-usually foolish will," she said, "but he is an unusually foolish boy"; and she smiled, quite merrily at her little sally. Like all the rest of her family, she was very stubborn when her mind was made up. So the thing was done as she wished it.

45   No provision was made for either my death or Ernest's—Miss Pontifex had settled it that we were neither of us going to die, and was too ill to go into details; she was so anxious, moreover, to sign her will while still able to do so that we had practically no alternative but to do as she told us. If she recovered we could see things put on a more satisfactory footing, and further discussion
50   would evidently impair her chances of recovery; it seemed then only too likely that it was a case of this will or no will at all.

When the will was signed I wrote a letter in duplicate, saying that I held all Miss Pontifex had left me in trust for Ernest except as regards £5000, but that he was not to come into the bequest, and was to know nothing whatever about

55 it directly or indirectly, till he was twenty-eight years old, and if he was
    bankrupt before he came into it the money was to be mine absolutely. At the
    foot of each letter Miss Pontifex wrote, "The above was my understanding
    when I made my will," and then signed her name. The solicitor and his clerk
    witnessed; I kept one copy myself and handed the other to Miss Pontifex's
60 solicitor.

1.   Paragraph six implies that Miss Pontifex thinks her nephew is

    (A)   a thief   (D)   financially immature

    (B)   a spendthrift   (E)   an enemy

    (C)   incompetent

2.   She wanted the narrator to

    (A)   pay 3,000 pounds in legacies and annuities

    (B)   take 2,000 pounds for himself as payment for being in charge of the boy's
    estate

    (C)   give the legacies and annuities to friends and servants

    (D)   Both (A) and (C)

    (E)   (A), (B), and (C)

3.   In the last paragraph, "bequest" probably means

    (A)   home

    (B)   family business

    (C)   arranged marriage

    (D)   inheritance

    (E)   burial plot

4.   We know from paragraph three that Miss Pontifex is realistic about her nephew
    because she itemizes the following:

    (A)   His grandfather left him money

    (B)   His father and mother will not help him with the money

    (C)   He will lose most of the money from his grandfather before he learns to
    manage money

    (D)   Both (A) and (B)

    (E)   (A), (B), and (C)

5.   From paragraph one, we may infer that the narrator and Miss Pontifex are

(A)   business partners   (D)   pupil and teacher

(B)   husband and wife   (E)   lovers

(C)   old friends

Questions 6–10 are based on the following passage. Read the passage carefully before you choose your answers. This passage is a portion of the NIDA InfoFacts on Drugged Driving, published by the National Institutes of Health and Human Services.

"Have one [drink] for the road" was, until recently, a commonly used phrase in American culture. It has only been within the past 20 years that as a Nation, we have begun to recognize the dangers associated with drunk driving. Through a multipronged and concerted effort involving many stakeholders,

5   including educators, media, legislators, law enforcement, and community organizations, such as Mothers Against Drunk Driving (MADD), the Nation has seen a decline in the numbers of people killed or injured due to drunk driving. It is now time that we recognize and address the similar dangers that can occur with drugged driving.

10   . . . the principal concern regarding drugged driving is that driving under the influence of any drug that acts on the brain could impair one's motor skills, reaction time, and judgment. Drugged driving is a public health concern because it puts not only the driver at risk, but passengers and others who share the road.

15   According to NHTSA, vehicle accidents are the leading cause of death among those aged 15 to 20.[1] It is generally accepted that because teens are the least experienced drivers as a group, they have a higher risk of being involved in an accident compared with more experienced drivers. When this lack of experience is combined with the use of marijuana or other substances that

20   impact cognitive and motor abilities, the results can be tragic.

NIDA's Monitoring the Future survey indicated that in 2004, 12.7 percent of high school seniors reported driving under the influence of marijuana, and 13.2 percent reported driving under the influence of alcohol in the two weeks

[1] National Highway Traffic Safety Administration. "Drugs and Human Performance Fact Sheet." U.S. Department of Transportation Report No. DOT HS 809 725, Washington, DC, 2004.

prior to completing the survey.[2] . . . The State of Maryland's Adolescent Survey indicates that 26.8 percent of the State's licensed, 12th-grade drivers reported driving under the influence of marijuana during 2001.[3]

. . . Drugs act on the brain and can alter perception, cognition, attention, balance, coordination, and other faculties required for safe driving. The effects of specific drugs of abuse differ depending on their mechanisms of action, the amount consumed, the history of the user, and other factors.

THC affects areas of the brain that control the body's movements, balance, coordination, memory, and judgment abilities, as well as sensations. Because these effects are multifaceted, more research is required to understand marijuana's impact on the ability of drivers to react to complex and unpredictable situations. However, we do know that:

- A meta-analysis of approximately 60 experimental studies, including laboratory, driving simulator, and on-road experiments, found that behavioral and cognitive skills related to driving performance were impaired in a dose-dependent fashion with increasing THC blood levels.[4]

- Evidence from both real and simulated driving studies indicates that marijuana can negatively impact a driver's attentiveness, perception of time and speed, and the ability to draw on information obtained through past experiences.

- Research shows that impairment increases significantly when marijuana use is combined with alcohol.[5]

- Studies have found that many drivers who test positive for alcohol also test positive for THC, making it clear that drinking and drugged driving are often linked behaviors.[6]

---

[2] National Institute on Drug Abuse (NIDA) website, http://www.drugabuse.gov/DrugPages/mtf. html. Monitoring the Future is funded by NIDA and conducted by the University of Michigan's Institute for Social Research. These findings are from the 2004 survey.

[3] Maryland Adolescent Survey, Conducted by the State Dept. of Education, http://www.msde. state.md.us/pdf_files/Final%202002%20MAS%20Report.pdf, 2002.

[4] G. Berghaus, N. Sheer, P. Schmidt. "Effects of Cannabis on Psychomotor Skills and Driving Performance–A Meta-Analysis of Experimental Studies." In: Proceedings–*13th International Conference on Alcohol, Drugs and Traffic Safety.* Eds. CN Kloeden, AJ McLean, NHMRC Road Accident Research Unit, The University of Adelaide, Adelaide, Australia, pp. 403–409, 1995.

[5] National Highway Traffic Safety Administration. Marijuana and Alcohol Combined Severely Impede Driving Performance. Ann Emer Med 35(4):398–399, 2000.

[6] O.H. Drummer, J. Gerostamoulos, H. Batziris, M. Chu, J.R. Caplehorn, M.D. Robertson, P. Swann. "The Incidence of Drugs in Drivers Killed in Australian Road Traffic Crashes," Forensic Sci Int 134:154–162, 2003.

- Prescription drugs: Many medications (e.g., benzodiazepines and opiate
50   analgesics) act on systems in the brain that could impair driving ability. In fact, many prescription drugs come with warnings against the operation of machinery—including vehicles—for a specified period of time after use. When prescription drugs are taken without medical supervision (i.e., when abused), impaired driving and other harmful reactions
55   can also result.

     In short, drugged driving is a dangerous activity that puts us all at risk.

6.   Which of the following is the best description of "drugged drivers" as described in this article?

    (A)   Drivers who are using prescription medications, marijuana, and/or any other drug that may impair judgment and performance

    (B)   Only teenage drivers who use marijuana and alcohol combined

    (C)   Drivers who are under age twenty-one and are using illegal drugs and/or alcohol

    (D)   Drivers who cause accidents that result in injuries or fatalities because their judgment and reaction time are inhibited by illegal drugs

    (E)   Drivers who have a medical condition that requires prescription drugs and therefore should not be consuming alcohol

7.   The tone of this article can best be described as

    (A)   anger   (D)   flippancy

    (B)   concern   (E)   regret

    (C)   sarcasm

8.   Which of the following statements can the reader make by simply looking at footnote 3?

    (A)   In 2002, the United States Department of Education conducted a survey of adolescents in Maryland in 2002.

    (B)   The 2002 survey of Maryland adolescents is posted on the Department of Education's website, but the results are not available there.

    (C)   It is possible to order a printed copy of the 2002 survey results by completing a mail-order form on http://www.msde.state.md.us/pdf_files/ Final%202002 %20MAS%20Report.pdf

(D) The Maryland Department of Education conducted a survey of adolescents across the nation and posted the results on their website in 2002.

(E) The Maryland Department of Education conducted a survey of adolescents in their state and posted it on their website in 2002.

9. In this article, the term "THC" is directly associated with

(A) driving

(B) marijuana

(C) alcohol

(D) prescription drugs

(E) the combined use of marijuana and alcohol

10. The sixth footnote informs the reader that

(A) An article about fatal automobile accidents in Australia appears in a book about forensic science

(B) An article about fatal automobile accidents in Australia appears on pages 154-162 in a 2003 journal

(C) Drummer, Gerostamoulos, Batziris, Chu, Caplehorn, Robertson, and Swann are forensic scientists who study such topics as drunk driving and drugged driving in Australia

(D) Drummer, Gerostamoulos, Batziris, Chu, Caplehorn, Robertson, and Swann were among the drivers killed in Australian traffic accidents

(E) The *Forensic Science International* (Forensic Sci Int) is a professional journal that focuses on drunk driving and drugged driving around the world

Questions 11–24 are based on the following passage. Read the passage carefully before choosing your answers.

Unjust laws exist: shall we be content to obey them, or shall we endeavor to amend them, and obey them until we have succeeded, or shall we transgress them at once? Men generally, under such a government as this, think that they ought to wait until they have persuaded the majority to alter them. They think
5   that, if they should resist, the remedy would be worse than the evil. But it is the fault of the government itself that the remedy *is* worse than the evil. *It* makes it worse. Why is it not more apt to anticipate and provide for reform? Why does it not cherish its wise minority? Why does it cry and resist before it is

hurt? Why does it not encourage its citizens to be on the alert to point out its
10 faults, and *do* better than it would have them? Why does it always crucify
Christ, and excommunicate Copernicus and Luther, and pronounce Washington and Franklin rebels?

If the injustice is part of the necessary friction of the machine of government, let it go, let it go: perchance it will wear smooth—certainly the machine
15 will wear out. If the injustice has a spring, or a pulley, or a rope, or a crank,
exclusively for itself, then perhaps you may consider whether the remedy will
not be worse than the evil; but if it is of such a nature that it requires you to be
the agent of injustice to another, then, I say, break the law. Let your life be a
counter-friction to stop the machine. What I have to do is to see, at any rate,
20 that I do not lend myself to the wrong which I condemn.

Under a government which imprisons any unjustly, the true place for a just
man is also a prison. The proper place today, the only place which Massachusetts has provided for her freer and less desponding spirits, is in her prisons, to
be put out and locked out of the State by her own act, as they have already put
25 themselves out by their principles. It is there that the fugitive slave, and the
Mexican prisoner on parole, and the Indian come to plead the wrongs of his
race should find them; on that separate, but more free and honorable, ground,
where the State places those who are not *with* her, but *against* her—the only
house in a slave State in which a free man can abide with honor. If any think
30 that their influence would be lost there, and their voices no longer afflict the
ear of the State, that they would not be as an enemy within its walls, they do
not know by how much more eloquently and effectively he can combat injustice who has experienced a little in his own person. Cast your whole vote, not a
strip of paper merely, but your whole influence. A minority is powerless while
35 it conforms to the majority; it is not even a minority then; but it is irresistible
when it clogs by its whole weight. If the alternative is to keep all just men in
prison, or give up war and slavery, the State will not hesitate which to choose.
If a thousand men were not to pay their tax-bills this year, that would not be a
violent and bloody measure, as it would be to pay them, and enable the State
40 to commit violence and shed innocent blood. This is, in fact, the definition of
a peaceable revolution, if any such is possible. If the tax-gatherer, or any other
public officer, asks me, as one has done, 'But what shall I do?' my answer is, 'If
you really wish to do anything, resign your office.' When the subject has
refused allegiance, and the officer has resigned his office, then the revolution is
45 accomplished. But even suppose blood should flow. Is there not a sort of blood

shed when the conscience is wounded? Through this wound a man's real manhood and immortality flow out, and he bleeds to an everlasting death. I see this blood flowing now.

11. In the second paragraph, the author refers to "the machine of government." How does this metaphor characterize the government as the author uses it?

    (A)   Efficient and reliable   (D)   Reparable

    (B)   Noisy and polluting   (E)   Labor-saving

    (C)   Single-minded and unfeeling

12. The opening paragraph poses a series of questions. What is the author's purpose?

    (A)   He states as questions the topics to be covered in the essay.

    (B)   He expects government officials to provide the reasons he seeks.

    (C)   He is satirically posing the questions to those with whom he disagrees.

    (D)   He is rhetorically stating what the government does and should not.

    (E)   He wants to polarize his readers between those who agree with him and those who do not.

13. In the passage, one goal of the speaker is to

    (A)   evoke the moral responsibility of the reader

    (B)   encourage an armed rebellion

    (C)   attract persecuted minorities to Massachusetts

    (D)   promote a political party

    (E)   reduce the tax burden

14. The passage contains all of the following EXCEPT

    (A)   a proposal for peaceful protest

    (B)   historical reference to other governments

    (C)   criticism of specific persons

    (D)   justification of bloodshed

    (E)   unanswered questions

15. Where is the "there" referred to in line 25?

    (A) Massachusetts   (D) Church

    (B) Prison   (E) The grave

    (C) Legislative building

16. Lines 34-36 are best restated as

    (A) a minority must maintain a difference from the majority, so it can disable the majority

    (B) a minority is an important part of the majority, without which the majority would collapse under its own weight

    (C) a majority exists only by actively contrasting the minority, and it is unconquerable when it acts in unison

    (D) a minority remaining in silence brings injustice upon itself, which it could stand against with its voice and unified action

    (E) a minority that complies to the will of the majority ceases to exist, but a minority that fully commits itself is unconquerable

17. According to the passage, what should the tax-gatherer do?

    (A) Steal the state's funds.   (D) Expect gunshots for greetings.

    (B) Submit counterfeit money.   (E) Sleep with one eye open.

    (C) Quit his job.

18. In lines 5-10, what is the antecedent of "it" and "its"?

    (A) Fault of the government   (D) Deceit of the government

    (B) Evil of the government   (E) Government

    (C) The governors

19. Contrast lines 19-20 with lines 21-22.

    (A) In lines 19-20, the author is content not to participate in injustice; but in lines 21-22, the existence of an injustice compels the author to give up his freedom in protest.

    (B) Lines 19-20 imply the author needs only react to what he sees; but lines 21-22 imply the author must react to all he knows.

    (C) Lines 19-20 advise neither a borrower nor a lender be; but lines 21-22 advise one to give up one's freedom for a man unjustly imprisoned.

(D) In lines 19-20, the author implies it is enough to condemn injustice; but in lines 21-22, the author says the only place for an honest man under a dishonest government is prison.

(E) Lines 19-20 advise a man to circumvent the wrongs of his state; but lines 21-22 advise him to meet them at every sacrifice to himself.

20. What does "cast your whole vote" (line 33) mean?

(A) Vote in every election, even the most local.

(B) Vote for the same party across the board.

(C) Run for office.

(D) Do everything you can to influence lawmaking.

(E) Vote as your conscience tells you.

21. It can be inferred from lines 22-25 that

(A) the author has been unjustly imprisoned

(B) the author has a loved one who is unjustly imprisoned

(C) the author is either in prison or not in Massachusetts

(D) Massachusetts' prisons are overcrowded

(E) Massachusetts has banished citizens that the author feels are principled

22. What change in tone would occur if, in the series of questions in the first paragraph, "it" were replaced with "they"?

(A) The paragraph would lose some of its impact.

(B) The paragraph would be less condemning and more of a general complaint.

(C) The paragraph would no longer lump all governments, past and present, into a convenient whipping post.

(D) The paragraph would be more accusatory, showing greater dissent.

(E) The paragraph would be more condescending, chastising a multitude instead of a single entity.

23. Identify the stages of the discussion through the passage.

(A) Question, answer, enact   (D) Criticize, suggest, inspire

(B) Goad, insult, attack   (E) Argue, reason, propose

(C) Taunt, imply, condemn

24.   What assumption lies behind lines 36-37?

(A)   The state is a democracy.

(B)   "All just men" will act simultaneously.

(C)   The prisons will not be large enough.

(D)   The women will not bail out the men.

(E)   "All just men" are a significant number.

Questions 25–38 are based on the following passage. Read the passage carefully before choosing your answers.

If ye be thus resolved, as it were injury to think ye were not, I know not what should withhold me from presenting ye with a fit instance wherein to show both that love of truth which ye eminently profess and that uprightness of your judgement which is not wont to be partial to yourselves by judging

5   over again that order which ye have ordained *to regulate printing. That no book, pamphlet, or paper shall be henceforth printed, unless the same be first approved and licensed by such,* or at least one of such as shall be thereto appointed. I warn that this will be primely to the discouragement of all learning and the stop of truth, not only by disexercising and blunting our abilities in what we know

10   already, but by hindering and cropping the discovery that might be yet further made both in religious and civil wisdom.

I deny not, but that it is of greatest concernment in the church and commonwealth to have a vigilant eye how books demean themselves, as well as men; and thereafter to confine, imprison and do sharpest justice on them as

15   malefactors: for books are not absolutely dead things but do contain a potency of life in them to be active as that soul whose progeny they are; nay, they do preserve as in a vial the purest efficacy and extraction of that living intellect that bred them. I know they are as lively and as vigorously productive as those fabulous dragon's teeth and being sown up and down, may chance to spring

20   up armed men. And yet on the other hand unless wariness be used, as good almost kill a man as kill a good book; who kills a man kills a reasonable creature, God's image; but he who destroys a good book, kills reason itself, kills the image of God, as it were in the eye. Many a man lives a burden to the earth; but a good book is the precious life-blood of a master-spirit, embalmed

25   and treasured up on purpose to a life beyond life. 'Tis true, no age can restore a life, whereof perhaps there is no great loss; and revolutions of ages do not oft recover the loss of a rejected truth, for the want of which whole nations fare far

worse. We should be wary therefore what persecution we raise against the living labours of public men, how we spill the seasoned life of man preserved and stored up in books; since we see a kind of homocide may be thus committed, sometimes a martyrdom, and if it extend to the whole impression, a kind of massacre, whereof the execution ends not in the slaying of an elemental life but strikes at that ethereal and fifth essence, the breath of reason itself, slays an immortality rather than a life.

Hear this revelation of the Apostle of Thessalonians: 'To the pure all things are pure,' not only meats and drinks, but all kind of knowledge whether of good or evil; the knowledge cannot defile, nor consequently the books, if the will and conscience be not defiled. For books are as meats and viands are, some of good, some of evil substance, and yet God in that unapocryphal vision, said without exception, 'Rise Peter, kill and eat,' leaving the choice to each man's discretion. Wholesome meats to a vitiated stomach differ little or nothing from unwholesome, and best books to a naughty mind are not unapplyable to occasions of evil. Bad meats will scarce breed good nourishment in the healthiest concoction; but herein the difference is of bad books, that they to a discreet and judicious reader serve in many respects to discover, to confute, to forewarn and to illustrate.

25. Which of the following is the grammatical antecedent of "them" in line 18?

   (A) Souls   (D) Books

   (B) Authors   (E) Children

   (C) Lives

26. The passage reads most like which of the following?

   (A) A letter   (D) A rebuttal

   (B) A lesson   (E) A sermon

   (C) A conversation

27. The author likens "killing" a book to killing a man. In what ways does the author imply that the former is worse?

   I.   Books live longer than men.

   II.   Books, as objects, are free of sin.

   III. Many men don't deserve to live.

(A)   I and III only   (D)   III only

(B)   I and II only   (E)   II only

(C)   II and III only

28.   How does the author use "Rise Peter, kill and eat" to argue that printing should not be regulated?

(A)   Just as Peter should strike down his own food, each man should destroy evil books.

(B)   Just as God let Peter choose what meat to eat, men should be able to choose freely what to read.

(C)   Just as Peter eats what he himself kills, men should read whatever books they find.

(D)   Just as men need to hunt for edible food, the human mind needs the quest for truth and wisdom.

(E)   Just as hunting has physical dangers, reading should have perils for the mind and soul.

29.   The passage compares books to all of the following EXCEPT

(A)   the image of God   (D)   reason

(B)   armed men   (E)   a vial of living intellect

(C)   a vault

30.   According to the passage, the regulation of printing will

(A)   result in a ban on books

(B)   create a black market

(C)   discourage scientific discovery

(D)   suppress the word of God

(E)   inhibit the distribution of knowledge

31.   The author's tone in the passage's opening (lines 1-5) is

(A)   scolding   (D)   pleading

(B)   sarcastic   (E)   agreeing

(C)   respectful

32. In the second paragraph, the author shifts from one stance to another. That shift is from

    (A) agreement to warning   (D) acknowledgment to justification

    (B) agreement to disagreement   (E) concern to wariness

    (C) acknowledgment to denial

33. How does the author feel about censorship?

    (A) He is against it in every form.

    (B) It should only apply to blasphemous texts.

    (C) It should be determined by the church, not the state.

    (D) It should occur after the book exists, not before the book is first circulated.

    (E) It is a necessary evil.

34. The sentence beginning "And yet on the other hand" (lines 20-23) serves primarily to

    (A) flatter the government officials being addressed

    (B) introduce the author's departure from agreeing with them

    (C) contradict the preceding part of the paragraph

    (D) start an unrelated topic

    (E) introduce the first metaphor

35. The author's argument would be more influential to a wider audience if he were to

    (A) quote prominent publishers

    (B) include graphs and illustrations

    (C) use puns and satire

    (D) use historic examples instead of religious ones

    (E) eliminate the transparently flattering introduction

36. The author's attitude toward the power of books in lines 24-25 is

    (A) envy   (D) respect

    (B) suspicion   (E) hatred

    (C) worship

37. What is the author's purpose in the repetition of the closing lines of the passage, ending with "to discover, to confute, to forewarn, and to illustrate"?

(A)   The author is emphasizing that reading is not man's only pastime.

(B)   The author points out that there are more ways to learn than from books.

(C)   The author is emphasizing that readers are more socially active in general.

(D)   The author points out that reading is not passive, that men read and react according to their natures.

(E)   The author is emphasizing that all knowledge, good and evil, expands the experiences of men.

38. The passage's longest sustained metaphor is that of books as

(A)   men   (D)   mummies

(B)   dragon's teeth   (E)   reason itself

(C)   meat

Questions 39–52 are based on the following passage. Read the passage carefully before choosing your answers.

Prohibition was the world's first enactment, written by the finger of God in the Garden of Eden to keep the way of life, to preserve the innocence and character of man. But under the cover of the first night, "in the cool of the day," there crept into the Garden a brewer by the name of Beelzebub, who told
5 the first man that God was a liar; that he could sin and not die; that the prohibition law upon the tree of life was an infringement upon his personal liberty and that the law had no right to dictate what a man should eat or drink or wear. The devil induced Adam to go into rebellion against the law of God in the name of personal liberty, and from that hour dates the fall of man.
10   We are hearing something of that same argument in this campaign against the serpent drink, and not only on the part of the enemy. There are many good men who look upon prohibition as an assault upon the personal liberty of the citizen; but it seems to us they do not keep clear the issues involved in this fight. They are not personal at all.
15   Personal liberty is a matter of personal choice, of personal right to eat or to drink. No prohibitory law ever adopted or proposed attempts to interfere with that right. It does not seek to compel a man to abstain; it does not say that he ought not, must not, or dare not drink. It passes only upon the social right of trade, traffic and sale. Whether a man drinks or abstains is entirely his

20 own affair, so long as he does not poison himself, compel society to cure him, support him when he is unable to take care of himself, lock him up when he is dangerous to be at large, bury him at the public expense when he is a corpse, or interfere with the personal liberty of others when he is exercising his own.

Men do not properly discriminate between a personal right and a social act.
25 Personal liberty relates to private conduct. If a man signs the temperance pledge he surrenders his personal liberty or personal privilege to drink; when he votes dry—to prohibit liquor traffic—it has nothing to do with the question of personal liberty.

You have a personal right to eat putrid meat; I have no right to sell it. If
30 your hog dies a natural death, or with the cholera, you have a personal right to grind it up into a sausage and eat it, but you have no right to offer it for public sale. A man has a personal right to corn his dead mule and serve it on his own table. You have as good a right to eat your cat as I have my chicken, or your dog as I have my pig. The Chinese in New York have a dog feast at their New
35 Year's celebration and the police have never interfered with their personal right. But if you opened a meat market and skinned dogs and cats or exposed horse sausage for public sale, the meat inspector would confiscate the entire supply, close up the place as a public nuisance and arrest you for selling what you had a personal right to eat.

40 To abstain is a personal act; to market, traffic and trade is a social act, limited by the social effect of the thing sold and the place where it is kept for sale. This distinction between total abstinence, which relates to personal liberty or personal conduct, and prohibition, which relates to social conduct and the State, is perfectly clear. The one is the act of the individual; the other is the act
45 of the State.

Total abstinence is the voluntary act of one man; it recognizes the right of choice of personal liberty. Prohibition is the act of the community, the State, the majority, which is the State, and is a matter of public policy, to conserve social and civic liberty by denying to an immoral and dangerous traffic the
50 right of public sale.

39. Which of the following does the author use as a synonym for "the majority"?

(A) The right   (D) The State

(B) The God-fearing populace   (E) Men

(C) Society

40. What does the author believe about "personal rights"?

   (A)   Personal rights must be agreed upon by society.

   (B)   Personal rights are confined to the privacy of the home.

   (C)   Personal rights are a fiction—societies have only personal privileges.

   (D)   Personal rights are forfeit when abused.

   (E)   Personal rights do not justify all social acts.

41. What means of argument is used in the fifth paragraph?

   (A)   A series of distinct metaphors

   (B)   A sustained metaphor

   (C)   Repetitious legal examples

   (D)   Satirical pseudo-legal examples

   (E)   Point-by-point counter-examples

42. The sentence beginning "You have a personal right" (line 29) is distinct from others in its paragraph in that it serves primarily to

   (A)   distinguish between personal rights and public acts

   (B)   associate liquor with putrid meat

   (C)   emphasize the difference between reader and author

   (D)   associate the author with the Prohibition movement

   (E)   mirandize the reader

43. The author's tone in the second paragraph can best be described as

   (A)   annoyed   (D)   impatient

   (B)   corrective   (E)   bored

   (C)   condescending

44. Which of the following is described as "immoral" (line 49)?

   (A)   Right   (D)   Traffic

   (B)   Sale   (E)   Liberty

   (C)   Public

45. What contradiction exists between the first and fifth paragraphs?

    (A) The first paragraph uses religious/literary examples, while the fifth paragraph uses legal examples.

    (B) The first paragraph takes liberties with its source to make an example, but the fifth does not.

    (C) The first paragraph assumes the reader is a Christian, while the fifth assumes the reader is a lawyer.

    (D) The first paragraph associates prohibition with eating, while the fifth associates it with sale.

    (E) The first paragraph is about fruit, while the fifth is about meat.

46. The author uses all of the following to refer to Satan EXCEPT

    (A) Beelzebub   (D) the enemy

    (B) a liar   (E) a brewer

    (C) the devil

47. What is the purpose of the sentence beginning "Whether a man drinks" (lines 19-23)?

    (A) To ridicule drinkers for comic effect

    (B) To exaggerate the evils of alcohol and so demean the opposition's credibility

    (C) To demonstrate that even a personal liberty can become a social concern

    (D) To explain the pervasiveness of personal liberties

    (E) To argue that personal liberties are inherently a social burden

48. According to the passage, the purpose of prohibition is to

    (A) conserve social and civic liberty

    (B) limit hazardous personal liberties

    (C) deny public sale to immoral and dangerous traffic

    (D) enforce the will of God on weak men

    (E) eliminate the profit from liquor consumption

49. In the first paragraph, the author implies that

    (A) Satan is a lawyer

    (B) Satan was correct

(C)   the Eden story is historic fact

(D)   the fruit is analogous to alcohol

(E)   Eden is abstinence

50.   Which of the following does the passage say is the distinction between total abstinence and prohibition?

   I.   One relates to personal conduct; the other relates to social conduct

   II.   One is the act of the individual; the other is the act of the State

   III.   One recognizes personal liberty; the other is a matter of public policy

   (A)   I and II only   (D)   I, II and III

   (B)   I and III only   (E)   II only

   (C)   II and III only

51.   In the context of the passage, what does "dry" mean?

   (A)   To be sober

   (B)   To have signed a temperance pledge

   (C)   To not offer alcohol

   (D)   To outlaw the sale of alcohol

   (E)   To thirst for alcohol

52.   What do the closing lines imply about the speaker?

   (A)   His principal concern is the safety of the public.

   (B)   He has a strong belief in God.

   (C)   He believes laws should uphold morality.

   (D)   He wants drinkers to brew their own intoxicants.

   (E)   He maintains the majority is always right.

Questions 53–60 are based on the following passage. Read the passage carefully before choosing your answers.

First, truly, to all them that, professing learning, inveigh against poetry, may justly be objected that they go very near to ungratefulness, to seek to deface that which, in the noblest nations and languages that are known, hath been the first lightgiver to ignorance, and first nurse, whose milk by little and little
5   enabled them to feed afterwards of toughest knowledges. And will they now

play the hedgehog, that, being received into the den, drive out his host? Or rather vipers, that with their birth kill their parents? Let learned Greece, in any of her manifold sciences be able to show me one book before Musaeus, Homer, and Hesiod, all three nothing but poets. Nay, let any history be brought that
10 can say any writers were there before them, if they were not men of the same skill, as Orpheus, Linus, and some other are named, who, having been the first of that country that made pens deliverers of their knowledge to their posterity, may justly challenge to be called their fathers in learning. For not only in time they had this priority—although in itself antiquity be venerable—but went
15 before them as causes, to draw with their charming sweetness the wild untamed wits to an admiration of knowledge. So as Amphion was said to move stones with his poetry to build Thebes, and Orpheus to be listened to by beasts,—indeed stony and beastly people. So among the Romans were Livius Andronicus and Ennius; so in the Italian language the first that made it aspire
20 to be a treasurehouse of science were the poets Dante, Boccace, and Petrarch; so in our English were Gower, and Chaucer, after whom, encouraged and delighted with their excellent foregoing, others have followed to beautify our mother-tongue, as well in the same kind as the other arts.

53. What is the author's tone in saying "all three (were) nothing but poets" (line 9)?
     (A)   Negative
     (B)   Condescending
     (C)   Satirical
     (D)   Mocking
     (E)   Harping

54. According to the passage, the significance of poetry to learning is that
     (A)   poetry helps break the monotony of more boring subjects
     (B)   rhyming aids the memorization required in other subjects
     (C)   poetry teaches the student that learning is fun
     (D)   poetry builds learning strengths needed for more difficult subjects
     (E)   poetry teaches the language, a prerequisite to all learning

55. The sentence beginning "Or rather vipers" (lines 6-7) serves primarily to
     (A)   associate the alleged ungratefulness with a most extreme example
     (B)   cloud the issue with proverbial references
     (C)   imply that others are guilty of the vipers' crime
     (D)   allude to the myth that snakes nurse from cows' udders
     (E)   link the accused with coldbloodedness

56. In the context of the passage, "wits" (line 16) means

(A) jokes   (D) senses of humor

(B) cares   (E) men

(C) minds

57. What does the passage attribute to Amphion?

(A) Being the first lightgiver to ignorance

(B) Recording on paper for prosperity

(C) Beautifying his mother tongue

(D) Cultivating sophisticated minds

(E) Building with stone blocks

58. As implied by the passage, which of the following groups of men speak one language among them?

I.   Dante, Boccace, and Petrarch

II.   Amphion, Thebes, and Orpheus

III. Homer, Hesiod, and Musaeus

(A) I only   (D) I and II only

(B) II only   (E) I and III only

(C) III only

59. What would be the effect of changing "aspire" to "attempt" in line 19?

(A) "Attempt" conveys the idea that this was a real, tangible task.

(B) "Attempt" clips the wings off the loftiness of "aspire."

(C) "Attempt" makes the sentence choppy in contrast to "aspire."

(D) "Attempt" negates the personification of "language."

(E) "Attempt" implies impending failure.

60. The passage's primary goal is to associate poetry with

(A) instruction   (D) communication

(B) language   (E) education

(C) history

STOP

This is the end of Section 1.
If time still remains, you may check your work only in this section.
Do not begin Section 2 until instructed to do so.

Section 2

TIME: 2 hours
          3 Essay Questions

Question 1 (Suggested time—40 minutes.) This question is one third of the total essay score.

The literary genre of fantasy is characterized by the existence of a fantasy realm in which an alternate mode of existence—an imaginary world—exists in severe disjunction with reality. Characteristics of the alternate world include:

the quality of the mythical and the imagined (think of unicorns, magical powers, spirits),

the achievable ideal (dreams and fantasies can be realized),

distortions of time (time is compressed or lengthened),

simplification of character,

expression of repressed desires,

and alternate values to reality (the world operates by a set of values different from those in reality).

For example, Lewis Caroll's *Alice in Wonderland* is a classic example of literary fantasy: Alice visits an alternate world in which time is distorted, fantastic creatures abound, and the everyday values of reality do not exist.

Such elements that constitute fantasy are also present in the non-literary: campaign speeches, product advertising, cartoon strips, children's toys. Select a topic that can be represented as an alternate world and write a well-organized essay explaining how at least two of the elements of literary fantasy are manifested in that alternate world. Be sure to use concrete details and explanations to back your thesis.

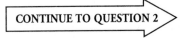

CONTINUE TO QUESTION 2

Question 2 (Suggested time—40 minutes.) This question is one-third of the total essay score.

To market a product successfully, it is necessary to appeal to the targeted consumer group. In addition to consumer needs, desires, personalities, spending habits, etc., advertisers need to tailor all aspects of the language to create an effective, appropriate advertisement.

HEY! Recognize this? [picture of the old Chevron] Sorry, wrong generation.

How about this? [picture of the new Chevron] Nice isn't it? Hard to believe it's from the same generation that spawned bell bottoms, platforms, the Village People, and expressions like "groovy" and "far out." Whoa, that was when our parents were cool.

But hey, we're a new generation, and now we're wearing Levis and flannel, cowboy boots and metal, and well, bell-bottoms and platforms. Like those classics, the Chevron is back, only it's not a car just for our parents anymore. It's our time now, and with the newly designed Chevron, we can express ourselves with power, speed, and sleek styling that shouts, "Hey, it's me!" Best of all, with the most standard features in its class, it still won't break the bank. So it'll leave you with enough money for all the CDs you need to listen to, concerts you need to attend, cities you need to visit, bridges you need to bungee-jump from...

Write a brief essay explaining why and how this ad is appropriate for the intended audience. Consider such elements as language, tone, syntax, and diction in your explanation.

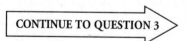

Question 3 *(Suggested reading time—15 minutes)*
(Suggested writing time—40 minutes)

Directions: The following prompt is based on the accompanying six sources.

This question requires you to synthesize a variety of sources into a coherent, well-written essay. *Refer to the sources to support your position; avoid mere paraphrase or summary. Your argument should be central; the sources should support this argument.*

Remember to attribute both direct and indirect sources.

Introduction: Obviously, a parent is an important part of a child's life. But in what ways does a parent influence a child, and how does that influence affect the child? What aspects of life does that influence impact?

Assignment: Read the following sources (including any introductory information) carefully. Then, in an essay that synthesizes at least three of the sources for support, take a position that defends, challenges, or qualifies the claim that a parent influences the physical and emotional development of a child.

You may refer to the sources by their titles (Source A, Source B, etc.) or by the descriptions in parentheses.

Source A (Maslow)

Source B (National Institute of Mental Health)

Source C (Eisenberg)

Source D (Office of National Drug Control Policy)

Source E (ChildStats)

Source F (President Bush)

Source A

Maslow, A. "A Theory of Human Motivation." *Psychological Review,* 50 (1943).

The following passage is excerpted from a book by Abraham Maslow, a classical psychologist who was best known for his research on human needs.

[An] indication of the child's need for safety is his preference for some kind of undisrupted routine or rhythm. He seems to want a predictable, orderly world. For instance, injustice, unfairness, or inconsistency in the parents seems to make a child feel anxious and unsafe. This attitude may be not so much because of the injustice *per se* or any particular pains involved, but rather because this treatment threatens to make the world look unreliable, or unsafe, or unpredictable. Young children seem to thrive better under a system which has at least a skeletal outline of rigidity, in which there is a schedule of a kind, some sort of routine, something that can be counted upon, not only for the present but also far into the future. Perhaps one could express this more accurately by saying that the child needs an organized world rather than an unorganized or unstructured one.

The central role of the parents and the normal family setup are indisputable. Quarreling, physical assault, separation, divorce or death within the family may be particularly terrifying. Also parental outbursts of rage or threats of punishment directed to the child, calling him names, speaking to him harshly, shaking him, handling him roughly, or actual physical punishment sometimes elicit such total panic and terror in the child that we must assume more is involved than the physical pain alone. While it is true that in some children this terror may represent also a fear of loss of parental love, it can also occur in completely rejected children, who seem to cling to the hating parents more for sheer safety and protection than because of hope of love.

Source B

National Institute of Mental Health. (2000). "Child and Adolescent Violence Research at the National Institute of Mental Health." (Publication No. 00-4706). Available at http://www.nimh.nih.gov/publicat/violenceresfact.cfm.

The following passage is excerpted from a National Institute of Mental Health overview that summarizes research into the causes, diagnosis, prevention, and treatment of child and adolescent violence.

The research on risk for aggressive, antisocial, and violent behavior includes multiple aspects and stages of life, beginning with interactions in the family. Such forces as weak bonding, ineffective parenting (poor monitoring, ineffective, excessively harsh, or inconsistent discipline, inadequate supervision), exposure to violence in the home, and a climate that supports aggression and violence puts children at risk for being violent later in life . . . .

. . . When antisocial behavior emerges later in childhood or adolescence, it is suspected that genetic factors contribute less, and such youths tend to engage in delinquent behavior primarily because of peer influences and lapses in parenting. The nature of the child's social environment regulates the degree to which heritable early predisposition results in later antisocial behavior. Highly adaptive parenting is likely to help children who may have a predisposition to antisocial behavior . . . .

Research has demonstrated that youths who engage in high levels of antisocial behavior are much more likely than other youths to have a biological parent who also engages in antisocial behavior. This association is believed to reflect both the genetic transmission of predisposing temperament and the maladaptive parenting of antisocial parents.

The importance of some aspects of parenting may vary at different ages. For example, inadequate supervision apparently plays a stronger role in late childhood and adolescence than in early childhood. There is evidence from many studies that parental use of physical punishment may play a direct role in the development of antisocial behavior in their children. In longitudinal studies, higher levels of parental supervision during childhood have been found to predict less antisocial behavior during adolescence. Other researchers have observed that parents often do not define antisocial behavior as something that should be discouraged, including such acts as youths bullying or hitting other children or engaging in "minor" delinquent acts such as shoplifting.

Research examining the mental health outcomes of child abuse and neglect has demonstrated that childhood victimization places children at increased risk for delinquency, adult criminality, and violent criminal behavior. Findings from early research on trauma suggest that traumatic stress can result in failure of systems essential to a person's management of stress response, arousal, memory, and personal identity that can affect functioning long after acute exposure to the trauma has ended. One might expect that the consequences of trauma can be even more profound and long lasting when they influence the physiology, behavior, and mental life of a developing child or adolescent.

Source C

Eisenberg, Leon. "What's Happening to American Families?" ERIC Digest (ED330496), 1991.

The following passage is excerpted from an article that focuses on changes in the structure and role of the American family.

Few issues vex Americans more than what has happened to the role of the family in caring for children. Almost one in four of the nation's youngsters under 18 lives with only one parent, almost always the mother. If the youngster is black, the ratio rises to one in two. The divorce ratio has tripled and the percentage of out-of-wedlock births among teenage women has doubled over the past 15 years.

Caring for infants is not just a dilemma for female-headed households. Whether or not the family is intact, more than half of all mothers with a preschool child are in the labor force, 50 percent more than the proportion employed out of the home a decade ago. The Labor Department reports that the number of women holding two or more jobs has increased five-fold since 1970.

What we need, we hear on all sides, is a return to the good old days when parents were responsible for their kids and kids obeyed their parents. We long for a return to an age when fundamental values were shared by all. If there WAS such an age, can we go back to it? No one doubts that today's family is harassed and overburdened. The question is: could what seemed to work then work now?

In the aftermath of the Industrial Revolution, the American family has been stripped of two of its traditional social functions: serving as a unit for economic production and as a school for the vocational training of children. The first function has been usurped by commercial firms, the second by the state. Two functions remain: first, the physical and emotional gratification of the family's adult members, and second, the socialization of the children into community mores and the promotion of their development. . . .

. . . economist Victor Fuchs has calculated that between 1960 and 1986, the opportunity for children to spend time with parents declined by 10 hours per week for the average white child, and 12 hours for the black child. The principal reason is the increase in the proportion of mothers holding paid jobs; not far behind is the increase in one-parent households. Fathers in intact families could offset the loss in hours of mothering by doing more fathering; there is little evidence that they do so. . . .

Parents of the past learned by modeling themselves not only on their parents, but on uncles, aunts, and grandparents at home or nearby. As they grew up, they learned how to care for younger siblings because they were expected to. The isolated nuclear family and the sharp sequestration of age groups in today's society combine to deprive today's children of these experiences.

. . . As society continues to evolve, so will the family. As the family changes, we will need to continue to monitor the state of our children.

Source D

Office of National Drug Control Policy. "Influence of Parents and Family on Children's Drug Use and Other Problem Behaviors: Review of the Literature." Available at http://www.whitehousedrugpolicy.gov/publications/prevent/parenting.

This passage is excerpted from an article that focuses on the family's influence on children's problem behaviors.

. . . A large body of research findings shows that the family contributes both risk and protective factors to the lives of adolescents; it affects both vulnerability and resilience to drug abuse.

Parent-family connectedness was measured through variables such as closeness to parent, perceived caring by the parent, satisfaction with the relationship with the parent, and feelings of being loved and wanted by family members. Other measures included the number of different activities engaged in with the mother or father during the past week; the physical presence of the parent before and after school, at bedtime, or at dinner; the parent's expectations for the teen to complete high school or college; and suicide attempts and/or completions by family members in the past year. . . .

. . . across all domains of risk, the role of parents and family in shaping the health of adolescents is critical. The protective role that perceived parental expectations play regarding adolescents' school attainment is a correlate of health and healthy behavior. Although the physical presence of a parent in the home at key times reduces risk (and especially substance use), of more significance is parental connectedness (e.g., feelings of warmth, love, and caring from parents). The home environment also helps shape health outcomes. Homes where adolescents have easy access to guns, alcohol, tobacco, and illicit substances contribute to the adolescent's increased risk of suicidality, involvement in interpersonal violence, and substance use. . . .

The parent's attitude and parental permissiveness toward the youth's use is a key factor in teenage drug use, as much as or more so than peer pressure. One 1993 study conducted by the Johnson Institute in Minneapolis found that when school-age youth are allowed to drink at home, they not only are more likely to use alcohol and other drugs outside the home, but also are more likely to develop serious behavioral and health problems related to substance use. The survey indicated that most parents allow for "supervised" underage drinking, which is a bigger factor in use and abuse than peer pressure. . . .

Family management practices and family communication patterns have a clear impact on a youth's behavior. The child raised with a warm and uncritical parenting style rather than a harsh, overly authoritarian or overly permissive style develops patterns of resiliency.

Source E

Federal Interagency Forum on Child and Family Statistics. "Beginning Kindergarteners' Knowledge and Skills." Available at http://www.childstats.gov/amchildren05/2000spe1.

The following information is excerpted from a publication that addresses the relationship between a mother's level of education and a child's proficiency upon entry to kindergarten.

As children enter kindergarten for the first time, they demonstrate a diverse range of cognitive knowledge, social skills, and approaches to learning. This indicator highlights their proficiency in several key skills needed to develop the ability to read. How well children read eventually affects how they learn and ultimately influences their chances for school success. Social skills and positive approaches to learning are also related to success in school and are equally important at this age. The depth and breadth of children's knowledge and skills are related to both developmental and experiential factors. These include child characteristics such as age, gender, and cognitive and sensory limitations and characteristics of the child's home environment and preschool experience. Mother's education is the background variable that is consistently related to children's knowledge and skills.

Percentage of Beginning Kindergartners With Selected Knowledge and Skills by Mother's Education, Fall 1998

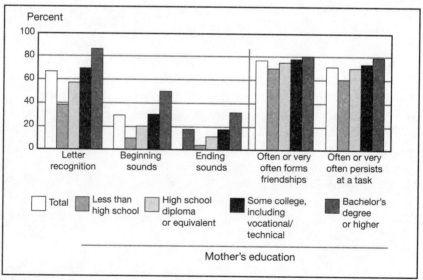

SOURCE: U.S. Department of Education, National Center for Education Statistics, Early Childhood Longitudinal Study, Kindergarten Class of 1998–99.

Emergent literacy—a child's understanding that the print in books has meaning—was assessed among incoming kindergartners in 1998. . . . Upon entry to kindergarten, 66 percent of children were proficient in recognizing letters. This skill varied by the level of the mother's education, from 38 percent of children with mothers who had not completed high school to 86 percent of those whose mothers had a bachelor's degree or higher.

. . . Proficiency in all . . . areas upon entry to kindergarten varies widely and is strongly related to the mother's level of education.

Source F

Bush, George W. "Parents' Day, 2003." Press Release. 25 July 2003. Office of the Press Secretary. Available at http://www.whitehouse.gov/news/releases/2003/07/20030725.html.

The following is excerpted from a press release issued in July 2003 by the White House for President George W. Bush.

A Proclamation

Children are a daily reminder of the blessings and responsibilities of life and a source of joy, pride, and fulfillment. Parents, stepparents, adoptive parents, and foster parents have the important responsibility of providing for, protecting, nurturing, teaching, and loving their children. On Parents' Day, we honor America's mothers and fathers and celebrate the values that bind families from one generation to the next and help define us as a Nation.

As a child's first teachers, parents are the most influential and effective instructors in a child's life. Through their words, actions, and sacrifices, parents are living examples for children. Young boys and girls watch their parents closely and imitate their behavior. Parents play a critical role in instilling responsibility, integrity, and other life lessons that shape the lives of America's future leaders.

My Administration is committed to supporting our Nation's families. We are working with faith-based and community organizations to promote healthy marriages, responsible parenting, and education. And we are committed to fully funding and supporting the Promoting Safe and Stable Families Program, which helps strengthen family bonds, promote adoption, and provide help for vulnerable children across our country.

Volunteer service is one way parents can spend time with their children while encouraging them to learn the value of helping others. . . . Parenting is one of the most rewarding and challenging endeavors in life. On this special day, we recognize the hard work and compassion of America's parents and celebrate the mothers and fathers who are positive role models for their children. I encourage parents to spend more time reading, talking, and volunteering with their children. I also urge parents to share the joys and wisdom of parenthood with new families in their communities and those planning families for the future.

NOW, THEREFORE, I, GEORGE W. BUSH, President of the United States of America, by virtue of the authority vested in me by the Constitution and laws of the United States and consistent with Public Law 103-362, as amended, do hereby proclaim Sunday, July 27, 2003, as Parents' Day. I encourage all Americans to express their respect and appreciation to parents everywhere for their contributions to their children, families, communities, and our Nation. I also call upon citizens to observe this day with appropriate programs, ceremonies, and activities.

IN WITNESS WHEREOF, I have hereunto set my hand this twenty-fifth day of July, in the year of our Lord two thousand three, and of the Independence of the United States of America the two hundred and twenty-eighth.

GEORGE W. BUSH

END OF EXAM

PRACTICE EXAM 3

AP English Language & Composition

Answer Key

Section 1

1.	**(D)**	21.	**(C)**	41.	**(C)**
2.	**(E)**	22.	**(B)**	42.	**(B)**
3.	**(D)**	23.	**(D)**	43.	**(B)**
4.	**(E)**	24.	**(E)**	44.	**(D)**
5.	**(C)**	25.	**(D)**	45.	**(D)**
6.	**(A)**	26.	**(E)**	46.	**(B)**
7.	**(B)**	27.	**(A)**	47.	**(C)**
8.	**(E)**	28.	**(B)**	48.	**(A)**
9.	**(B)**	29.	**(C)**	49.	**(D)**
10.	**(B)**	30.	**(E)**	50.	**(D)**
11.	**(C)**	31.	**(C)**	51.	**(D)**
12.	**(D)**	32.	**(A)**	52.	**(C)**
13.	**(A)**	33.	**(D)**	53.	**(C)**
14.	**(C)**	34.	**(B)**	54.	**(D)**
15.	**(B)**	35.	**(D)**	55.	**(A)**
16.	**(E)**	36.	**(C)**	56.	**(C)**
17.	**(C)**	37.	**(D)**	57.	**(E)**
18.	**(E)**	38.	**(A)**	58.	**(E)**
19.	**(A)**	39.	**(D)**	59.	**(B)**
20.	**(D)**	40.	**(E)**	60.	**(E)**

PRACTICE EXAM 3

AP English Language & Composition

Detailed Explanations of Answers

Section 1

1. **(D)**   The correct answer is (D) since it was mentioned previously that she would like him to make his financial mistakes before inheriting her money. While she calls him "foolish," Miss Pontifex gives no evidence of thinking him (A), (B), (C), or (E), all of these choices being far too negative to describe her feelings about him and, therefore, incorrect answers.

2. **(E)**   As we see in paragraph six, (A), (B), and (C) are all listed as her desires to the narrator making (E) the correct answer. (A), (B), and (C) are all incorrect because each supplies only part of the correct answer. (D) is incorrect since it omits one of the three requests Miss Pontifex makes of the narrator.

3. **(D)**   (D) is the correct answer since the passage deals with both Miss Pontifex's money and her death. While (A), (B), (C), and (E) deal with family matters, they do not necessarily include the money she wants to leave to her nephew.

4. **(E)**   By re-reading the paragraph, we see that (A), (B), and (C) are all mentioned, thereby making (E) the correct answer. While (D) includes two of the three, omitting the third choice causes it to be incorrect. (A), (B), and (C) are each incorrect since each mentions only one part of Miss Pontifex's being realistic about her nephew instead of all three.

5. **(C)**   (C) is the correct answer; Miss Pontifex refers to their "long and close intimacy." While she has asked him to be in charge of her nephew's estate, there is no indication that they have other business, causing (A) to be incorrect. There is also no indication in the passage to lead to the conclusion of that they are (B), (D), or (E), making each of these incorrect answers.

6. **(A)**   Lines 10–12 specifically state that "under the influence of any drug that acts on the brain could impair one's motor skills, reaction time, and judgment." It refers to the use of marijuana and prescription drugs in particular, as well as the use of

alcohol in combination with such drugs. Although especially concerned about teenage drivers who use these substances, the author does not limit the term "drugged drivers" to (B) only teenage drivers who use marijuana and alcohol combined, (C) drivers who are under age twenty-one and are using illegal drugs and/or alcohol, (D) drivers who cause accidents that result in injuries or fatalities because their judgment and reaction time are inhibited by illegal drugs, or (E) drivers who have a medical condition that requires prescription drugs and therefore should not be consuming alcohol.

7. **(B)** Throughout the article, concern is evident. The first paragraph says, "It is now time that we recognize and address the similar dangers that can occur with drugged driving," and the last sentence is "In short, drugged driving is a dangerous activity that puts us all at risk." The author frequently uses such words as "risk" and cites statistics to help prove the gravity of the issue. Although the author's concern is evident, nowhere does he/she appear to be (A) angry, (C) sarcastic, (D) flippant, or (E) regretful.

8. **(E)** The footnote specifically states that the cited survey was conducted by the Maryland Department of Education, and the date on the website is 2002. Therefore, choice (E) is correct. The Maryland Department of Education—not the United States Department of Education—conducted the survey; so (A) is wrong. You cannot tell simply by looking at the footnote exactly what information is available on this website; thus, (B) is not correct. Likewise, nothing in the footnote indicates that (C) it is possible to order a printed copy of the survey or that a mail-order form is available there. And the footnote cites the Maryland Adolescent Survey, implying that the survey is limited to adolescents of that state, rather than (E) adolescents across the nation.

9. **(B)** Although this article does not specifically define or explain THC, this term is directly related to marijuana. THC is mentioned for the first time in line 31; this sentence is followed by a comment that more research on marijuana is required. The information in lines 36–39 came from the source cited in footnote 4, the title of which includes the word "cannabis" (marijuana). The article does discuss (A) driving, (C) alcohol, (D) prescription drugs, and (E) the combined use of marijuana and alcohol; however, only marijuana is directly associated with the term "THC."

10. **(B)** This footnote cites an article titled "The Incidence of Drugs in Drivers Killed in Australian Road Traffic Crashes," which appeared in 2000 on pages 154 through 162 in volume 134 of the *Forensic Science International*. It was written by Drummer, Gerostamoulos, Batziris, Chu, Caplehorn, Robertson, and Swann. The only correct answer choice is (B). The footnote does not cite (A) a book about forensic science. The footnote does not tell us whether or not the authors are forensic scientists, and it does not tell us what topics they study. All we know is that they wrote at least one article about drug-related fatal traffic accidents in Australia. Therefore, choice (C) is not correct. Drummer, Gerostamoulos, Batziris, Chu, Caplehorn, Robertson, and Swann were the writers of the article—not (D) among the drivers killed in Australian traffic accidents. And this footnote does not tell us what the focus of the journal

is—only that this one specific article is about drug-related fatal traffic accidents in Australia; therefore, choice (E) is wrong.

11. **(C)** The author suggests that "injustice is part of the necessary friction" of government, implying that government does not react to the injustices it encounters. This gives the impression of a lack of awareness and concern. The idea that your life should "be a counter-friction to stop the machine" implies that the machine cannot be operated, that it is going about its purpose and can only be sabotaged. For these reasons, the answer is (C) "single-minded and unfeeling." The passage says nothing favorable about the "machine," eliminating (A) "efficient and reliable" and (E) "labor-saving." The author finds the government as efficient as being lost but making great time. The passage also is not optimistic about the "machine," as notable in the "let your life be a counter-friction" quotation; so (D) "reparable" is incorrect. Nowhere does the author complain literally about machines; so (B) "noisy and polluting" is also incorrect.

12. **(D)** A quick scan of these questions will tell you that these are not "topics to be covered in the essay"; so (A) is incorrect. Also, one will note that these are the legitimate concerns of the author, so (C) "He is satirically posing the questions of those he disagrees with" is incorrect. At no point in the essay does the author antagonize his reading audience; so (E) "He wants to polarize his readers…" is incorrect. The idea of (B), that the author "expects…the reasons," seems possible at first with the beginning questions, but the last question, "Why does it always crucify Christ,…pronounce Washington and Franklin rebels?" obviously is accosting different governments of different centuries. These questions of the author do not function truly as questions—they have no addressee and expect no answers. The author is complaining about the traditional abuses of government, even "good" government. (D) "He is rhetorically stating what the government does and should not" is the correct answer.

13. **(A)** The speaker's primary goal is to address the injustices of the state so they may be undone. He would obviously prefer a simple tax revolt; so (B) "encourage an armed revolution" is incorrect. However, this is a means, not an end; so "reduce the tax burden" (E) is incorrect also. The author never refers to the taxes as weighty or unfair, only misused. He would certainly not "attract persecuted minorities to Massachusetts" (C), because Massachusetts supposedly "imprisons unjustly." The author cannot be said to "promote a political party" (D), because his proposal of a tax revolt would not exchange a single elected official for another person. The author seeks to "evoke the moral responsibility of the reader" (A), as in "Under a government which imprisons any unjustly, the true place for a just man is also a prison."

14. **(C)** The passage suggests that men not pay their taxes, which is "a proposal of peaceful protest" (A). The passage refers to the governments of Christ, Copernicus, and Washington, which are "historical references to other governments" (B). The passage states, "But even suppose blood should flow. Is there not a sort of blood shed when the conscience is wounded?," or "justification for bloodshed" (D). The passage opens with a series of rhetorical questions, which are "unanswered questions" (E). By elimination, the answer is "criticism of specific persons," (C), which never occurs in the passage.

15. **(B)**   The passage reads "…in her prisons…It is there that…," so the correct answer is (B) "prison." The same paragraph refers to (A) "Massachusetts," but at best you would have to say "Massachusetts prisons" to capture the same meaning. Neither (C) "legislative building," (D) "church," nor (E) "the grave," occurs in the paragraph to be potential antecedents.

16. **(E)**   The lines being paraphrased are "A minority is powerless while it conforms to the majority; it is not even a minority then; but it is irresistible when it clogs by its whole weight." (A) "A minority…so it can disable the majority" is an inaccurate paraphrase because the minority should clog the "machine" of government, not assault the majority. (B) "A minority is an important part of the majority…" is obviously wrong. The minority is an important part of the people, but, by definition, not any part of the majority. (C) "A majority exists…" is incorrect because it transposes "minority" and "majority." (D) "A minority…brings injustice upon itself" is incorrect because lines 34-36 say nothing of the kind. The answer is (E) "A minority that complies to the will of the majority ceases to exist, but a minority that fully commits itself to impeding the unjust action of the majority is unconquerable" because it accurately hits all the points of the original.

17. **(C)**   The author says to the tax-gatherer "if you really wish to do anything, resign your office," which is (C) "quit his job." The author never suggests (A) "steal the state's funds" or (B) "submit counterfeit money." Nor does the author threaten the officer, as (D) "expect gunshots for greetings" and (E) "sleep with one eye open" suggest.

18. **(E)**   First (C) "the governors" can be eliminated because it is plural while "it" and "its" need a singular antecedent. Line 10 refers to "its citizens," which allows us to eliminate (A) "fault of…," (B) "evil of…," and (D) "deceit of…" because, while governments can have citizens, the same cannot be said of faults, evils and deceits. Now it will be important to note the author's distinction between "the government" and "government." The use of "the" implies the specification of a specific one or example, while its conspicuous absence implies a generalization. If you heard someone say, "The man is prone to violence," you would respond, "Lock him up" or "Get him help"; but if that person had said, "Man is prone to violence," you would respond, "Is it the culture or the species?" The paragraph refers to the different governments of Christ, Copernicus, and Washington as if they were one or as if he were stating a general truth. Therefore, "its" meaning is best captured by (E), "government."

19. **(A)**   The question asks you to contrast "What I have to do is to see, at any rate, that I do not lend myself to the wrong which I condemn" with "Under a government which imprisons any unjustly, the true place for a just man is also a prison." (B) "…only react to what he sees…" takes "to see" from the original in the too literal sense of vision when the author meant "to see" as in "to make sure." Similarly, "…neither borrower nor lender be…" (C) takes "lend" too literally when the author used "lend myself" to mean "aid." (D) "…it is enough to condemn justice…" is incorrect because, in the original, the author insists that beyond condemning injustice, he must not assist its function. (E) "… advise a man to circumvent the wrongs of his

state…" is incorrect because the author nowhere advises avoidance of problems—he always advises protesting to them, whether by strike or opposition. "In lines 19-20, the author is content not to participate in injustice; but in lines 21-22, the existence of an injustice compels the author to give up his freedom in protest." (A) accurately paraphrases the conflict of the original lines.

20. **(D)**   The entire sentence referred to in this question is "Cast your whole vote, not a strip of paper merely, but your whole influence." The key word is "influence," which helps to identify (D) "do everything you can to influence lawmaking" as the correct answer. "Vote in every election…" (A) does not convey the "whole influence" of a person, and neither does (B) "vote…across the board" or (E) "vote…your conscience." "Run for office" (C) suggests one's whole influence is given, but nowhere does the passage imply that the author is suggesting everyone run for office.

21. **(C)**   While (A) "the author has been unjustly imprisoned" or (B) "the author has a loved one…imprisoned" are conceivable, they are not inferred by lines 22-25. Nowhere is it suggested that (D) "Massachusetts' prisons are overcrowded." When the passage says the state "put out and locked out" some citizens, it is metaphorically referring to imprisonment (note line 23 "in her prisons"), not the banishment suggested by (E) "…banished citizens…" While one may argue that imprisonment is a form of banishment, the correct answer must reflect most precisely what the passage's lines imply. These lines say the principled men in Massachusetts should be in prison; thus, the answer is (C) "the author is either in prison or not in Massachusetts."

22. **(B)**   The change from "it" to "they" would not significantly alter the strength of the argument, so (A) "…lose impact" is incorrect. Another problem with (A) is a problem for (C) "…no longer lump all governments…"; while they refer to changes that may or may not be accurate, they are not "changes in tone" as the question requires. "…More accusatory…" (D) and (E) "…more condescending…" claim changes in tone, but these changes do not occur with the stated substitution. The correct answer is (B) "…less condemning and more of a general complaint:" by not lumping the governments into one, as (C) mentioned, the accusation becomes buckshot, covering several targets instead of a single strike at a single entity.

23. **(D)**   Because the questions of the opening paragraph are never answered, (A) "question, answer, enact" is incorrect. Because the opening paragraph does not intend to address the government, it cannot be said to prod anyone or anything into action; so (B) "goad, insult, attack" is incorrect. Similarly, (C) "taunt, imply, condemn" is incorrect because the government must be addressed to be taunted. "Argue, reason, propose" (E) is a reasonable answer; but (D) is better and correct because the opening of the passage is best described as criticizing. Also, the passage does more than merely "suggest" and "propose." It follows through to "inspire" action.

24. **(E)**   These lines do not necessarily assume (A) "the State is a democracy" because any government gets its power from the tolerance of the people. While (B) "…all…act simultaneously" would be the best means of enacting the author's pro-

posal, it would not be necessary to its success. To say that "the prisons won't be large enough" (C) is to assume the government has little imagination concerning where to put people and how else to punish them. "The women will not bail out the men" (D) ignores the option of prisoners to refuse bail. The assumption behind lines 36-37 is (E) "'all just men' are a significant number" of which the government will need to take notice. "All just men" is best in quotation marks because it is, as the author defines them, implicitly "those who agree with me."

25. **(D)** The clause begins at line 15 with "for books are…," and so "books" (D) is the correct answer. Books are bred by "authors"; (B), so that is not the correct option. "Souls" (A), "lives" (C), and "children" (E) do not occur in the sentence as plurals and so cannot be the antecedent of "them."

26. **(E)** The passage lacks the personal tone of both "a letter" (A) and "a conversation" (C). The author is reacting to an event "ye have ordained" (line 5) but not in a point by point way like one would react to an argument in the form of "a rebuttal" (D). The religious nature of the discussion makes the passage most like "a sermon" (E). Because a sermon is a form of "a lesson" (B), that answer seems correct but (E) is more detailed and more accurate.

27. **(A)** The passage says in lines 23-25, "Many a man lives a burden to the earth; but a good book…(has) a life beyond life," which affirms both statement I and statement III. Lines 35-36 say, "books are…some of good, some of evil substance," which contradicts statement II. Therefore, the only correct answer is (A) "I and III only."

28. **(B)** The passage says that the significance of God's command was "leaving the choice to each man's discretion" (lines 40-41). This does not support "…each man's task, not the government's, to destroy evil books" (A) because it concerns consumption as in eating or reading, not destruction as in killing or banning. "Read whatever books…" (C) ignores the choice by limiting the choosing to one—everything. (D) conveys an interesting idea that has nothing to do with the passage. (E) "…perils for the mind and soul" has the ring of something with which the author might agree; but he never suggests this. The correct answer "men should be able to choose" (B) is exactly the argument made by the passage.

29. **(C)** The passage says, "he who destroys a good book…kills reason itself, kills the image of God," (lines 22-23) verifying (D) and (A) respectively. Lines 16-18 say books "do preserve as in a vial…that living intellect that bred them," which verifies option (E) "a vial of living intellect." A less direct connection is made in lines 19-20, "(Books) are…may spring up armed men," verifying (B). The word "vault" does not occur anywhere in the passage; so the answer is "a vault" (C).

30. **(E)** The author makes a warning in lines 7-11 that does not suggest (A) "…a ban on all books" or (B) "…a black market." He worries that regulation will "hinder…discovery…in religious and civil wisdom," but to hinder is not the same as to (C) "discourage…" To make something more difficult is not automatically the same

as to make it less desirable. The author is not concerned that religion will be a target as (D) "suppress the word of God" suggests. One of his concerns is that regulation will "(blunt) our abilities in what we know already," as in (E) "inhibit the distribution of knowledge."

31. **(C)** The author seems to be addressing a legislative body, and is very tactful and diplomatic. He is not (A) "scolding" or (B) "sarcastic." The author does not concede any agreement (E) until the following paragraph. Although he is making an appeal (D), the author should not be characterized as "pleading," which implies self-deprecation. His tone maintains his own personal audience's "love of truth (and)...uprightness of...judgement" (lines 3-4).

32. **(A)** The author begins the second paragraph by not only acknowledging the dangers of books, "I deny not..." (line 12), but also by agreeing that some books should be "confine(d), imprison(ed)" (line 14). "Acknowledgment to denial" (C) and "acknowledgment to justification" (D) are incorrect because "acknowledgment" is not strong enough to describe the author's concession. "Concern to wariness" (E) is inaccurate because line 12's "it is of concernment to the church" is not the author's concern but the author's acknowledgment of the church's concern. The paragraph proceeds to suggest that by killing books, you also kill good books. The author's position is not distant enough to be "disagreement" (B). The answer is "agreement to warning" (A).

33. **(D)** The author's true feelings about censorship are expressed in the beginning of the second paragraph, "it is of the greatest concernment in the church and commonwealth to have a vigilant eye how books demean themselves, as well as men; and thereafter to confine...and do sharpest justice on them as malefactors" (lines 12-15). He is not (A) "...against it in every form," nor does he find it (E) "...a necessary evil." He has an approval of censorship that is not limited to religion as (B) "...apply to blasphemous texts" and (C) "...determine by the church" suggest. His belief is most accurately expressed by (D) "it should occur after the books exists, not before the book is first circulated." The ordinance that the author is reacting to forbids the publishing of books that have not been "approved" by the state.

34. **(B)** The sentence beginning "And yet on the other hand..." does not (A) "flatter..." anyone; nor does it (E) "introduce the first metaphor" or the second or the third. This sentence begins a change, but not to (D) "...an unrelated topic." It begins to show the potential hazards of regulation, not by (C) "contradict(ing) the preceding..." but by explaining the consequences of improper banning. The sentence serves primarily to (B) "introduce the author's departure from agreement."

35. **(D)** Any group that would ban books is not likely to be influenced by (A) "quote(d) prominent publishers." The topic is too serious to approach it with (C) "...puns and satire." Because the issue is truly a matter of principle rather than science or commerce, (B) "...graphs..." is not advisable. It is inaccurate to characterize the introduction as (E) "...transparently flattering..."; and, as it is, the introduction

cannot harm the argument. The best proposed change to the essay is (D) "use historic examples instead of religious ones," which would release the limitation of appealing to only Christian faiths.

36. **(C)** The passage in lines 24-25 says, "a good book is the precious life-blood of a master-spirit, embalmed and treasured up on purpose to a life beyond life." The attitude conveyed is certainly positive, eliminating (A) "envy," (B) "suspicion," and (E) "hatred," but we must now distinguish between worship and respect. The lines refer to a purpose without specifying or even remotely describing it. Usually one respects a power, an ability or an authority, but these lines do not emphasize these concepts. The lines have images of death and afterlife, emphasizing religion and suggesting a tone of (C) "worship."

37. **(D)** The closing lines address what men get out of reading, eliminating (A) "...reading is not man's only pastime" and (B) "...more ways to learn than from books." Similarly, the author is not (C) "...emphasizing that readers are more socially active..." (E) implies that all experience, like all reading, can be positive, but the author would rather emphasize that evil reading can be reacted to in a constructive way. (D) "the author points out that reading is not passive, that men read and react according to their natures" is correct because reading does not "happen" to men. Men are in action when they read.

38. **(A)** The passage only briefly uses the metaphors of (B) "dragon's teeth," (D) "mummies," and (E) "reason itself." While the metaphor of (C) "meat" is used throughout the third paragraph, (A) "men" is used in more lines and in more ways, as the offspring of men, as armed men, as the image of God, and the running metaphor describing the death of men with images of homicide, martyrdom, and massacre.

39. **(D)** In lines 47-48, the passage says, "Prohibition is the act of the community, the State, the majority, which is the State...," verifying (D) "the State." The passage does not use the words of (A) "the right" or (B) "the Godfearing populace." (C) "society" is never used as a synonym for the majority. While the passage tends toward gender bias, the author does not go so far as to equate the majority with (E) "men."

40. **(E)** The author never goes so far as to denounce the legitimacy of personal rights. He does not annihilate all of them by saying they (C) "...are a fiction...." He does not depopulate personal rights by saying they (A) "...must be agreed upon..." or that they (D) "...are forfeit when abused." The author does not restrict personal rights (B) "...to the privacy of the home"; he simply argues that (E) "Personal rights do not justify all social acts"—namely, that the right to eat rotting meat does not create the right to sell rotting meat.

41. **(C)** The fifth paragraph uses examples, not metaphors, eliminating (A) "a series..." and (B) "a sustained...." The examples are in earnest, not (D) "satirical..."; but they are not (E) "point by point counter-examples." The examples of the fifth

paragraph, while many, only make one point among them; so they cannot be said to be point by point. They are (C) "repetitious legal examples."

42. **(B)** The sentence beginning "You have a personal right...," (line 29) serves primarily to (B) "associate liquor with putrid meat." The paragraph (A) "distinguish(es) between personal rights and public acts" again and again, but never with so extreme an example as putrid meat. The sentence does not (C) "emphasize the difference between reader and author" because the "you" and the "I" are examples, not distinctions of roles. (D) "associate the author..." is incorrect because the author is in no way seeking to distance himself from his audience. (E) "mirandize the reader" is incorrect because, for the same reason just stated, the author does not assume any authority over the reader.

43. **(B)** The author's tone in the second paragraph is neither (A) "annoyed" nor (E) "bored." There is no sense of him being (D) "impatient," rather there is an atmosphere that a moment's explanation will clear the air. The author's reference to "many good men" dispels the idea that he is being (C) "condescending." The overall tone that simple explanation will convince the many good men that there is no assault on personal liberty is best described as (B) "corrective."

44. **(D)** Line 49 describes (D) "traffic" as immoral, "denying to an immoral and dangerous traffic the right of public sale," not (A) "right," (B) "sale," (E) "liberty," or (C) "public" (which is an adjective).

45. **(D)** Certain differences exist between the first and fifth paragraphs, such as (A) "...religious/literary (vs) legal...," (B) "...takes liberties (vs) not," and (E) "...fruit (vs) meat." However, these differences, while true, do not necessarily mean there is a conflict. Because the paragraphs do not undermine each others' points, they do not truly conflict. (D) "the first paragraph associates prohibition with eating, while the fifth associates it with sale" as eating or consumption. The fifth paragraph labors to convey the idea that prohibition does not limit the personal right to eat, while the first paragraph calls God's forbiddance of eating the fruit of the tree of knowledge "prohibition." (C) is incorrect because in using varying examples, the author does not assume anything about the reader.

46. **(B)** The first paragraph alternately refers to Satan as (A) "Beelzebub," (C) "the devil," and (E) "a brewer." The second paragraph refers to those against prohibition as (D) "the enemy," but there is a secondary meaning implying that "the enemy" is Satan and that he is also against prohibition. The answer is (B) "a liar," which occurs in the first paragraph but is Satan's reference to God.

47. **(C)** The purpose of the sentence beginning "Whether a man drinks" (lines 19-23) is (C) "to demonstrate that even a personal liberty can become a social concern." The sentence is not guilty of (B) "exaggerat(ion)," nor of implying the inevitability of (E) "...personal liberties are inherently a social burden." The sentence is almost comical in its lengthy list, but it does not go so far as (A) "to ridicule drinkers..." The sentence does demonstrate "...the pervasiveness of personal liberties," but its primary purpose is (C).

48. **(A)** The passage never claims that the law should or does (B) "limit hazardous personal liberties." While allowing people to drink, but not allowing the sale of liquor, may seem to intend (E) "eliminate the profit…," the passage never makes that statement. Nor does the passage outwardly claim that prohibition (D) "enforce(s) the will of God on weak men." The passage claims that prohibition (C) "den(ies) public sale to immoral and dangerous traffic," but that is a definition, not its purpose. The purpose of prohibition, as taken from lines 48-49, is to (A) "conserve social and civic liberty."

49. **(D)** In the first paragraph, the author, to a limited degree, characterizes Satan as a lawyer but never truly implies that (A) "Satan is a lawyer." The concessions of later paragraphs may suggest that (B) "Satan was correct," but the first paragraph does not. The author uses the Eden story as a form of truth without necessarily implying that (C) "the Eden story is historic fact." The first paragraph may imply that Eden was abstinence, but it does not imply that paradise can be regained by avoiding alcohol, that (E) "Eden is abstinence." The author definitely implies that (D) "the fruit is analogous to alcohol," that drinking alcohol is another fall, when he refers to the devil as "a brewer" (line 4).

50. **(D)** Lines 42-43 state, "total abstinence…relates to…personal conduct, and prohibition…relates to social conduct," which verifies statement I. Lines 44-45 state, "one is the act of the individual; the other is the act of the State," which verifies statement II. Lines 46-48 state, "abstinence…recognizes…personal liberty… Prohibition…is a matter of public policy," which verifies statement III. The answer is (D) all of the above.

51. **(D)** The passage does not define "dry" as (A) "…sober" or as (E) "to thirst for alcohol." The passage specifically distinguishes between (B) "(having) signed a temperance pledge" and "dry" in the fourth paragraph. Also, the passage never refers to (C) "to not offer alcohol." Lines 26-27 state, "when he votes dry—to prohibit liquor traffic." The answer is (D) "to outlaw the sale of alcohol."

52. **(C)** The author's belief or disbelief in God is not referred to in the closing lines of the passage, eliminating (B) "He has a strong belief in God." Nowhere does the passage suggest that the author (D) "…wants drinkers to brew their own intoxicants." In the closing lines, the author uses the will of the majority to justify prohibition, but does not (E) "…maint(ain that) the majority is always right." The author expresses (A) "…concern…(for) the safety of the public," but this concern is not implied to be primary. Line 49 refers to "an immoral and dangerous traffic," which implies that the immorality of the product is a reason to restrain it from public sale. The correct answer is that the author (C) "…believes laws should uphold morality."

53. **(C)** The passage intends to exalt poetry; so (A) "negative" is not the tone of line 9. Similarly, the line "all three nothing else but poets" is neither (E) "harping" nor (B) "condescending." The passage is not being serious, but its function is more sophisticated than (D) "mocking." The line is making fun of the idea that these men might be referred to as "nothing else but poets." It is (C) "satiri(zing)" both the attitude and the language.

54. **(D)** The passage does not claim that poetry is more interesting than other subjects; so (A) "poetry helps break the monotony…" is incorrect. Poetry is not limited to rhyming and the author never even refers to the convention; so (B) "rhyming aids…" is incorrect. The passage does not use the word "fun" or anything of a similar meaning; so (C) "poetry teaches the student that learning is fun" is incorrect. While it is an interesting argument that (E) "poetry teaches the language…," it is not one that the passage makes. The answer is (D) "poetry builds learning strengths…," as found in lines 4-5 "(poetry's) milk by little and little enabled them to feed afterwards on tougher knowledges."

55. **(A)** The sentence beginning "Or rather the vipers" is not meant to (D) "allude to the myth that snakes nurse from cows' udders." This test does not require outside knowledge of that sort, only reading and comprehension skills. The sentence might be distantly said to (C) "imply that others are guilty…" and (E) "link the accused with coldbloodedness," but the clearer, more direct function of the sentence is to (A) "associate the alleged ungratefulness with a most extreme example." The sentence does not (B) "cloud the issue with proverbial references," but it might be said to cloud the issue with exaggeration.

56. **(C)** The word "wits" in line 16 is not used in the sense of amusement, which eliminates (A) "jokes" and (D) "senses of humor." The sentence is a discussion of education; so (B) "cares" is incorrect; but both (C) and (E) have potential to be the answer. The sentence reads "wild untamed wits," which is obviously not a reference to savage (E) "men," but uneducated (C) "minds."

57. **(E)** The passage refers to poetry as (A) "being the first lightgiver to ignorance" in lines 3-4 and as (D) "cultivating sophisticated minds" in lines 15-16. Orpheus and Linus are credited with (B) "recording on paper for prosperity" in lines 11-12. Chaucer, Gower, and others are said to (C) "beautify his mother tongue" in the closing lines of the passage. In lines 16-17, Amphion is attributed with writing poetry so moving that he used it to (E) "(build) with stone blocks."

58. **(E)** Lines 7-9 refer to Homer, Hesiod, and Musaeus as being from Greece, verifying statement III. Dante, Boccace, and Petrarch are said to aspire to alter Italian in lines 19-20, verifying statement I. Amphion, Thebes, and Orpheus are mentioned in the same sentence in lines 16-18, but Thebes is a city, not a man, disqualifying statement II. The correct answer is (E) "I and III only."

59. **(B)** A change from "aspire" to "attempt" in line 18 would not (C) "…make the sentence choppy…" While the word "attempt" admits the possibility of failure, (E) "'attempt' implies impending failure" exaggerates the significance of that possibility. The word "attempt" does not (D) "…negate the personification of 'language'" because it continues to attribute action and intent to "language." While (A) "'attempt' conveys the idea that this was a real, tangible task," the more significant change in tone and effect is (B) "'attempt' clips the wings off the loftiness of 'aspire'."

60. **(E)** In lines 4-5, the author associates poetry with (A) "instruction." In the closing lines, poetry is associated with (B) "language." Lines 9-10 associate poetry with (C) "history." In lines 21-22, poetry is associated with (D) "communication." Because all of these are true and because they have a cumulative effect, (E) "education" is the answer. "Education" represents all forms of learning, and it is the passage's primary goal to associate poetry with all forms of learning.

Model Student Response to Essay Question 1:

It seems rare that a young girl of any generation since the invention of the Barbie doll has not been exposed to the phenomenon. With the birth and decline of other less-memorable fads, Barbie has maintained a seemingly immortal position in the toy industry. Barbie's world, however, is an artificial storybook world, a fantastic microcosm of American culture in which the classical elements of literary fantasy can be discerned. As a surrogate world, "Barbie-dom" is characterized by the achievable ideal, and values alternate to those present in reality.

To young girls, Barbie represents an achievable ideal. It cannot be denied that Barbie indeed has it all—every possible symbol of material possession that figures into the American dream can be found in the world of Barbie: her own Corvette, a multilevel mansion, swimming pool, candy store, fast food franchise, a wardrobe of immeasurable size, a steady boyfriend, and a bevy of adoring plastic friends from the same mold. In a nutshell, she is an all-American beauty who dwells in a luxurious world in which every aspect of life is picture-perfect, and moreover, ultimately attainable. As a symbol of the American dream of materialism, Barbie demonstrates that a girl can have anything her heart desires (with the added bonus of no parental supervision).

On a similar note, Barbie's world also operates by values alternate to those present in reality. In her world, the work ethic does not exist and life is instead led in hedonistic pursuit of fun. Time can be frittered away at the poolside or shopping because Barbie does not need to work for her money. Represented in this fantasy is a mode of living by which Barbie attains everything she desires; but we ask ourselves, *how* does she get it all? For we only see the end rewards in the forms of cars, clothing, and fast-food chains, but are kept ignorant of the processes by which they are attained. Anything Barbie could ever need is begotten by way of wish fulfillment rather than hard work; in reality, as is sometimes all-too-painfully obvious, nothing is obtained that easily.

Ultimately, the world of Barbie can be described as unreal, imagined, idealistic and escapist—in short, a fantasy. With her materially-dictated, pleasure-driven lifestyle untainted by the work ethic, Barbie offers the young girl a world of fantasy in which alternate values predominate and impossible ideals are achieved. Barbie, in her material wealth, is the manifestation of an American dream begotten in fantasy, a dream ultimately unattainable in the world of reality.

Analysis of Student Response to Essay Question 1:

This essay effectively accomplishes the assigned task: to represent a non-literary topic or text as a fantasy by illustrating how at least two elements of classic literary fantasy are manifested in an alternate world. By selecting an appropriate topic and by using concrete examples and detailed explanations, the writer demonstrates an understanding of the essay question and the elements of literary fantasy. In this case, the writer chooses to represent the world of the Barbie doll and illustrates, with concrete details, how the fantastic elements of the achievable ideal and values, alternate to those in reality, characterize "Barbie-dom" as an alternative world.

As defined by the essay question, an imaginary world in literary fantasy represents the "achievable ideal" in that dreams and fantasies are fulfilled. In other words, what we dream about or wish for in our everyday fantasies can be realized in the alternative worlds represented in fantasy. Here, the writer depicts how the American dream of ideal materialism and luxury is realized in Barbie's world: her car, wardrobe, and home represent the material possessions of this dream, which, in Barbie's alternate mode of existence, are indubitably attainable. By way of these examples, Barbie, as a girl who "can have anything her heart desires," is empowered with wish fulfillment. We can recognize wish fulfillment as a means to achieve the ultimate dream.

The imaginary world in literary fantasy operates by a set of values surrogate to those in everyday life. Conventional laws, rules and morals may be altered, reversed, or may even be nonexistent. The writer demonstrates how the work ethic does not exist in Barbie's world. Barbie is able to attain material possessions without the hard work that is normally necessary; since Barbie does not need to work for her money, she can spend her life in "hedonistic pursuit of fun."

The essay itself is well-ordered, with the thesis clearly stated in the first paragraph and support of the thesis organized in the body. The two chosen elements of literary fantasy are each well-represented and accorded ample analysis in their respective portions of the body. The concluding paragraph reiterates the thesis and summarizes the points made in the essay in a clear and effective manner: "With her materially-dictated, pleasure-driven lifestyle, untainted by the work ethic, Barbie offers the young girl a world of fantasy in which alternate values predominate and impossible ideals are achieved."

Model Student Response to Essay Question 2:

When trying to reach a specific audience in advertising, one approach is to establish a rapport with the members of that audience through appropriate tone and language. In this case, I chose to adopt a casual, conversational tone to address my intended audience: potential car buyers in their early to mid-twenties. Such a tone is not always conducive to proper grammar or sentence structure and, moreover, would not be suitable for all advertising situations (i.e., marketing investment products to serious investors). Here, however, an easygoing, friendly tone evokes an atmosphere of familiarity, akin to speaking with friends in a twenty-something peer group. The tone puts the reader more at ease and less resistant to a sales message. My ultimate goal is to present the product in a manner that is more like a friend recommending a car, as opposed to a hard-sell sales pitch.

Opening the ad with an emphatic "Hey!" serves to capture the reader's attention much in the manner of calling to a friend (Hey, Joe!). Following with a direct question to the reader (Recognize this?) further emphasizes the tone of familiarity and insinuates a sense of reader involvement.

Informal language and syntax are appropriate companions to the casual tone of the ad. Using such words and phrases as "Hey," "cool," and "living it up" mimics the conventions of informal conversation and everyday slang and bridges the communication gap. The same effect is evoked with the sentence beginning, "But hey, we're a new generation, and it's the age of, well...."

To further identify with the audience, the use of the first person nominative case (we) and the possessive case (our) situates myself as a member of the peer group. I make references to the things "we" want and how this is "our" time. By mentioning current popular trends, such as flannel, platforms, and bellbottoms, I am treading on common ground with the twenty-something peer group. This, along with the affable tone, serves to render less apparent my role as an advertiser trying to sell the product to the consumer and, instead, makes it seem more like a friend recommending the car.

Adopting a casual, familiar tone, using informal language, and identifying with the audience are ways to set a rapport with the audience that facilitates the advertising message. My ultimate goal is to reach the twenty-something consumer by speaking in the language and tone characteristic of this group and by referring to common desires and interests. The desired effect is a more intimate sense of familiarity between myself (the advertiser) and the potential buyer. This approach allows me to present the product to the audience in a manner that is engaging, comfortable, and less obtrusive than a hard-sell sales pitch.

Analysis of Student Response to Essay Question 2:

While advertising and marketing know-how are not required to answer the essay question, an appropriate response should demonstrate a cognizant understanding of the elements of language. As both the advertisement and essay illustrate, the literary elements of tone, diction, language, and syntax can be adapted in advertising to reach a particular audience. Furthermore, the writer furnishes a comprehensive response by explaining both how and why the advertisement is appropriate for its intended audience.

The goal of the advertisement, as stated by the writer, is to present the product in the manner of a friend's recommendation to the targeted audience of twenty-something consumers. To clarify this, the writer explains the choice of a casual tone to establish a rapport with the audience. By capturing the reader's attention with "Hey!" and addressing the reader of the ad with a direct question, the writer establishes an "easygoing, friendly tone," which evokes an air of familiarity and "puts the reader more at ease and less resistant to a sales message." Here, the writer demonstrates both how the casual tone is established and why such a tone is appropriate.

The writer further explains how the use of informal language and syntax ("hey" and "cool" and "it's the age of, well,") complements the casual tone and mimics the slang and conversational style of the twenty-something consumer group in order to "bridge the communication gap." Use of the first person nominative case "we" and the possessive case "our" serves to situate the writer as a member of the audience's peer group. Such an effect is strengthened by reference to popular trends, such as bellbottoms and platform shoes. By such methods, the writer explains, a rapport is established with the audience, which facilitates delivery of the advertising message in the manner of a friend recommending a product to another friend.

Model Student Response to Essay Question 3:

We all have many influences in our lives, and those influences may change as we grow and develop. However, parents almost always play a major role in a person's life. The influences of a parent in a child's life are numerous, and they can be both positive and negative.

Parents affect our performance at school. Schools expect all students to get along with one another; however, children whose parents are antisocial are not likely to possess adequate skills to meet those expectations (Source B), since children almost always imitate their parent's behavior (Source F). Additionally, a parent's level of education may affect a child's academic performance. The ChildStats web site correlates mothers' education level with young children's proficiency in the skills they need even at the kindergarten level (Source E). One can speculate from these figures that the less educated mother may simply not have the knowledge to help her children learn what they need to know, but other factors (e.g., home environment) may also be involved. Children who come from unhappy homes are not likely to care much about doing well at school—and may not be able to perform well even if they do care.

Parents influence the way we look at the world and what we expect in life. Maslow pointed out that children expect and need some type of predictable schedule (Source A). When parents fail to provide an orderly routine, the child may learn to perceive the world as chaotic and unpredictable, even as an adult. Orderliness and predictability encompass parental supervision and rules. Source D promotes "a warm and uncritical parenting style" as a means of developing a flexible individual, implying that those who grow up in a warm home atmosphere are likely to perceive themselves as able to perform successfully in a variety of situations and to feel secure about the outcome. Those who lack parental supervision are probably not going to feel as successful or secure about themselves because they will feel uncertain about what may happen.

Parents influence the type of person an individual becomes. President George W. Bush reminded Americans of "the values that bind families from one generation to the next" (Source F). However, these values are not always positive. Little good can come from having weak or abusive parents. As Source B indicates, the child who has a weak bond with parents and suffers abuse may become violent as an adult. And physical abuse as we grow up may cause us to feel life-long rejection. Feeling connected to one's family is a key to feeling good about oneself and about life in general. And that connectedness includes "feelings of warmth, love, and caring from parents" (Source D). Obviously, the way our parents treat us affects our self-image, and our self-image plays a key role in the type of individuals we become.

In his press release, President Bush referred to children as "a source of joy, pride, and fulfillment" (Source F). His viewpoint is idealistic and sometimes unrealistic. Although parents are undoubtedly major influences in our lives, not every parent welcomes the responsibility of raising a child; in that case, the child may not be successful in school, and he or she may grow up to be insecure and have a low self-esteem. In contrast, the individual who is fortunate enough to have educated, warm, and caring parents is likely to be success-oriented and secure.

Analysis of Student Response to Essay Question 3:

The student's response addresses the main challenge of the question (a synthesis of at least three sources for support and a position that defends, challenges, or qualifies the claim that a parent influences the physical and emotional development of a child). The writer begins with an introductory paragraph that starts with the broad topic of influences in our lives, and narrows to the specific topic of parental influences. The writer addresses three ways parents influence a child's life, and devotes one paragraph to each of those ways. The writer effectively synthesizes the sources to support the position of the essay by quoting or paraphrasing the sources to prove each point. For example, the second paragraph paraphrases, " . . . children whose parents are antisocial are not likely to possess adequate skills to meet those expectations (Source B), since children almost always imitate their parent's behavior (Source F)." And in the third paragraph the writer quotes a source: "Source D promotes 'a warm and uncritical parenting style.' " Each reference is clearly attributed. The conclusion echoes the main ideas of the essay's body. The essay's language and development are effective, and the writer's position is supported with well-chosen examples (some drawn from the writer's own viewpoint rather than the sources). Overall, this essay is an effective response to the prompt.

APPENDICES

AP English Language & Composition

Punctuation

Try to read this paragraph.

take some more tea the march hare said to alice very earnestly ive had nothing yet alice replied in an offended tone so i cant take more you mean you cant take less said the hatter its very easy to take more than nothing lewis carroll

Now try again.

"Take some more tea," the March Hare said to Alice, very earnestly.

"I've had nothing yet," Alice replied in an offended tone, "so I can't take more."

"You mean you can't take less," said the Hatter. "It's very easy to take more than nothing."

—Lewis Carroll

This example illustrates to what extent punctuation helps the reader understand what the writer is trying to say. The most important role of punctuation is clarification.

In speech, words are accompanied by gesture, voice, tone, and rhythm that help convey a desired meaning. In writing, it is punctuation alone that must do the same job.

There are many rules about how to use the various punctuation marks. These are sometimes difficult to understand, because they are described with so much grammatical terminology. Therefore, this discussion of punctuation will avoid as much terminology as possible. If you still find the rules confusing, and your method of punctuation is somewhat random, try to remember that most punctuation takes the place of pauses in speech.

Keeping this in mind, read your sentences aloud as you write; if you punctuate according to the pauses in your voice, you will do much better than if you put in your commas, periods, and dashes either at random or where they look good.

Stops

There are three ways to end a sentence:

1. a period
2. a question mark
3. an exclamation point

The Period

Periods end all sentences that are not questions or exclamations. In speech, the end of a sentence is indicated with a full pause. The period is the written counterpart of this pause.

Go get me my paper. I'm anxious to see the news.

Into each life some rain must fall. Last night some fell into mine.

The moon is round. The stars look small.

Mary and Janet welcomed the newcomer. She was noticeably happy.

When a question is intended as a suggestion and the listener is not expected to answer or when a question is asked indirectly as part of a sentence, a period is also used.

Mimi wondered if the parade would ever end.

May we hear from you soon.

Will you please send the flowers you advertised.

We'll never know who the culprit was.

Periods also follow most abbreviations and contractions.

Wed.	Dr.	Jr.	Sr.
etc.	Jan.	Mr.	Mr.
Esq.	cont.	a.m.	A.D.

Periods (or parentheses) are also used after a letter or number in a series.

a. apples	1. president
b. oranges	2. vice president
c. pears	3. secretary

Errors to Avoid

Be sure to omit the period after a quotation mark preceded by a period. Only one stop is necessary to end a sentence.

She said, "Hold my hand." (no period after the final quotation mark)

"Don't go into the park until later."

"It's not my fault," he said. "She would have taken the car anyway."

After many abbreviations, particularly those of organizations or agencies, no period is used (check in a dictionary if in doubt).

AFL-CIO	NAACP	GM
FBI	NATO	IBM
TV	UN	SEC

The Question Mark

Use a question mark to end a direct question even if it is not in the form of a question. The question mark in writing denotes the rising tone of voice used to indicate a question in speech. If you read the following two sentences aloud, you will see the difference in tone between a statement and a question composed of the same words.

Mary is here.

Mary is here?

Here are some more examples of correct use of the question mark. Pay special attention to the way it is used with other punctuation.

Where will we go next?

Would you like coffee or tea?

"Won't you," he asked, "please lend me a hand?"

"Will they ever give us our freedom?" the prisoner asked.

"To be or not to be?" was the question asked by Hamlet.

Who asked, "When?"

Question marks indicate a full stop and lend a different emphasis to a sentence than do commas. Compare these pairs of sentences.

Was the sonata by Beethoven? or Brahms? or Chopin?

Was the sonata by Beethoven, or Brahms, or Chopin?

Did they walk to the park? climb the small hill? take the bus to town? or go skating out back?

Did they walk to town, climb the small hill, take the bus to town, or go skating out back?

Sometimes question marks are placed in parentheses. This indicates doubt or uncertainty about the facts being reported.

The bombing started at 3 a.m. (?)

She said the dress cost $200,000 (?)

Hippocrates (460(?)-(?)377 B.C.) is said to be the father of modern medicine.

The Exclamation Point

An exclamation point ends an emphatic statement. It should be used only to express strong emotions, such as surprise, disbelief, or admiration. If it is used too often for mild expressions of emotion, it loses its effectiveness.

Let go of me!

Help! Fire!

It was a wonderful day!

Who shouted "Fire!" *(Notice no question mark is necessary)*

Fantastic!

"Unbelievable!" she gasped. *(Notice no comma is necessary)*

Where else can I go! *(The use of the exclamation point shows that this is a strong statement even though it is worded like a question.)*

Do not overuse exclamation points. The following is an example of the overuse of exclamation points:

Dear Susan,

> *I was so glad to see you last week! You looked better than ever! Our talk meant so much to me! I can hardly wait until we get together again! Could you believe how long it has been! Let's never let that happen again! Please write as soon as you get the chance! I can hardly wait to hear from you!*

> > *Your friend,*
> > *Nora*

INTERJECTIONS

An interjection is a word or group of words used as an exclamation to express emotion. It need not be followed by an exclamation point. Often an interjection is followed by a comma (see **The Comma**) if it is not very intense. Technically, the interjection has no grammatical relation to other words in the sentence; yet it is still considered a part of speech.

Examples:

Oh dear, I forgot my keys again.

Ah! Now do you understand?

Ouch! I didn't realize that the stove was hot.

Oh, excuse me. I didn't realize that you were next on line.

Pauses

There are five ways to indicate a pause shorter than a period.

1. dash
2. colon
3. parentheses
4. semicolon
5. comma

The Dash

Use the dash (—)to indicate a sudden or unexpected break in the normal flow of the sentence. It can also be used in place of parentheses or of commas if the meaning is clarified. Usually the dash gives special emphasis to the material it sets off. On a typewriter, two hyphens (--) indicate a dash.

Could you—I hate to ask!—help me with these boxes?

When we left town—a day never to be forgotten—they had a record snowfall.

She said—we all heard it—"The safe is not locked."

These are the three ladies—Mrs. Jackson, Miss Harris, and Ms. Forrest—you hoped to meet last week.

The sight of the Andromeda Galaxy—especially when seen for the first time—is astounding.

That day was the longest in her life—or so it seemed to her.

A dash is often used to summarize a series of ideas that have already been expressed.

Freedom of speech, freedom to vote, and freedom of assembly—these are the cornerstones of democracy.

Carbohydrates, fats, and proteins—these are the basic kinds of food we need.

Jones, who first suggested we go; Marshall, who made all the arrangements; and Kline, who finally took us there—these were the three men I admired most for their courage.

James, Howard, Marianne, Angela, Catherine—all were displeased with the decision of the teacher.

The dash is also used to note the author of a quotation that is set off in the text.

Nothing is good or bad but thinking makes it so.
>—William Shakespeare

Under every grief and pine
Runs a joy with silken twine.
>—William Blake

The Colon

The colon (:) is the sign of a pause about midway in length between the semicolon and the period. It can often be replaced by a comma and sometimes by a period. Although used less frequently now than it was 50 to 75 years ago, the colon is still convenient to use, for it signals to the reader that more information is to come on the subject of concern. The colon can also create a slight dramatic tension.

It is used to introduce a word, a phrase, or a complete statement (clause) that emphasizes, illustrates, or exemplifies what has already been stated.

He had only one desire in life: to play baseball.

The weather that day was the most unusual I'd ever seen: It snowed and rained while the sun was still shining.

In his speech, the president surprised us by his final point: the conventional grading system would be replaced next year.

Jean thought of only two things the last half hour of the hike home: a bath and a bed.

Notice that the word following the colon can start with either a capital or a small letter. Use a capital letter if the word following the colon begins another complete sentence. When the words following the colon are part of the sentence preceding the colon, use a small letter.

May I offer you a suggestion: don't drive without your seat belts fastened.

The thought continued to perplex him: Where will I go next?

When introducing a series that illustrates or emphasizes what has already been stated, use the colon.

Only a few of the graduates were able to be there: Jamison, Mearns, Linkley, and Commoner.

For Omar Khayyam, a Persian poet, three things are necessary for a paradise on earth: a loaf of bread, a jug of wine, and one's beloved.

In the basement, he kept some equipment for his experiments: the test tubes, some chemical agents, three sunlamps, and the drill.

Long quotations set off from the rest of the text by indentation rather than quotation marks are generally introduced with a colon.

The first line of Lincoln's Gettysburg address is familiar to most Americans:

> Four score and seven years ago our fathers brought forth on this continent a new nation, conceived in liberty and dedicated to the proposition that all men are created equal.

I quote from Shakespeare's *Sonnets*:

> When I do count the clock that tells the time,
> And see the brave day sunk in hideous night;
> When I behold the violet past prime,
> And sable curls all silver'd o'er with white …

It is also customary to end a business letter salutation with a colon.

Dear Senator Jordan:

To Whom It May Concern:

Gentlemen:

Dear Sir or Madam:

In informal letters, use a comma.

Dear Chi-Leng,

Dear Father,

The colon is also used in introducing a list.

Please send the following:

1. 50 index cards
2. 4 typewriter ribbons
3. 8 erasers

Prepare the recipe as follows:

1. Slice the oranges thinly.
2. Arrange them in a circle around the strawberries.
3. Pour the liqueur over both fruits.

At least three ladies will have to be there to help:

1. Mrs. Goldman, who will greet the guests;
2. Harriet Sacher, who will serve the lunch; and
3. my sister, who will do whatever else needs to be done.

Finally, the colon is used between numbers when writing the time, between the volume and number or volume and page number of a journal, and between the chapter and verse in the Bible.

4:30 P.M.

The Nation, 34:8

Genesis 5:18

Parentheses

To set off material that is only loosely connected to the central meaning of the sentence, use parentheses [( )].

Most men (at least, most that I know) like wine, women, and song but have too much work and not enough time for such enjoyments.

On Tuesday evenings and Thursday afternoons (the times I don't have classes), the television programs are not too exciting.

Last year at Vail (we go there every year), the skiing was the best I've ever seen.

In New York (I've lived there all my life and ought to know), you have to have a license for a gun.

What must be done to think clearly and calmly (is it even possible?) and then make the decision?

Watch out for other punctuation when you use parentheses. Punctuation that refers to the material enclosed in the parentheses occurs inside the marks. Punctuation belonging to the rest of the sentence comes outside the parentheses.

I thought I knew the poem by heart (boy, was I wrong!).

For a long time (too long as far as I'm concerned), women were thought to be inferior to men.

We must always strive to tell the truth. (Are we even sure we know what truth is?)

When I first saw a rose (don't you think it's the most beautiful flower?), I thought it must be man-made.

The Semicolon

Semicolons (;) are sometimes called mild periods. They indicate a pause midway in length between the comma and the colon. Writing that contains many semicolons is usually in a dignified, formal style. To use them correctly, it is necessary to be able to recognize main clauses—complete ideas. When two main clauses occur in a single sentence without a connecting word *(and, but, or, nor, for)*, the appropriate mark of punctuation is the semicolon.

It is not a good idea for you to leave the country right now; you should actually try to stay as long as you possibly can.

Music lightens life; literature deepens it.

In the past, boy babies were often dressed in blue; girls, in pink. *("Were often dressed" is understood in the second part of the sentence.)*

Can't you see it's no good to go on alone; we'll starve to death if we keep traveling this way much longer.

Burgundy and maroon are very similar colors; scarlet is altogether different.

Notice how the use of the comma, period, and semicolon gives a sentence a slightly different meaning.

Music lightens life; literature deepens it.

Just as music lightens life, literature deepens it.

Music lightens life. Literature deepens it.

The semicolon lends a certain balance to writing that would otherwise be difficult to achieve. Nonetheless, you should be careful not to overuse it. A comma can just as well join parts of a sentence with two main ideas; the semicolon is particularly appropriate if there is a striking contrast in the two ideas expressed.

Ask not what your country can do for you; ask what you can do for your country.

It started out as an ordinary day; it ended being the most extraordinary of her life.

Our power to apprehend truth is limited; to seek it, limitless.

If any one of the following words or phrases is used to join together compound sentences, it is generally preceded by a semicolon.

then	however	thus	furthermore
hence	indeed	consequently	also
that is	nevertheless	anyhow	in addition

in fact	on the other hand	likewise	moreover
still	meanwhile	instead	besides
otherwise	in other words	henceforth	for example
therefore	at the same time	even now	

> For a long time, people thought that women were inferior to men; *even now* it is not an easy attitude to overcome.

> Being clever and cynical, he succeeded in becoming president of the company; *meanwhile,* his wife left him.

> Cigarette smoking has never interested me; *furthermore,* I couldn't care less if anyone else smokes or not.

> Some say Bach was the greatest composer of all time; *yet* he still managed to have an ordinary life in other ways: he and his wife had twenty children.

> We left wishing we could have stayed much longer; *in other words,* they showed us a good time.

When a series of complicated items is listed or if there is internal punctuation in a series, the semicolon is sometimes used to make the meaning clearer:

> You can use your new car for many things: to drive to town or to the country; to impress your friends and neighbors; to protect yourself from rain on a trip away from home; and to borrow against should you need money right away.

> The scores from yesterday's games came in late last night: Pirates-6, Zoomers-3; Caterpillars-12, Steelys-8; Crashers-9, Links-8; and Greens-15, Uptowns-4.

> In October a bag of potatoes cost 69¢; in December, 99¢; in February, $1.09; and in April, $1.39. I wonder if this inflation will ever stop.

The semicolon is placed outside quotation marks or parentheses, unless it is a part of the material enclosed in those marks.

> I used to call him "my lord and master"; it made him laugh every time.

> The weather was cold for that time of year (I was shivering wherever I went); nevertheless, we set out to hike to the top of that mountain.

The Comma

Of all the marks of punctuation, the comma (,) has the most uses. Before you tackle the main principles that guide its usage, be sure that you have an elementary understanding of sentence structure. There are actually only a few rules and conventions to follow when using commas; the rest is common sense. The worst abuse of commas comes from those who overuse them or who place them illogically. If you are ever in doubt as to whether or not to use a comma, do not use it.

IN A SERIES

When more than one adjective (an adjective series) describes a noun, use a comma to separate and emphasize each adjective.

the long, dark passageway

another confusing, sleepless night

an elaborate, complex plan

the haunting, melodic sound

the old, gray, crumpled hat

In these instances, the comma takes the place of "and." To test if the comma is needed, try inserting "and" between the adjectives in question. If it is logical, you should use a comma. The following are examples of adjectives that describe an adjective-noun combination that has come to be thought of almost as one word. In such cases, the adjective in front of the adjective-noun combination needs no comma.

a stately *oak tree*	my worst *report card*
an exceptional *wine glass*	a borrowed *record player*
a successful *garage sale*	a porcelain *dinner plate*

If you insert "and" between the adjectives in the above examples, it will not make sense.

The comma is also used to separate words, phrases, and whole ideas (clauses); it still takes the place of "and" when used this way.

an apple, a pear, a fig, and a banana

a lovely lady, an indecent dress, and many admirers

She lowered the shade, closed the curtain, turned off the light, and went to bed.

John, Frank, and my Uncle Harry all thought it was a questionable theory.

The only question that exists about the use of commas in a series is whether or not one should be used before the final item. Usually "and" or "or" precedes the final item, and many writers do not include the comma before the final "and" or "or." However, it is advisable to use the comma, because often its omission can be confusing—in such cases as these, for instance.

NO: Would you like to shop at Saks, Lord and Taylor and Macy's?

NO: He got on his horse, tracked a rabbit and a deer and rode on to Canton.

NO: We planned the trip with Mary and Harold, Susan, Dick and Joan, Gregory and Jean and Charles. *(Is it Gregory and Jean or Jean and Charles or Gregory and Jean and Charles?)*

WITH A LONG INTRODUCTORY PHRASE

Usually if a phrase of more than five or six words precedes the subject at the beginning of a sentence, a comma is used to set it off.

After last night's fiasco at the disco, she couldn't bear the thought of looking at him again.

Whenever I try to talk about politics, my husband leaves the room.

When it comes to actual facts, every generation makes the same mistakes as the preceding one.

Provided you have said nothing, they will never guess who you are.

It is not necessary to use a comma with a short sentence.

In January she will go to Switzerland.

After I rest I'll feel better.

At Grandma's we had a big dinner.

During the day no one is home.

If an introductory phrase includes a verb form that is being used as another part of speech (a "verbal"), it must be followed by a comma. Try to make sense of the following sentences without commas.

NO: When eating Mary never looked up from her plate.

YES: When eating, Mary never looked up from her plate.

NO: Because of her desire to follow her faith in James wavered.

YES: Because of her desire to follow, her faith in James wavered.

NO: Having decided to leave Mary James wrote her a letter.

YES: Having decided to leave Mary, James wrote her a letter.

Above all, common sense is the best guideline when trying to decide whether or not to use a comma after an introductory phrase. Does the comma make the meaning clearer? If it does, use it; if not, there is no reason to insert it.

TO SEPARATE SENTENCES WITH TWO MAIN IDEAS (COMPOUND SENTENCES)

To understand this use of the comma, you need to have studied sentence structure and be able to recognize compound sentences.

When a sentence contains more than two subjects and verbs (clauses) and the two clauses are joined by a connecting word *(and, but, or, yet, for, nor),* use a comma before the connecting word to show that another clause is coming.

I thought I knew the poem by heart, but he showed me three lines I had forgotten.

Are we really interested in helping the children, or are we more concerned with protecting our good names?

Jim knows you are disappointed, and he has known it for a long time.

Living has its good points to be sure, yet I will not mind when it is over.

If the two parts of the sentence are short and closely related, it is not necessary to use a comma.

He threw the ball and the dog ran after it.

Jane played the piano and Charles danced.

Errors to Avoid

Be careful not to confuse a compound sentence with a sentence that has a compound verb and a single subject. If the subject is the same for both verbs, there is no need for a comma.

> NO: Charles sent some flowers, and wrote a long letter explaining why he had not been able to come.

> NO: Last Thursday we went to the concert with Julia, and afterward dined at an old Italian restaurant.

> NO: For the third time, the teacher explained that the literacy level of high school students was much lower than it had been in previous years, and, this time, wrote the statistics on the board for everyone to see.

TO SET OFF INTERRUPTING MATERIAL

There are so many different kinds of interruptions that can occur in a sentence that a list of them all would be quite lengthy. In general, words and phrases that stop the flow of the sentence or are unnecessary for the main idea are set off by commas.

Abbreviations after names

Did you invite John Paul, Jr., and his sister?

Martha Harris, Ph.D., will be the speaker tonight.

Interjections: An exclamation added without grammatical connection.

Oh, I'm so glad to see you.

I tried so hard, alas, to do it.

Hey, let me out of here.

No, I will not let you out.

Direct address

Roy, won't you open the door for the dog?

I can't understand, Mother, what you are trying to say.

May I ask, Mr. President, why you called us together?

Hey, lady, watch out for the car!

Tag questions: A question that repeats the helping verb and is in the negative.

I'm really hungry, aren't you?

Jerry looks like his father, doesn't he?

You'll come early, won't you?

We are expected at nine, aren't we?

Mr. Jones can chair the meeting, can't he?

Geographical names and addresses

The concert will be held in Chicago, Illinois, on August 12.

They visited Tours, France, last summer.

The letter was addressed to Ms. Marion Heartwell, 1881 Pine Lane, Palo Alto, California 95824. *(No comma is used before a zip code.)*

Transitional words and phrases

On the other hand, I hope he gets better.

In addition, the phone rang six times this afternoon.

I'm, nevertheless, going to the beach on Sunday.

You'll find, therefore, no one more loyal to you than I.

To tell the truth, I don't know what to believe.

Parenthetical words and phrases

You will become, I believe, a great statesman.

We know, of course, that this is the only thing to do.

In fact, I planted corn last summer.

The Mannes affair was, to put it mildly, a surprise.

Bathing suits, generally speaking, are getting smaller.

Unusual word order

The dress, new and crisp, hung in the closet. *(Normal word order: The new, crisp dress hung in the closet.)*

Intently, she stared out the window. *(Normal word order: She stared intently out the window.)*

NONRESTRICTIVE ELEMENTS
(NOT ESSENTIAL TO THE MEANING)

Parts of a sentence that modify other parts are sometimes essential to the meaning of the sentence and sometimes not. When a modifying word or group of words is not vital to the meaning of the sentence, it is set off by commas. Since it does not restrict the meaning of the words it modifies, it is called "nonrestrictive." Modifiers that are essential to the meaning of the sentence are called "restrictive" and are not set off by commas. Compare the following pairs of sentences:

The girl *who wrote the story* is my sister. (essential)

My sister, *the girl who wrote the story,* has always been drawn to adventure. (nonessential)

John Milton's famous poem *"Paradise Lost"* tells a remarkable story. (essential—Milton has written other poems)

Dante's great work, *"The Divine Comedy,"* marked the beginning of the Renaissance and the end of the Dark Ages. (nonessential—Dante wrote only one great work)

My parakeet *Simian* has an extensive vocabulary. (essential—because there are no commas, the writer must have more than one parakeet)

My parakeet, *Simian,* has an extensive vocabulary. (nonessential—the writer must have only one parakeet, whose name is Simian)

The people *who arrived late* were not seated. (essential)

George, *who arrived late,* was not seated. (nonessential)

She always listened to her sister *Jean.* (essential—she has more than one sister)

She always listened to her husband, *Jack.* (nonessential—obviously, she has only one husband)

TO SET OFF DIRECT QUOTATIONS

Most direct quotes or quoted materials are set off from the rest of the sentence by commas.

"Please read your part more loudly," the director insisted.

"I won't know what to do," said Michael, "if you leave me now."

The teacher said sternly, "I will not dismiss this class until I have silence."

Mark looked up from his work, smiled, and said, "We'll be with you in a moment."

Be careful not to set off indirect quotations or quotes that are used as subjects or complements.

"To be or not to be" is the famous beginning of a soliloquy in Shakespeare's *Hamlet.* (subject)

Back then my favorite song was *"A Summer Place."* (complement)

She said she would never come back. (indirect quote)

"Place two tablespoons of chocolate in this pan" were her first words to her apprentice in the kitchen. (subject)

TO SET OFF CONTRASTING ELEMENTS

Her intelligence, *not her beauty,* got her the job.

Your plan will take you further from, *rather than closer to,* your destination.

It was a reasonable, *though not appealing,* idea.

James wanted an active, *not a passive,* partner.

IN DATES

Both forms of the date are acceptable.

She will arrive on April 6, 1992.

He left on 5 December 1990.

In January 1987 he handed in his resignation.

In January 1987, he handed in his resignation.

Appendix B

Spelling

At first glance, one would expect *blew* and *sew* to rhyme. Instead, *sew* rhymes with *so*. If words were spelled the way they sound, one would expect *so* to rhyme with *do* instead of *dough* and would never expect *do* to rhyme with *blew*. Confusing, isn't it?

Words are not always spelled phonetically, and it sometimes seems that spelling is totally illogical. However, in spelling there is usually only one correct form.

It is important to learn to spell properly. Poor spelling is usually a sign of haste or carelessness, and it is often taken as a sign of ignorance or illiteracy. Yet learning to spell correctly is indeed more difficult for some people than for others. In any case, it can be mastered with time and patience.

There are many helpful practices to improve spelling: using the dictionary, keeping a list of words that cause difficulty, familiarizing oneself with word origin, and studying the word list and the rules in this chapter.

If a writer has absolutely no idea how to spell a word, he or she obviously cannot look it up. Yet in most spelling problems, the writer has a general idea of the spelling but is not certain. Even if only the first few letters of the word are known, the writer should be able to find it in the dictionary.

Example: To check the spelling of the word *miscellaneous*.

The writer probably knows that *misc-* compose the first four letters of the word and might even know a few more by sounding the word out. Although phonetics is not a reliable source for spelling, it can be helpful when using the dictionary. In this particular problem, it most likely is the ending *-aneous* that gives the writer difficulty. Since in the English language there are few words beginning with the letters *misc-*, the writer should have little trouble finding *miscellaneous* in the dictionary.

Example: To check the spelling of *occasionally*.

Here, the writer is probably concerned with the number of *c*'s and *s*'s. If one looks up the word with the beginning *oca-*, there is no listing. The next logical choice is to check the word with two *c*'s, which will be found a few entries later. One can even skim the page when a general idea of the spelling is known.

When using the dictionary, be sure also that you have found the desired word, not a homonym or a word with a similar form, by checking the word's definition.

So checking spelling is a matter of trial and error; use the dictionary when you are not sure—and even when you feel certain.

Word Analysis

A basic knowledge of the English language, especially familiarity with its numerous prefixes, can help build vocabulary and also strengthen spelling skills. For example, if one knows that *inter-* means *between* and that *intra-* means *within,* one is not likely to spell *intramural* as *intermural.* (The former means within the limits of a city, a college, etc.)

The following table lists some common Latin and Greek prefixes, which form part of the foundation of the English language.

PREFIX	MEANING	ENGLISH EXAMPLE
ab-, a-, abs-	away, from	abstain
ad-	to, toward	adjacent
ante-	before	antecedent
anti-	against	antidote
bi-	two	bisect
cata-, cat-, cath-	down	cataclysm
circum-	around	circumlocution
contra-	against	contrary
de-	down, from	decline
di-	twice	diatonic
dis-, di-	apart, away	dissolve
epi-, ep-, eph-	upon, among	epidemic
ex-, e-	out of, from	extricate
hyper-	beyond, over	hyperactive
hypo-	under, down, less	hypodermic
in-	in, into	instill
inter-	among, between	intercede
intra-	within	intramural
meta-, met-	beyond, along with	metaphysics
mono-	one	monolith
non-	no, not	nonsense
ob-	against	obstruct
para-, par-	beside	parallel
per-	through	permeate
pre-	before	prehistoric
pro-	before	project
super-	above	superior
tele-, tel-	far	television
trans-	across	transpose
ultra-	beyond	ultraviolet

Spelling Lists

There are some words that consistently give writers trouble. The list below contains about 100 words that are commonly misspelled. In studying this list, readers will find that certain words are more troublesome than others. These in particular should be reviewed.

100 COMMONLY MISSPELLED WORDS

accommodate	February	professor
achievement	height	prominent
acquire	immediately	pursue
among	interest	quiet
apparent	its, it's	receive
arguing	led	procedure
argument	lose	profession
athletics	losing	receiving
belief	marriage	recommend
believe	mere	referring
beneficial	necessary	remember
benefited	occasion	repetition
bureau	occurred	rhythm
business	occurrence	sense
category	occurring	separate
comparative	opinion	separation
conscious	opportunity	similar
controversial	parallel	studying
define	particular	succeed
definitely	performance	succession
definition	personal	surprise
describe	personnel	technique
description	possession	than
despair	possible	their, they're, there
disastrous	practical	then
effect	precede	thorough
embarrass	prejudice	to, too, two
environment	prepare	tomorrow
exaggerate	prevalent	transferred
existence	principal	unnecessary
existent	principle	villain
experience	privilege	write
explanation	probably	writing
fascinate	proceed	

As a handy reference, it is a good idea to set aside an area in a notebook to list problem words. Add to it any new words that are persistent spelling problems.

Spelling Rules

Prefixes

Prefixes (such as *dis-*, *mis-*, *in-*, *un-*, and *re-*) are added to words without doubling or dropping letters.

dis + appear = disappear
dis + service = disservice
dis + solved = dissolved
dis + satisfied = dissatisfied
mis + information = misinformation
mis + spelled = misspelled
mis + understand = misunderstand
in + capable = incapable
in + definite = indefinite
in + numerable = innumerable
un + usual = unusual
un + seen = unseen
un + named = unnamed
re + elect = reelect
re + search = research

Suffixes

When forming adverbs from adjectives ending in *al,* the ending becomes *ally.*

normal	normally	real	really
occasional	occasionally	legal	legally
royal	royally		

Words ending in *n* keep the *n* when adding *ness.*

openness   stubbornness   suddenness   brazenness

All words ending in *ful* have only one *l.*

cupful	cheerful
forgetful	doleful
mouthful	graceful
helpful	meaningful
spoonful	handful

Add *ment* without changing the root word's spelling.

> adjust + ment = adjustment
>
> develop + ment = development
>
> amaze + ment = amazement

Silent *e.*

When a suffix beginning with a vowel is added, a word ending in a silent *e* generally drops the *e.*

Example:

> admire + able = admirable
>
> allure + ing = alluring
>
> believe + able = believable
>
> come + ing = coming
>
> dare + ing = daring
>
> deplore + able = deplorable
>
> desire + ous = desirous
>
> explore + ation = exploration
>
> fame + ous = famous
>
> imagine + able = imaginable
>
> move + able = movable
>
> note + able = notable

However, the word retains the *e* when a suffix beginning with a consonant is added.

Example:

> arrange + ment = arrangement
>
> glee + ful = gleeful
>
> like + ness = likeness
>
> spite + ful = spiteful
>
> time + less = timeless

With *judgment, acknowledgment,* and other words formed by adding *ment* to a word with a *dge* ending, the final *e* is usually dropped, although it is equally correct to retain it.

When adding *ous* or *able* to a word ending in *ge* or *ce,* keep the final *e* when adding the suffix. The *e* is retained to keep the soft sound of the *c* or *g.*

courageous	manageable	outrageous
changeable	advantageous	traceable

IE + EI

In words with *ie* or *ei* in which the sound is e, (long *ee*), use *i* before *e* except after *c*.

Examples: i before *e:*

believe	pier	shield	wield
chief	priest	siege	yield
niece	reprieve		

Examples: Except after *c:*

ceiling   conceit   conceive   deceive   perceive   receive

The following words are some exceptions to the rule and must be committed to memory.

either	conscience	weird	reign
leisure	height	freight	weigh
neither	forfeit		
seize	neighbor		

Except before *ing*, final *y* usually changes to *i*.

rely + ance = reliance
study + ing = studying
modify + er = modifier
modify + ing = modifying
amplify + ed = amplified
amplify + ing = amplifying

When preceded by a vowel, final *y* does not change to *i*.

annoying, annoyed
destroying, destroyed, destroyer
journeyman, journeyed, journeyer

Doubling the Final Consonant

In one-syllable words that end in a single consonant preceded by a single vowel, double the final consonant before adding a suffix that begins with a vowel.

Example:

drop + ing = drop(p)ing
clap + ed = clap(p)ed
man + ish = man(n)ish
snap + ed = snap(p)ed
quit + ing = quit(t)ing

However, when a suffix begins with a consonant, do not double the final consonant before adding the suffix.

Example:

> man + hood = manhood
> glad + ly = gladly
> bad + ly = badly
> fat + ness = fatness
> sin + ful = sinful

This is also the case in multisyllabic words that are accented on the final syllable and have endings as described above.

Example:

> admit + ed = admitted
> begin + ing = beginning
> commit + ed = committed
> > BUT
> commit + ment = commitment

However, in words with this type of ending, in which the final syllable is not accented, the final consonant is not doubled.

Example:

> happen + ing = happening
> profit + able = profitable
> comfort + ed = comforted
> refer + ence = reference
> confer + ence = conference

Only three words end in *ceed* in English. They are *exceed, proceed,* and *succeed.* All other "seed-sounding" words (except *supersede*) end in *cede.*

intercede	recede
concede	accede
secede	precede

Proofreading

The best way to improve spelling is to reread what has been written. In fact, many other writing problems can be avoided as well if the writer carefully rereads and revises. Remember, poor spelling is not something that must be tolerated. With a little work, it can be greatly improved.

ANSWER SHEETS

AP English Language & Composition

ANSWER SHEETS
AP English Language & Composition

Exam 1

Section I

1. Ⓐ Ⓑ Ⓒ Ⓓ Ⓔ	21. Ⓐ Ⓑ Ⓒ Ⓓ Ⓔ	41. Ⓐ Ⓑ Ⓒ Ⓓ Ⓔ
2. Ⓐ Ⓑ Ⓒ Ⓓ Ⓔ	22. Ⓐ Ⓑ Ⓒ Ⓓ Ⓔ	42. Ⓐ Ⓑ Ⓒ Ⓓ Ⓔ
3. Ⓐ Ⓑ Ⓒ Ⓓ Ⓔ	23. Ⓐ Ⓑ Ⓒ Ⓓ Ⓔ	43. Ⓐ Ⓑ Ⓒ Ⓓ Ⓔ
4. Ⓐ Ⓑ Ⓒ Ⓓ Ⓔ	24. Ⓐ Ⓑ Ⓒ Ⓓ Ⓔ	44. Ⓐ Ⓑ Ⓒ Ⓓ Ⓔ
5. Ⓐ Ⓑ Ⓒ Ⓓ Ⓔ	25. Ⓐ Ⓑ Ⓒ Ⓓ Ⓔ	45. Ⓐ Ⓑ Ⓒ Ⓓ Ⓔ
6. Ⓐ Ⓑ Ⓒ Ⓓ Ⓔ	26. Ⓐ Ⓑ Ⓒ Ⓓ Ⓔ	46. Ⓐ Ⓑ Ⓒ Ⓓ Ⓔ
7. Ⓐ Ⓑ Ⓒ Ⓓ Ⓔ	27. Ⓐ Ⓑ Ⓒ Ⓓ Ⓔ	47. Ⓐ Ⓑ Ⓒ Ⓓ Ⓔ
8. Ⓐ Ⓑ Ⓒ Ⓓ Ⓔ	28. Ⓐ Ⓑ Ⓒ Ⓓ Ⓔ	48. Ⓐ Ⓑ Ⓒ Ⓓ Ⓔ
9. Ⓐ Ⓑ Ⓒ Ⓓ Ⓔ	29. Ⓐ Ⓑ Ⓒ Ⓓ Ⓔ	49. Ⓐ Ⓑ Ⓒ Ⓓ Ⓔ
10. Ⓐ Ⓑ Ⓒ Ⓓ Ⓔ	30. Ⓐ Ⓑ Ⓒ Ⓓ Ⓔ	50. Ⓐ Ⓑ Ⓒ Ⓓ Ⓔ
11. Ⓐ Ⓑ Ⓒ Ⓓ Ⓔ	31. Ⓐ Ⓑ Ⓒ Ⓓ Ⓔ	51. Ⓐ Ⓑ Ⓒ Ⓓ Ⓔ
12. Ⓐ Ⓑ Ⓒ Ⓓ Ⓔ	32. Ⓐ Ⓑ Ⓒ Ⓓ Ⓔ	52. Ⓐ Ⓑ Ⓒ Ⓓ Ⓔ
13. Ⓐ Ⓑ Ⓒ Ⓓ Ⓔ	33. Ⓐ Ⓑ Ⓒ Ⓓ Ⓔ	53. Ⓐ Ⓑ Ⓒ Ⓓ Ⓔ
14. Ⓐ Ⓑ Ⓒ Ⓓ Ⓔ	34. Ⓐ Ⓑ Ⓒ Ⓓ Ⓔ	54. Ⓐ Ⓑ Ⓒ Ⓓ Ⓔ
15. Ⓐ Ⓑ Ⓒ Ⓓ Ⓔ	35. Ⓐ Ⓑ Ⓒ Ⓓ Ⓔ	55. Ⓐ Ⓑ Ⓒ Ⓓ Ⓔ
16. Ⓐ Ⓑ Ⓒ Ⓓ Ⓔ	36. Ⓐ Ⓑ Ⓒ Ⓓ Ⓔ	56. Ⓐ Ⓑ Ⓒ Ⓓ Ⓔ
17. Ⓐ Ⓑ Ⓒ Ⓓ Ⓔ	37. Ⓐ Ⓑ Ⓒ Ⓓ Ⓔ	57. Ⓐ Ⓑ Ⓒ Ⓓ Ⓔ
18. Ⓐ Ⓑ Ⓒ Ⓓ Ⓔ	38. Ⓐ Ⓑ Ⓒ Ⓓ Ⓔ	58. Ⓐ Ⓑ Ⓒ Ⓓ Ⓔ
19. Ⓐ Ⓑ Ⓒ Ⓓ Ⓔ	39. Ⓐ Ⓑ Ⓒ Ⓓ Ⓔ	59. Ⓐ Ⓑ Ⓒ Ⓓ Ⓔ
20. Ⓐ Ⓑ Ⓒ Ⓓ Ⓔ	40. Ⓐ Ⓑ Ⓒ Ⓓ Ⓔ	60. Ⓐ Ⓑ Ⓒ Ⓓ Ⓔ

Section 2

Use the following page to prepare your essays. During the official exam, you will be given 12 lined pages for your essays.

ANSWER SHEETS

AP English Language & Composition

Exam 2

Section I

1. Ⓐ Ⓑ Ⓒ Ⓓ Ⓔ	21. Ⓐ Ⓑ Ⓒ Ⓓ Ⓔ	41. Ⓐ Ⓑ Ⓒ Ⓓ Ⓔ
2. Ⓐ Ⓑ Ⓒ Ⓓ Ⓔ	22. Ⓐ Ⓑ Ⓒ Ⓓ Ⓔ	42. Ⓐ Ⓑ Ⓒ Ⓓ Ⓔ
3. Ⓐ Ⓑ Ⓒ Ⓓ Ⓔ	23. Ⓐ Ⓑ Ⓒ Ⓓ Ⓔ	43. Ⓐ Ⓑ Ⓒ Ⓓ Ⓔ
4. Ⓐ Ⓑ Ⓒ Ⓓ Ⓔ	24. Ⓐ Ⓑ Ⓒ Ⓓ Ⓔ	44. Ⓐ Ⓑ Ⓒ Ⓓ Ⓔ
5. Ⓐ Ⓑ Ⓒ Ⓓ Ⓔ	25. Ⓐ Ⓑ Ⓒ Ⓓ Ⓔ	45. Ⓐ Ⓑ Ⓒ Ⓓ Ⓔ
6. Ⓐ Ⓑ Ⓒ Ⓓ Ⓔ	26. Ⓐ Ⓑ Ⓒ Ⓓ Ⓔ	46. Ⓐ Ⓑ Ⓒ Ⓓ Ⓔ
7. Ⓐ Ⓑ Ⓒ Ⓓ Ⓔ	27. Ⓐ Ⓑ Ⓒ Ⓓ Ⓔ	47. Ⓐ Ⓑ Ⓒ Ⓓ Ⓔ
8. Ⓐ Ⓑ Ⓒ Ⓓ Ⓔ	28. Ⓐ Ⓑ Ⓒ Ⓓ Ⓔ	48. Ⓐ Ⓑ Ⓒ Ⓓ Ⓔ
9. Ⓐ Ⓑ Ⓒ Ⓓ Ⓔ	29. Ⓐ Ⓑ Ⓒ Ⓓ Ⓔ	49. Ⓐ Ⓑ Ⓒ Ⓓ Ⓔ
10. Ⓐ Ⓑ Ⓒ Ⓓ Ⓔ	30. Ⓐ Ⓑ Ⓒ Ⓓ Ⓔ	50. Ⓐ Ⓑ Ⓒ Ⓓ Ⓔ
11. Ⓐ Ⓑ Ⓒ Ⓓ Ⓔ	31. Ⓐ Ⓑ Ⓒ Ⓓ Ⓔ	51. Ⓐ Ⓑ Ⓒ Ⓓ Ⓔ
12. Ⓐ Ⓑ Ⓒ Ⓓ Ⓔ	32. Ⓐ Ⓑ Ⓒ Ⓓ Ⓔ	52. Ⓐ Ⓑ Ⓒ Ⓓ Ⓔ
13. Ⓐ Ⓑ Ⓒ Ⓓ Ⓔ	33. Ⓐ Ⓑ Ⓒ Ⓓ Ⓔ	53. Ⓐ Ⓑ Ⓒ Ⓓ Ⓔ
14. Ⓐ Ⓑ Ⓒ Ⓓ Ⓔ	34. Ⓐ Ⓑ Ⓒ Ⓓ Ⓔ	54. Ⓐ Ⓑ Ⓒ Ⓓ Ⓔ
15. Ⓐ Ⓑ Ⓒ Ⓓ Ⓔ	35. Ⓐ Ⓑ Ⓒ Ⓓ Ⓔ	55. Ⓐ Ⓑ Ⓒ Ⓓ Ⓔ
16. Ⓐ Ⓑ Ⓒ Ⓓ Ⓔ	36. Ⓐ Ⓑ Ⓒ Ⓓ Ⓔ	56. Ⓐ Ⓑ Ⓒ Ⓓ Ⓔ
17. Ⓐ Ⓑ Ⓒ Ⓓ Ⓔ	37. Ⓐ Ⓑ Ⓒ Ⓓ Ⓔ	57. Ⓐ Ⓑ Ⓒ Ⓓ Ⓔ
18. Ⓐ Ⓑ Ⓒ Ⓓ Ⓔ	38. Ⓐ Ⓑ Ⓒ Ⓓ Ⓔ	58. Ⓐ Ⓑ Ⓒ Ⓓ Ⓔ
19. Ⓐ Ⓑ Ⓒ Ⓓ Ⓔ	39. Ⓐ Ⓑ Ⓒ Ⓓ Ⓔ	59. Ⓐ Ⓑ Ⓒ Ⓓ Ⓔ
20. Ⓐ Ⓑ Ⓒ Ⓓ Ⓔ	40. Ⓐ Ⓑ Ⓒ Ⓓ Ⓔ	60. Ⓐ Ⓑ Ⓒ Ⓓ Ⓔ

Section 2

Use the following page to prepare your essays. During the official exam, you will be given 12 lined pages for your essays.

_____

_____

_____

_____

_____

_____

_____

_____

_____

_____

_____

_____

_____

_____

_____

_____

_____

ANSWER SHEETS

AP English Language & Composition

Exam 3

Section I

1. Ⓐ Ⓑ Ⓒ Ⓓ Ⓔ	21. Ⓐ Ⓑ Ⓒ Ⓓ Ⓔ	41. Ⓐ Ⓑ Ⓒ Ⓓ Ⓔ
2. Ⓐ Ⓑ Ⓒ Ⓓ Ⓔ	22. Ⓐ Ⓑ Ⓒ Ⓓ Ⓔ	42. Ⓐ Ⓑ Ⓒ Ⓓ Ⓔ
3. Ⓐ Ⓑ Ⓒ Ⓓ Ⓔ	23. Ⓐ Ⓑ Ⓒ Ⓓ Ⓔ	43. Ⓐ Ⓑ Ⓒ Ⓓ Ⓔ
4. Ⓐ Ⓑ Ⓒ Ⓓ Ⓔ	24. Ⓐ Ⓑ Ⓒ Ⓓ Ⓔ	44. Ⓐ Ⓑ Ⓒ Ⓓ Ⓔ
5. Ⓐ Ⓑ Ⓒ Ⓓ Ⓔ	25. Ⓐ Ⓑ Ⓒ Ⓓ Ⓔ	45. Ⓐ Ⓑ Ⓒ Ⓓ Ⓔ
6. Ⓐ Ⓑ Ⓒ Ⓓ Ⓔ	26. Ⓐ Ⓑ Ⓒ Ⓓ Ⓔ	46. Ⓐ Ⓑ Ⓒ Ⓓ Ⓔ
7. Ⓐ Ⓑ Ⓒ Ⓓ Ⓔ	27. Ⓐ Ⓑ Ⓒ Ⓓ Ⓔ	47. Ⓐ Ⓑ Ⓒ Ⓓ Ⓔ
8. Ⓐ Ⓑ Ⓒ Ⓓ Ⓔ	28. Ⓐ Ⓑ Ⓒ Ⓓ Ⓔ	48. Ⓐ Ⓑ Ⓒ Ⓓ Ⓔ
9. Ⓐ Ⓑ Ⓒ Ⓓ Ⓔ	29. Ⓐ Ⓑ Ⓒ Ⓓ Ⓔ	49. Ⓐ Ⓑ Ⓒ Ⓓ Ⓔ
10. Ⓐ Ⓑ Ⓒ Ⓓ Ⓔ	30. Ⓐ Ⓑ Ⓒ Ⓓ Ⓔ	50. Ⓐ Ⓑ Ⓒ Ⓓ Ⓔ
11. Ⓐ Ⓑ Ⓒ Ⓓ Ⓔ	31. Ⓐ Ⓑ Ⓒ Ⓓ Ⓔ	51. Ⓐ Ⓑ Ⓒ Ⓓ Ⓔ
12. Ⓐ Ⓑ Ⓒ Ⓓ Ⓔ	32. Ⓐ Ⓑ Ⓒ Ⓓ Ⓔ	52. Ⓐ Ⓑ Ⓒ Ⓓ Ⓔ
13. Ⓐ Ⓑ Ⓒ Ⓓ Ⓔ	33. Ⓐ Ⓑ Ⓒ Ⓓ Ⓔ	53. Ⓐ Ⓑ Ⓒ Ⓓ Ⓔ
14. Ⓐ Ⓑ Ⓒ Ⓓ Ⓔ	34. Ⓐ Ⓑ Ⓒ Ⓓ Ⓔ	54. Ⓐ Ⓑ Ⓒ Ⓓ Ⓔ
15. Ⓐ Ⓑ Ⓒ Ⓓ Ⓔ	35. Ⓐ Ⓑ Ⓒ Ⓓ Ⓔ	55. Ⓐ Ⓑ Ⓒ Ⓓ Ⓔ
16. Ⓐ Ⓑ Ⓒ Ⓓ Ⓔ	36. Ⓐ Ⓑ Ⓒ Ⓓ Ⓔ	56. Ⓐ Ⓑ Ⓒ Ⓓ Ⓔ
17. Ⓐ Ⓑ Ⓒ Ⓓ Ⓔ	37. Ⓐ Ⓑ Ⓒ Ⓓ Ⓔ	57. Ⓐ Ⓑ Ⓒ Ⓓ Ⓔ
18. Ⓐ Ⓑ Ⓒ Ⓓ Ⓔ	38. Ⓐ Ⓑ Ⓒ Ⓓ Ⓔ	58. Ⓐ Ⓑ Ⓒ Ⓓ Ⓔ
19. Ⓐ Ⓑ Ⓒ Ⓓ Ⓔ	39. Ⓐ Ⓑ Ⓒ Ⓓ Ⓔ	59. Ⓐ Ⓑ Ⓒ Ⓓ Ⓔ
20. Ⓐ Ⓑ Ⓒ Ⓓ Ⓔ	40. Ⓐ Ⓑ Ⓒ Ⓓ Ⓔ	60. Ⓐ Ⓑ Ⓒ Ⓓ Ⓔ

Section 2

Use the following page to prepare your essays. During the official exam, you will be given 12 lined pages for your essays.

Notes

Notes

Notes

Notes

Available at your local bookstore or order directly from us by sending in coupon below.

MAXnotes®
REA's Literature Study Guides

MAXnotes® are student-friendly. They offer a fresh look at masterpieces of literature, presented in a lively and interesting fashion. **MAXnotes**® offer the essentials of what you should know about the work, including outlines, explanations and discussions of the plot, character lists, analyses, and historical context. **MAXnotes**® are designed to help you think independently about literary works by raising various issues and thought-provoking ideas and questions. Written by literary experts who currently teach the subject, **MAXnotes**® enhance your understanding and enjoyment of the work.

Available **MAXnotes**® include the following:

Absalom, Absalom!	Henry IV, Part I	Othello
The Aeneid of Virgil	Henry V	Paradise
Animal Farm	The House on Mango Street	Paradise Lost
Antony and Cleopatra	Huckleberry Finn	A Passage to India
As I Lay Dying	I Know Why the Caged	Plato's Republic
As You Like It	Bird Sings	Portrait of a Lady
The Autobiography of	The Iliad	A Portrait of the Artist
Malcolm X	Invisible Man	as a Young Man
The Awakening	Jane Eyre	Pride and Prejudice
Beloved	Jazz	A Raisin in the Sun
Beowulf	The Joy Luck Club	Richard II
Billy Budd	Jude the Obscure	Romeo and Juliet
The Bluest Eye, A Novel	Julius Caesar	The Scarlet Letter
Brave New World	King Lear	Sir Gawain and the
The Canterbury Tales	Leaves of Grass	Green Knight
The Catcher in the Rye	Les Misérables	Slaughterhouse-Five
The Color Purple	Lord of the Flies	Song of Solomon
The Crucible	Macbeth	The Sound and the Fury
Death in Venice	The Merchant of Venice	The Stranger
Death of a Salesman	Metamorphoses of Ovid	Sula
Dickens Dictionary	Metamorphosis	The Sun Also Rises
The Divine Comedy I: Inferno	Middlemarch	A Tale of Two Cities
Dubliners	A Midsummer Night's Dream	The Taming of the Shrew
The Edible Woman	Moby-Dick	Tar Baby
Emma	Moll Flanders	The Tempest
Euripides' Medea & Electra	Mrs. Dalloway	Tess of the D'Urbervilles
Frankenstein	Much Ado About Nothing	Their Eyes Were Watching God
Gone with the Wind	Mules and Men	Things Fall Apart
The Grapes of Wrath	My Antonia	To Kill a Mockingbird
Great Expectations	Native Son	To the Lighthouse
The Great Gatsby	1984	Twelfth Night
Gulliver's Travels	The Odyssey	Uncle Tom's Cabin
Handmaid's Tale	Oedipus Trilogy	Waiting for Godot
Hamlet	Of Mice and Men	Wuthering Heights
Hard Times	On the Road	Guide to Literary Terms
Heart of Darkness		

Research & Education Association
61 Ethel Road W., Piscataway, NJ 08854
Phone: (732) 819-8880   **website: www.rea.com**

Please send me more information about your MAXnotes® books.

Name _____

Address _____

City _____ State _____ Zip _____

REA's Test Preps
The Best in Test Preparation

- REA "Test Preps" are **far more** comprehensive than any other test preparation series
- Each book contains up to **eight** full-length practice tests based on the most recent exams
- **Every** type of question likely to be given on the exams is included
- Answers are accompanied by **full** and **detailed** explanations

REA publishes over 70 Test Preparation volumes in several series. They include:

Advanced Placement Exams (APs)
Art History
Biology
Calculus AB & BC
Chemistry
Economics
English Language & Composition
English Literature & Composition
European History
French Language
Government & Politics
Latin
Physics B & C
Psychology
Spanish Language
Statistics
United States History
World History

College-Level Examination Program (CLEP)
Analyzing and Interpreting Literature
College Algebra
Freshman College Composition
General Examinations
General Examinations Review
History of the United States I
History of the United States II
Introduction to Educational Psychology
Human Growth and Development
Introductory Psychology
Introductory Sociology
Principles of Management
Principles of Marketing
Spanish
Western Civilization I
Western Civilization II

SAT Subject Tests
Biology E/M
Chemistry
French
German
Literature
Mathematics Level 1, 2
Physics
Spanish
United States History

Graduate Record Exams (GREs)
Biology
Chemistry
Computer Science
General
Literature in English
Mathematics
Physics
Psychology

ACT - ACT Assessment
ASVAB - Armed Services Vocational Aptitude Battery
CBEST - California Basic Educational Skills Test
CDL - Commercial Driver License Exam
CLAST - College Level Academic Skills Test
COOP & HSPT - Catholic High School Admission Tests
ELM - California State University Entry Level Mathematics Exam
FE (EIT) - Fundamentals of Engineering Exams - For Both AM & PM Exams

FTCE - Florida Teacher Certification Examinations
GED - (U.S. Edition)
GMAT - Graduate Management Admission Test
LSAT - Law School Admission Test
MAT - Miller Analogies Test
MCAT - Medical College Admission Test
MTEL - Massachusetts Tests for Educator Licensure
NJ HSPA - New Jersey High School Proficiency Assessment
NYSTCE - New York State Teacher Certification Examinations
PRAXIS PLT - Principles of Learning & Teaching Tests
PRAXIS PPST - Pre-Professional Skills Tests
PSAT/NMSQT
SAT
TExES - Texas Examinations of Educator Standards
THEA - Texas Higher Education Assessment
TOEFL - Test of English as a Foreign Language
TOEIC - Test of English for International Communication
USMLE Steps 1,2,3 - U.S. Medical Licensing Exams

Research & Education Association
61 Ethel Road W., Piscataway, NJ 08854
Phone: (732) 819-8880   **website: www.rea.com**

Please send me more information about your Test Prep books.

Name _____

Address _____

City _____ State _____ Zip _____

REA's Test Prep Books Are The Best!
(a sample of the <u>hundreds of letters</u> REA receives each year)

" I am writing to congratulate you on preparing an exceptional study guide.
In five years of teaching this course I have never encountered a more thorough,
comprehensive, concise and realistic preparation for this examination. "

Teacher, Davie, FL

" I have found your publications, *The Best Test Preparation...,* to be exactly that. "

Teacher, Aptos, CA

" I used your *CLEP Introductory Sociology* book and rank it 99% — thank you! "

Student, Jerusalem, Israel

" Your *GMAT* book greatly helped me on the test. Thank you. "

Student, Oxford, OH

" I recently got the *French SAT II* Exam book from REA. I congratulate
you on first-rate French practice tests."

Instructor, Los Angeles, CA

" Your *AP English Literature and Composition* book is most impressive."

Student, Montgomery, AL

" The REA *LSAT* Test Preparation guide is a winner! "

Instructor, Spartanburg, SC

(more on front page)